VIRGINIA WOOLF

CRITICAL ISSUES SERIES

General Editors: John Peck and Martin Coyle

Published

Virginia Woolf	*Linden Peach*
Henry James	*Jeremy Tambling*

In preparation

Jane Austen	*Robert Clark*
William Shakespeare	*Richard Dutton*
Geoffrey Chaucer	*Ruth Evans*
George Eliot	*Pauline Nestor*
Charles Dickens	*Lyn Pykett*
James Joyce	*Kiernan Ryan*
D. H. Lawrence	*Rick Rylance*
William Wordsworth	*John Williams*

Critical Issues

Virginia Woolf

Linden Peach

First published 2000 by
MACMILLAN PRESS LTD
Houndmills, Basingstoke, Hampshire RG21 6XS
and London
Companies and representatives
throughout the world

ISBN 0–333–68730–2 hardcover
ISBN 0–333–68731–0 paperback

A catalogue record for this book is available
from the British Library.

This book is printed on paper suitable for recycling and
made from fully managed and sustained forest sources.

10   9   8   7   6   5   4   3   2   1
09   08   07   06   05   04   03   02   01   00

Printed in Hong Kong

Published in the United States of America by
ST. MARTIN'S PRESS, INC.,
Scholarly and Reference Division
175 Fifth Avenue, New York, N.Y. 10010

ISBN 0–312–22889–9 hardcover
ISBN 0–312–22891–0 paperback

For Cynthia and Angela

Contents

Acknowledgements

I seem to have lived with the ideas in this book for so long and discussed them with so many colleagues and students that it is impossible to acknowledge everyone who has contributed in some way to it, and particularly to the refining of my thoughts. But I would certainly like to thank Angela for her encouragement and support, for always being ready to discuss ideas and for believing in the project. I should like to acknowledge colleagues and students in the Department of English and Drama at Loughborough University who have been more help to me than perhaps they realised, and the organisers of the 1930s Conference at Anglia Polytechnic University, Cambridge, where I first aired some of the ideas on which this study is based and where I was able to benefit from informed and useful discussion of them. I am particularly grateful to Martin Coyle and John Peck for their painstaking attention to earlier drafts of this book and for their invaluable advice and criticism. Special thanks are due also to Margaret Bartley and Gabriella Stiles at the Publishers and to Valery Rose for seeing the book through production. I should also like to thank the staff of the Interlibrary Loans Department, the Pilkington Library, Loughborough University, for their speedy and efficient assistance.

Some of the material on cryptanalysis in Chapter 2 and on *The Waves* in Chapter 7 appeared in my essay 'No Longer a View: Virginia Woolf in the 1930s and the 1930s in Virginia Woolf', in *Women Writers of the 1930s: Gender, Politics and History*, edited by Maroula Joannou (Edinburgh: Edinburgh University Press, 1999).

1

Introduction

The subject of this book is as much history in the work of Virginia Woolf as Virginia Woolf's work in history. Its principal premise is that literature contributes to the way in which our view of history is shaped and determined, reflecting the interest of New Historicism in history as a narrative and as a product of particular social and political contexts. As Jeffrey Cox and Larry Reynolds have pointed out:

> For the most part new historicism can be distinguished from 'old' historicism by its lack of faith in 'objectivity' and 'permanence' and its stress not upon the direct recreation of the past, but rather the processes by which the past is constructed or invented... it rejects the idea of 'History' as a directly accessible, unitary past, and substitutes for it the conception of 'histories', an ongoing series of human constructions, each representing the past at particular present moments for particular present purposes.[1]

However, New Historicism should not be seen only in relation to 'old' historicism or History which it frequently misrepresents as being less interested in the construction of historiography than it actually is. Drawing on poststructuralist, including feminist, theories of discourse and Marxist theories of ideology, New Historicism was originally, and to some extent still is, interventionist, challenging the ahistorical bias of New Criticism, myth criticism and deconstructionism.

In 1984, Iain Wright complained that a few decades earlier poststructuralist approaches to literary criticism had prevented the formulation of new conceptions of literary history.[2] Fresh recognition of the limitless instability of language and meaning in poststructuralist literary criticism inspired the kind of 'joyous affirmation' which Jacques Derrida discovered in the 'free play' of words[3] – an emphasis upon the way in which language operates as a system of internal differences rather than as a system of positive terms or presences. The poststructuralist argument that dominant Western traditions had privileged their own perspectives in seeking absolute or guaranteed meanings in language should have provided the basis for a critique of traditional history, particularly of its overemphasis upon universal principles rather than relativism and upon progressive human self-development. Jonathan Culler argues that Derridian deconstructionism had the potential to couple 'a philosophical critique of history and historical understanding with the specification that discourse is historical and meaning historically determined ...'.[4] However, if deconstruction should have encouraged critics to think in terms of histories rather than history, to challenge the homogenising assumptions of 'old' historicism and to ask in whose interests and with what bias are historical narratives written, this was not often the case. The affirmation of free play and indeterminate meaning which became the linchpin of much deconstructionist criticism in practice seemed to deny the existence of any historical determined 'reality'. Despite the fact that things were changing in the academic discipline of History, among many deconstructionists History, equated with the worship of origins and with guaranteed meanings, was stigmatised as 'destructive of individual freedom and creativity'.[5]

While the battle to revise the concept of History has been won, a number of New Historicists, perhaps influenced by the more extreme modes of deconstructionist criticism, remain unconvinced by Culler's assertion that in deconstruction the concept of discourse as historically determined and a philosophical critique of history might together provide the basis of a revisionist historical method. Culler's arguments, however, have been taken up by others, including Lee Patterson:

> Thus deconstruction, far from either denying the reality of history or its availability to knowledge, is a critical practice that seeks to understand how 'reality' is put in place by discursive means. When Derrida notoriously says that 'there is nothing outside the text', he is restating the position held by many sociocultural historians, that reality is culturally or discursively produced, that – in Jonathan Culler's words – 'the realities with which politics is concerned, and the forms in which

they are manipulated, are inseparable from discursive structures and systems of signification'. While of course such a program *could* lead us to submerge agency into structure, nothing requires us to do so.[6]

This contention does not persuade Jeremy Hawthorn, who thinks that, for all his carefulness, Patterson 'hesitates between two irreconcilable positions'.[7] Patterson appears to posit two contradictory concepts of history: one that is outside discourse – 'the reality of history' – and one that is formulated by discourse. But Iain Wright, drawing on the work of Hans-Georg Gadamer,[8] argues that the models of the past presented by traditional history – 'as inert specimens beneath the scientist-historian's microscope' – and by deconstructionism, at least in its extreme form – 'as empty sites for deconstructive revelry' – are not the only options. He maintains, as Patterson seems to be suggesting, that without sacrificing our own historical identity or assuming that the past is a historical object that can objectively reveal its historical value, we could 'conceive of our relationship to a text of the past as a *dialogue*' in which the interlocutor is 'prepared to learn from the other'.[9] The realities with which politics is concerned may be manipulated by discursive systems but we are being addressed by them as much as addressing them.

II

The realities with which politics is concerned and the forms in which they are manipulated are recurring concerns in Virginia Woolf's fiction. Indeed, Hawthorn, in a discussion of *Between the Acts*, suggests that in some respects Woolf appears postmodernist.[10] What he means by this is that, although Woolf is a writer for whom 'hardly anything...is presented independently of a sense of its placing within a process of historical change or continuity...',[11] her work, as Elizabeth Abel in a psychoanalytic critical study says, is 'thick with a variety of pasts'.[12] Indeed, the way in which Woolf renders the past through the memories of a variety of characters is part of her method to represent and explore the diversity of history. But Woolf is also concerned with the relationship between the plurality of history and the way in which some histories are privileged over others. In other words, her work seems to be located at the very juncture between deconstruction and New Historicism for which

Culler and Patterson argue. New Historicism provides an apposite approach to her work in which the past, if it is not the product of discourse, is certainly mediated by it and has to be carefully uncovered.

The dialogical relationship between the claims of history and historicity which has revolutionised historicism in theory and which needs to be brought to any discussion of literary history is actually raised as an issue in Woolf's work itself. Of principal interest in her fiction is the relationship between the present and the past. Indeed, it tackles what has become an issue in the practice of New Historicist criticism generally, the extent to which a critique of history as a dialogue between two historical situations tends toward what Roland Barthes called the 'ordering of that which is intelligible in our own time'.[13] In both her diary and in *Jacob's Room*, for example, Woolf grapples, as Judith Hattaway says, with 'the impossibility of seeing the whole significance of the War'.[14] But the novel's constant shifts in perspective turn the impossibility of seeing the whole significance of any historical event into the book's principal subject.

The potential and the limitations of the terms within which Woolf pursued the rival claims of history and historicity become clear when we try to read her work alongside that of theorists such as Hayden White, with whose view of history Jeremy Hawthorn has argued there are many parallels,[15] and Michel Foucault. Although White's views actually seem much closer to the concept of historiography by which Angela Carter was engaged, White, Woolf and Carter all see history as accessible only through partial and partisan narratives in which it is realised. For White, 'history' is an 'emplotment', quite literally a story of the world imposed upon it by historians. Not only, he argues, is there no objective, external criterion by which the truth of a narrative may be established, but it is also impossible to distinguish between different historical accounts.

White's work alerts us to Woolf's interest in the partisan nature of interpretations of the past. It is certainly true to say that the view of the period between the end of the First World War and 1923 in *Mrs Dalloway* is 'poetic', to employ White's own term for history as a narrative prose structure.[16] But the dialogic nature of her novels, while positioning readers in the difficulties of interpretation, invites different perspectives to be compared and contrasted in a performative act that does privilege some viewpoints over others. For example, in *Mrs Dalloway* the reader is invited to compare Septimus' view of himself, the opinions of two doctors and his wife's responses to him. Guided by the nuances of the narrator's account, the reader is likely to arrive at a sympathetic view of Septimus as a victim of war and a more critical view of the perspectives of his wife and the doctors. In order to do so, the reader needs some understanding of the period, of the way in which the war did not end for many in 1918 (rendering at least one voice in the novel blatantly ironic) and of dominant cultural views of masculinity and mental illness. It is, for example, important to recognise how in this period, as Eric Leed has pointed out, different views of the veteran after 1919 reflected not only different views of the war 'but different conceptualisations of the social order'.[17]

Woolf's work, however, is located in an awareness of historicity that in many respects is closer to Foucault's than White's. Woolf is positioned between an old 'historicist' viewpoint, tied to a concept of the permanence of originary meaning, and a 'textual' view of history which releases it from the conditions of its birth. Her approach is more dialectical than is allowed for in either of these two polarised positions and is akin to Foucault's position on the nature of those statements which constitute various discourses in society, be they history, medicine, or religion:

> The statement, then, must not be treated as an event that occurred in a particular time and place, and that the most one can do is recall it – and celebrate it from afar off – in an act of memory. But neither is it an ideal form that can be actualised in any body, at any time, in any circumstances and in any material conditions.[18]

In Woolf's work, the historical event is

> Too repeatable to be entirely identifiable with the spatio-temporal co-ordinates of its birth (it is more than the place and date of its appearance), too bound up with what surrounds it and supports it to be free as a pure form . . . it is endowed with a certain modifiable heaviness, a weight relative to the field in which it is placed, a constancy that allows of various uses, a temporal permanence that does not sleep on its own past.[19]

Her own proximity to the position which Foucault describes here is evident in the way in which events from the pasts with which they are concerned enter her texts. As in the case of the marching boy soldiers to the Tomb of the Unknown Warrior in *Mrs Dalloway*, the text preserves what surrounds and supports the event. But in the way the soldiers are viewed critically by a character who observes them and by the narrator, it is clear that Woolf recognises that the weight of the event is relative and modifiable. The soldiers marching to the wreath-laying ceremony in *Mrs Dalloway* acquire significance because it is the repetition of a poignant event that occurred years earlier, but in the eyes of the narrator it has already been modified by the new, later context – it has not been allowed to 'sleep on its own past'.

The exploration of the relationship between history and historicity in Woolf's fiction is posited on an understanding of what constitutes a text that is, also, close to Foucault's. Foucault viewed a text, such as the wreath-laying ceremony, as 'a node within a network'.[20] In other words, 'texts' such as this ceremony are not simply established within a network of references but are brought into being by them. At the heart of any text, Foucault argues, is an interpretation and reinterpretation of events that have no existence either inside or outside of the text independent of its interpretative framework. Of particular relevance to Woolf's work is Foucault's argument that an event is always located in 'a complex group of relations', that these are constantly changing and that with them the event itself will change.[21]

III

The range of spatial metaphors currently employed in contemporary theory – for example, 'position', 'location', 'centre–margin', 'global–local', 'liminal space', 'third space' – reflects the extent and the importance of a further paradigmatic shift which has occurred concerning the role of history in social theory. Since the nineteenth century, history has occupied a privileged position in Western thought and has informed and shaped many of the discourses around notions of identity. The development of identity has been seen as a largely historical process in which the significance of geography has been underestimated. The American postmodern geographer Edward Soja pointed out in the late 1980s that Marxism had 'stashed away the geographical imagination in some superstructural attic to gather the dust of discarded and somewhat tainted memories' while 'Geography isolated itself in a tight little island of its own'.[22]

But the intersection of history, biography and society, theorised now as much in terms of the socio-spatial as the socio-temporal, provides us with a framework within which to reclaim the under-recognised spatiality of Woolf's literary imagination.

According to the Marxist theorist Fredric Jameson, the characteristic of social and cultural life in the latter half of the twentieth century is its domination by the logic of spatial organisation rather than time. That this was the direction which social life was taking was apparent in the early decades of the twentieth century and was certainly obvious to Virginia Woolf. As I hope to show in the subsequent chapters, her fiction explores the figurative nature of space – particularly the extent to which space repeats and is structured by the real determinants of social relations. But this is not to suggest that her novels can be reduced to socio-spatial critiques. They recognise the difficulty of determining whether the spaces they invoke are 'real', 'imaginary', 'symbolic' or 'metaphor-concepts'.

Of course, most of the spaces that the novels invoke are urban or semi-urban spaces. And to the organisation of urban space, as Michel de Certeau has pointed out, there are two imaginary dimensions: the rational organisation that must repress all the physical, mental and political pollution that would compromise it, and the ruses and combinations of power that have no immediately obvious identity.[23] Structuralism has allowed us to render each of these aspects of cultural space synchronically. That is to say, it has allowed us to recognise, in the apparently discontinuous nature of the urban, coherent patterns and systems. New Historicism, on the other hand, has enabled us to render each of these aspects of urban space diachronically – through time.[24] These dual mappings of urban space are particularly relevant to an appreciation of how Woolf's novels function as 'discursive events', breaking the deep structures of metaphor in which space is gendered. Symbolism and metaphors which imbue space with cultural meanings are perceived as particularly important. Women in Woolf's fiction enter and are seen as having entered new locations (streets, shops and offices) and different social positions in a changing socio-political milieu. The novels explore the relevance of these different locations for women's identities and the role that the cartography of gendered relations, in which private and public had been so clearly separated, played in shaping them. Previously in fiction the concepts of 'private' and 'public' had been subject to limited exploration in relation to the metaphorical aspects of space. The separation of the public and private as dichotomous spaces was seen as reproducing socio-cultural categories. But Woolf's fiction opens up the interconnections between them and explores the significance of space generally in the transformation of identities. Michael Bakhtin's concept of the chronotope confronts us in any attempt to discuss the spatio-temporal dimension of Woolf's work, particularly her realisation that events are always embedded, as Foucault says, in a complex web of power relationships. The chronotope is literally the time–space unit in a narrative, and what is distinctive about Bakhtin's concept is that neither time nor space is privileged:

> In the literary artistic chronotope, spatial and temporal indicators are fused into one carefully thought-out, concrete whole. Time, as it were, thickens, takes on flesh, becomes artistically visible; likewise, space becomes charged and responsive to the movements of time, plot and history.[25]

Bakhtin's concept of the chronotope offers an especially suggestive approach to Woolf's fiction because of the way he links transformations within the chronotope to changes in people's conception of space and time. However, Woolf recognises that when a chronotope changes over time, the spatio-temporal shift that occurs has implications for the dialogical relationship between past and present. Thus, when an event from the past enters the present, there is often a dialectic between 'the spatio-temporal co-ordinates of its birth' and the spatio-temporal shift that occurs as it is accommodated in a new milieu. But at the same time there is the suggestion that it will be relocated again at some future point in a further spatio-temporal shift. Hence, as we shall see, Peter Walsh's encounter with the marching young soldiers participating in the wreath-laying ceremony in *Mrs Dalloway* is a chronotope through which new attitudes emerge but which do not achieve fixity, for they themselves will be subject to further modification in a future spatio-temporal context. The inescapable context for these transformations within the chronotope is social change, but in Woolf's fiction this is linked to metaphorical conceptions of time and space. These conceptions, formed in historically changing modes of life, have come to be recognised as more significant to Woolf's novels than used to be the case. But insufficient attention has been paid to Woolf's interest in how particular metaphorical conceptions of time and space are privileged over others in dominant discursive formations and in how, transmitted through discourse, they acquire a mode of life beyond the spatio-temporal co-ordinates of their birth.

IV

The following chapters (which I summarise briefly here) explore the sophisticated nature of Woolf's political thought as evidenced in each of her novels. Her first two novels – *The Voyage Out* and *Night and Day* – are seen as more innovative than critics have generally allowed, subverting the male-oriented narrative of voyage and the romance respectively. It is argued in Chapter 3 that the discourses around 'romance', 'marriage' and 'domesticity' are 'precarious ensembles' and that both novels present cryptographically what these discourses conceal, such as relationships between women and anxieties about empire – the diminishing and diminished status of the empire in the early twentieth century is alluded to throughout *The Voyage Out*. Not only are the boundaries between love and friendship and between intimacy and homoeroticism challenged in these novels but, anticipating Michel Foucault, they are related to concepts of power. While Woolf's use of male and imperialist adventure genres has been related to her concern with gender differences, the relevance of these intertexts to Woolf's concern with Englishness and empire has been overlooked. In correcting this oversight, Chapter 3 argues that, as in Conrad's *Heart of Darkness*, the real horror is viewed as at the heart of 'civilisation'. Thus *The Voyage Out* is seen as taking its central character Rachel not just into her own sexuality but into elements of her country of which she was previously unaware.

Night and Day, it is argued, is a more cryptically subversive novel than *The Voyage Out*. The cryptic nature of the text as a whole is reinforced by its preoccupation with silence and its concern with the need to break linguistic structures, issues that recur in Woolf's later fiction. The bridge between Woolf's first two novels and her first novel of the 1920s, *Jacob's Room*, is discussed in Chapter 4, provided by her short story 'Kew Gardens'. While critics have focused on the fragmentariness with which reality is presented in the story, I suggest that its allusive references to war should lead the reader to reconsider the suggestiveness with which the story presents 'reality'.

As a rejoinder to John McCrae's Poem 'In Flanders Fields', *Jacob's Room* (Chapter 4) is approached as a rueful glance backward to the hothouse culture in which the young officer class of the First World War was brought up and how their privileged lives were a curse rather than a blessing. Woolf, it is argued, presents a critique of pre-war England, or an aspect of it, without sacrificing the subtlety of its discursive formations. Like much of Woolf's work, the novel is seen as subverting existing genres but it is also reconsidered as a rejoinder to Edward Marsh's memoir of Rupert Brooke. The discussion takes issue with those critics who have accused Woolf of essentialising masculinity, missing the point that she is concerned with a particular generation of males from a particular class and thus with the essentialising nature of a particular upbringing and set of attitudes. I also suggest that critics who have read the repeated references to Greek culture as underscoring its patriarchy have missed the point that the novel is concerned not with Greek culture *per se* but with the way in which it has been appropriated in Victorian and pre-war England in support of particular definitions of Englishness and masculinity. The novel, I argue, is posited on a mourning that is more real than that to be found in war-time memoirs and obituaries. Particular importance is attached to the way in which Jacob is presented through the observations of different women, but the focus is on its analysis of the social discourses of womanhood, and the way in which they entrap different types of women in different socio-political situations. The novel thus not only anticipates the links between Fascism and patriarchy in *Three Guineas* but reflects the arguments and the tenor of Woolf's essay on the Plumage Bill.

The discussion of *Mrs Dalloway* in Chapter 5 challenges the view that the novel creates problems for the reader because it appears to consist of two unconnected narratives. It suggests that the different narrative threads are connected in their exploration of the dominant fictions of post-war Britain and what is hidden within or by these fictions. The multivalent narrative is seen as central to the novel's engagement with the difficulties of writing history. The movement in the narrative between different minds and viewpoints is shown as mirroring the way in which the critique of the past in the text is a dialogue between different historical situations. Crucial to the novel is a dialogue between post-and pre-war England, particularly the contradiction in post-war British life between withdrawal from imperialist expansion, anxieties about empire and about the war on the one hand, and a perceived need to preserve the ideologies that informed and sustained empire, Englishness and masculinity on the other. The chapter also places the novel's themes in the context of discourses about same-sex relationships and the formation of gender identity. It takes issue with the thesis that a more conservative 'feminine' England emerged after the war, arguing that *Mrs Dalloway* distinguishes between a feminine England and an England in which there is a preponderance of women, and sees the novel as engaging with the spectacle of modernity in the 1920s. The spatial geography of the novel, it is argued, reflects Britain's position at the cusp of two socio-economic orders and that the attitude toward modernity in the book is ambiguous. In particular, I argue that the novel recognises the complicated relationship that existed in post-war Britain between the emergent conservative middle class and the more overtly political high Toryism. In discussing *Mrs Dalloway*, it is important to distinguish between what critics have labelled 'conservative nationalism' and what in relation to Woolf's novel we might call 'national conservatism'. The latter worried Woolf because of the way in which Englishness appeared to be locked into the homophobic and militaristic ideologies that she argued in *Jacob's Room* led Britain to war.

The basis of the discussion of *To the Lighthouse* in Chapter 6 is that it is an interruption of *Jacob's Room*, either developing aspects of that earlier novel or pursuing alternatives to some of the issues raised and perspectives employed. The preoccupation in criticism with the way in which the novel provided Woolf with a vehicle for exorcising her mother's ghost has meant that its concern with the cultural construction of women as Woman has been overlooked. The chapter focuses on the novel's concern with discourses of 'womanhood', 'motherhood', and 'masculinity' and with the occluded *crypta* within family and mother-child relationships. In this sense, the novel is part of Woolf's exploration of gender in the post-war period.

Orlando and *The Waves* are linked as apologues, an appropriate form for Woolf to have chosen to pursue her ideas about cultural discourses. Particular attention is paid in Chapter 7 to the use of carnival in *Orlando* and the way in which Woolf fuses the carnivalesque in the novel with what might appear to be the surrealistic aspects of Modernism. It is argued that *Orlando* is the product of a wide range of reading from which Woolf derived an approach to history that anticipates Foucault's *The Archaeology of Knowledge*. In *Orlando* Woolf permits herself freedom from history and from the historians' histories, focusing instead on how a masculine social memory has shaped the processes of memory for women and how these influences may be resisted.

Anticipating postmodern theories of the nation state, Woolf eschews the historicism that dominated discussion of nationhood in the nineteenth century and examines nationhood as a form of social and textual affiliation. *Orlando* reconfigures the role of history in the formation of national identity and particularly the way in which a nation's past is frequently presented in terms of continuous lines of development to a necessary future. More particularly, it is argued that *Orlando* is an example of a metropolitan intervention in the debate about imperialism and that there are cryptic references to the cultural representation of the East and Ireland and to international relations with Turkey in the 1920s. Two areas of cultural life are satirised – the way in which gender is perceived in absolute and essential terms, and the myth of a self-contained and pure 'English-ness'. Woolf thus returns to a recurring theme in her fiction – that what is rendered as 'Other' is an important part of the definition of Englishness.

While *A Room of One's Own* is normally regarded as a lecture, I argue that, in the way it exemplifies the experiences of women and records the social conditions that obstruct them – employing mockery, satire, fantasy, irony – it is actually a fusion of the lecture and the apologue. This concern with presenting the 'truth' of related cultural assumptions is pursued in the discussion of *The Waves*. While criticism has generally seen *The Waves* as a Modernist experiment, the basis of the discussion here is that Woolf sought to explore the extent to which individual consciousness is determined by the *a priori*. The novel is compared with *Jacob's Room* but like *Orlando* is seen as drawing on turbulent international events of the 1920s, in this case the movement for independence in India. Whereas earlier novels have been concerned largely with the formation of a mentality intended to serve empire, this novel is primarily concerned with the impact of the demise of empire upon a class whose identity was bound up with notions of colonialism, Englishness and masculinity.

The discussion of *The Years* (Chapter 8) takes issue with the view that it is a social-realist text. What critics have taken for traditional social realism in *The Years*, it is argued here, is the manifestation of social discourses that determine individual subjectivity. These discourses are in turn linked to particular narratives of history. When we think of the novel as being concerned with the construction of history and experience, particularly female experience, it appears to be a less radical shift in her *oeuvre* than critics who have seized on its apparent verisimilitude have suggested. The cryptic details of family are discussed in the context of how they undermine the public face of the family and the novel is seen as occupying a space opened up by the dialectic between several principal and interrelated narratives of family available to writers in the 1920s and 1930s. Bakhtin's concept of the chronotope is suggested as providing a particularly appropriate model within which to discuss the Victorian preoccupation with public space in *The Years*, and especially with control and the loss of control. The concept of a 'controlled decontrol' in British emotional life is linked in the discussion of the novel to the Victorian fear of boundarylessness.

The short story 'The Shooting Party', I suggest in Chapter 9, marks the transition from *The Years* to *Between the Acts* in its fusion of the apocalyptic and the dark carnivalesque. In both texts there is a sense of a traditional upper-middle-class English life coming to an end. In Woolf's final novel, the end of European civilisation is linked to the end of the European concept of history. But despite the sombreness of its subject, I argue that the novel has a strong theatrical element and blurs the boundaries between prose narrative and drama. The influence of being on the threshold of war is evident in the text in a number of ways, not least the way in which ordinary words, details and events are raised to the level of symbol and the way in which different chronotopes enter into people's minds and consciousness. The pageant which is at the heart of the novel presents not only a critique of Englishness and empire but an exploration of some of the issues pertaining to the concepts of history and historiography. Preceding this analysis of Woolf's political thought, however, is a chapter on 'Contexts' where I look at the reception and critical history of the texts as well as at Woolf's own history.

2

Contexts

'Politics be damned!' issued clearly from the body on the left-hand side, and, as these words were uttered, the mouths, noses, chins, little moustaches, tweed caps, rough boots, shooting coats, and check stockings of the two speakers became clearer and clearer....
Virginia Woolf, 'Solid Objects'[1]

I

Many of the features of Woolf's fiction that appeared radical to her contemporaries, even though they were not unique to her – its challenges to realism, disruptions of linearity, multi-voiced narratives and the articulation of inner consciousness – have now become commonplace in postmodern fiction. Only habitual readers of very traditional realist writing – which still maintains a powerful hold over contemporary, especially popular, fiction – will find Woolf's novels as challenging and as difficult as some of her reviewers. But if the previously radical has now become commonplace, it is important not to homogenise non-realistic fiction. One of the negative consequences of the popularity of postmodern writing is that critics often place works that employ the broad features of modernism and postmodernism on the same bookshelf, ignoring the distinctiveness that lies in the articulation of specific occluded experiences and the subtle, localised innovations within the wider framework. For example, the works of the African-American novelist Toni Morrison, who included a study of Woolf's work in her Master's thesis, have much in common with modernist and postmodern European fiction; Morrison was undoubtedly influenced by the articulation of inner consciousness and the multivalence within Woolf's fiction. But only

14

the most cursory reading of her work could overlook the fact that Morrison's challenge to realism, linearity and closure is driven by African-American concerns and experiences even though the narrative strategies themselves are not unique to black writing. It is through her articulation of previously occluded subjects, narratives and voices, and the way her writing is informed by black ontology while endlessly complicating and deferring the definition of African-American, that Morrison extends the possibilities of the novel form. Similarly, we must be careful not to allow Woolf's fiction to be consumed by an homogenising concept of modernist art that blurs the boundaries between writers who employ ostensibly similar strategies but in different ways, to fulfil different needs and to meet different goals.

The experimental nature of Woolf's work, together with the critical tendency to emphasise the formal features of such experimentation, has been responsible for the prevailing view of her as a writer more concerned with artistic form than with political content. In suggesting that Woolf is a 'political' novelist – or more of a political novelist than critics have generally acknowledged until recently – I mean that she is a writer who, like Toni Morrison for whom she became a mentor figure, uses literary form, style and technique to achieve 'political' as well as aesthetic ends – in her case to implement modernist, feminist and satiric goals. The subject of this book is the critical issues arising from the intersection of space, political history and the 'imaginary' in Virginia Woolf's fiction and, in particular, how in exploring the links between these concepts – each of which for Woolf was the tip of an iceberg – her fiction anticipates and challenges some of the concerns and debates in modern critical and social theory. To my mind, the configuration of space, political history and the 'imaginary' is at the heart of Woolf's thinking as a 'political' novelist.

Even now, the description of Woolf as a 'political thinker' is not an incontestable formulation. An American scholar has recently observed that it is still necessary to confront the popular image of Woolf, in England and America anyway, as 'an upscale Laura Ashley English female *objet d'art*, as collectible as a faded bit of lawn and lace, faintly printed with wildflowers and certainly harmless'.[2] Recent scholarship, however, suggests that Woolf has been perceived differently not only by different generations but in different countries. Despite the fact that there is more international exchange of scholarship and ideas than ever before through international publishing houses, conferences, visiting scholarships, and the internet, there remains, as Vera and Ansgar Nünning have pointed out, 'an obvious divergence in national traditions of Woolf studies'.[3]

In British criticism, the image of Woolf as an eccentric, ladylike artist, out of touch with other writers and her own times, and too much influenced by her upper-middle-class origins, has been a long time dying. But Hermione Lee's major biography finally confirms the different portrait that has been emerging in Anglo-American criticism since the 1970s of an independently minded critic who transformed the feminist and pacifist traditions she appropriated, and in her fiction as in her radical essays such as *A Room of One's Own* and *Three Guineas* challenged many of the prevailing conventions and ideologies of her day.[4] As the American scholar Mark Hussey has observed, 'one of the most welcome and significant effects of the scholarship on Virginia Woolf since the early 1970s has been to correct the "official version" promulgated in her own country of Woolf as an exquisite stylist whose interest in what has traditionally been allowed as "politics" was negligible.'[5] Woolf is more confidently seen in recent criticism as exceeding the dominant political thinking of her time and as transcending what has too often been presented as a stranglehold exerted over her by an idle, mannered clique.

In Germany, Woolf's early and late novels have received less attention than her experimental, modernist works. The old cliché of Woolf as a modernist writer or even as an apolitical aesthete has proved to be much more lasting there than anywhere else, and German critics have refrained until recently from the application of theory to Woolf's writing.[6] The same cannot be said for French literary criticism after 1970, however, where, Pierre-Eric Villeneuve points out, the steer for Woolf criticism was her 'femininity and that connection between the body and text that inevitably essentializes Woolf's place, making her one of the foremothers of the feminist discourse so popular in France [in the 1980s]'.[7] However, there has also been a tendency in France to focus on Woolf's life rather than on her feminist texts, following Hélène Cixous' infamous declaration 'that although I recognise the greatness of the writing, Woolf represents the "woman dead", "the woman killed" and therefore it doesn't speak to me because what I want to work on is "the woman alive and to come"'.[8]

In America, Jane Marcus maintains, Woolf has been held hostage by American feminist critics and her reputation has followed the curve of the fortunes of feminism.[9] Believing that 'the mistaken image of "theory" as itself élitist and hostile to values of bourgeois humanism has tended to mark Woolf as alien, difficult, snobby and out of touch with real, material or historical concerns', Marcus argues for greater recognition of Woolf as 'a writer worthy of world-scale interest as a social thinker'.[10] Despite the title of her paper, Marcus does not review many American critics on Woolf. Mark Hussey, on the other hand, argues that one myth that feminist writers in America, including Jane Marcus herself, have done much to dispel is that she was apolitical.[11] Certainly the important works revisioning Woolf as a political writer, such as Alex Zwerdling's study, emerged from American presses in the 1980s.[12]

II

As is now well known, attacks on the Bloomsbury group with which Woolf became associated for its alleged élitist nature and narrowing influence began in England in the 1930s from F. R. and Q. D. Leavis and from Wyndham Lewis. The term 'Bloomsbury Group' was first coined in 1910 as a joke, but by 1914 Woolf herself was using it in more serious vein.[13] The group began to meet the year after the family moved from Hyde Park Gate, Kensington, to the then unfashionable Bloomsbury following the death of their father. Woolf's mother had died in 1895 when she was 13, after which she suffered her first nervous breakdown. In 1905, her brother Thoby began holding Thursday evenings at home with his Cambridge friends and the group eventually expanded to include Clive Bell, Lytton Strachey, Roger Fry and E. M. Forster as well as other non-Bloomsbury people such as T. S. Eliot, Katherine Mansfield and Hugh Walpole.

The Leavises' negative view of the Bloomsbury group became established in Britain in the 1940s and 1950s because the political culture of the time indulged an ideal of an organic past 'in which speech was natural and vigorous, in which life was deeply felt and morally simple and unalloyed'.[14] The Bloomsbury group, along with industrial and urban insincerity, were seen as having contributed to the cultural decline of the past:

> Articulateness and unreality cultivated together: callousness disguising itself in articulateness; conceit casting itself safely in a confined sense of high sophistication; the uncertainty as to whether one is serious or not taking itself for ironic pose; who has not at some time observed the process?[15]

There is undoubtedly a class element (as well as a kind of intellectual snobbery) in the attack upon Woolf. Leavis and the critics associated with *Scrutiny* came from the middle class, while the members of the Bloomsbury group, like the earlier generation of university teachers whom F. R. Leavis and his own teacher I. A. Richards replaced at Cambridge University, were from the upper-middle class. In their crusade to make literature morally and socially relevant only a handful of authors were deemed morally serious enough to be incorporated into the English canon: Jane Austen, George Eliot, Henry James, Joseph Conrad, D. H. Lawrence and eventually Dickens for *Hard Times*. As Marion Shaw points out, the Leavises' attacks on Woolf and the Bloomsbury group damaged her reputation in the eyes of generations of students who were tutored in the *Scrutiny* critical ideology and many of them who went on in turn to become teachers disseminated the *Scrutiny* view of Woolf to further generations of readers.[16]

The American critic Jane Marcus, hardly able to contain her frustration that 'pernicious' criticism of Woolf in Britain has brought together critics and writers as diverse as Angela Carter, Terry Eagleton and Tom Paulin, suspects that the marginalising of Woolf in all but the academic niche of women's writing preserves 'the hegemony of those very professors at Oxbridge and its branches abroad she railed against in her work....'[17] The kind of 'pernicious' criticism she has in mind is exemplified by Tom Paulin's writings on Woolf. He concludes an article written on the fiftieth anniversary of her death thus:

> Her fiction and her two supposed feminist polemics – *A Room of One's Own* and *Three Guineas* – uphold the British empire and the existing state of society.... Woolf is no feminist, but she is a committed snob, a racist, an imperialist, and a sloppy amateur writer who for some reason has attracted huge numbers of admirers.[18]

Paulin's views of Woolf are clearly mediated by his opinion of the Bloomsbury group and 'the atmosphere of high culture' that he sees as surrounding it, views that again return us to the attacks upon the group in the 1930s and 1940s.

Alex Zwerdling presents a different picture of this group from its British critics. While acknowledging that some of the shallower members of the group may have had a negative influence on Woolf, he argues that 'for a young woman born and raised by the rules in Victorian England and denied a university education, the group offered an extraordinary opportunity for mental expansion'.[19] This is not to deny that Woolf's early life offered her intellectual opportunities that were not available to many women of her day. Although her gender denied her the Cambridge University education enjoyed by her brothers, Thoby and Adrian, she had the benefits of private Greek lessons with Janet Case and access to the library of her own father, an eminent biographer and editor of the *Dictionary of National Biography*. Moreover, as Zwerdling says, 'if we count both the inner circle of Bloomsbury and its satellites, we can see that Woolf's private university included not only writers but painters, art critics, political theorists, practical politicians, economists, feminist reformers, philosophers, and psychoanalysts'.[20] During the war it met in the 1917 Club, a venue for various political groups, and Clive Bell even considered taking over *The Egoist* and making it a Bloomsbury Review. In terms of Woolf's political and historical education, the influences of John Maynard Keynes, Beatrice and Sidney Webb, Lytton Strachey and Ethel Smyth are singled out by Zwerdling as particularly important.

The Bloomsbury group was influential in enabling Woolf to look critically at her father's library – her diet of home reading included the great male biographies and histories of the nineteenth century – the staple of upper-class Victorian culture. But it also nurtured a critique of how Victorian letters produced young men 'with what E. M. Forster described as well-developed bodies, fairly well-developed minds and under-developed hearts'.[21] In this respect, Lytton Strachey's *Eminent Victorians* (1918) was particularly important. Neither history nor biography in the sense that Woolf may have gleaned from her father's library, Strachey's monograph was a polemic against the Victorian establishment and its culture. Its influence is clearly discernible in the critique of colonialism in her first novel, *The Voyage Out* – the essay on Gordon is an attack on imperialism and empire – and in *Jacob's Room*, a critique *pace* the Bloomsbury group of how Victorian culture and the Victorian education system conspired to produce a certain kind of unfeeling, upper-class masculinity which Woolf believed led Britain into the First World War.

The Bloomsbury group were seen very differently by its contemporaries across the channel from those at home. The Parisian intellectual scene was an important centre for the diffusion of Bloomsbury aesthetics and values. There were obvious parallels with *La Nouvelle Revue Française*, the intellectual élite surrounding André Gides and Jacques Rivière between the wars. But most important of all, the Bloomsbury group maintained links with French culture, initiated with the Post-Impressionist Exhibition in 1910 and strengthened by the group's participation at the Entretiens of Pontigny in 1923 and 1925.[22] Woolf's interest in French literature clearly provided important influences on her work in the mid-1920s. As is well known, *To the Lighthouse* is indebted to Marcel Proust's *A la recherche du temps perdu* (1913–27). Like his work, which appeared in England volume by volume, Woolf's novel is about Time Lost and Time Regained and it is possible to discern close connections between the two works in the evocation of seascapes, the loss and 'rememory' of a loved one and, of course, the Post-Impressionist style. Woolf's critical reception in France was mediated, as in England, through the opinions held of the Bloomsbury group, but between the wars the group was held in higher regard in France than in Britain.

III

From Zwerdling's and Hermione Lee's studies, there thus emerges a picture of Virginia and Leonard Woolf developing 'a private network of intellectual peers and associates who were not "Bloomsbury" but whose varied interests helped to strengthen their links with the wider culture'.[23] This portrait accords with facts that are too often forgotten: that she taught working-class men and women at evening class, presided over meetings of the Women's Co-operative Guild held in her own house, worked for women's suffrage, and wrote in favour of pacifist and feminist causes. However, while all this is presented positively in Zwerdling's study, Hermione Lee's biography conveys a more ambivalent and complicated picture. There is no doubt that Woolf's teaching at Morley College from 1905 to 1907, for example, was evidence of her interest in forging links with wider society and contributed to her appreciation of the world beyond Bloomsbury. But while the experience of teaching English Composition and a course on 'English history from the beginning' was initially uplifting, she eventually found teaching a mixed-sex group that included a 'difficult elderly Socialist' and 'anaemic shop girls' hard work.[24] This was not, however, simply a matter of the difficulty of communicating across social barriers. Woolf was too independently minded to be seduced by arch philosophies that come with capital letters or with naïve versions of philanthropy that leave the root causes of social injustice unchanged. At one point in her first novel, *The Voyage Out*, the 'politically' minded Evelyn Murgatroyd tries to elicit the support and friendship of the heroine, Rachel:

> 'I belong to a club in London. It meets every Saturday, so it's called the Saturday Club. We're supposed to talk about art, but I'm sick of talking about art – what's the good of it? With all kinds of real things going on round one? It isn't as if they'd got anything to say about art, either. So what I'm going to tell 'em is that we've talked enough about art, and we'd better talk about life for a change. Questions that really matter to people's lives, the White Slave Traffic, Women's Suffrage, the Insurance Bill, and so on. And when we've made up our mind what we want to do we could form ourselves into a society for doing it .... I am certain that if people like ourselves were to take things in hand instead of leaving it to policemen and magistrates, we could put a stop to – prostitution' – she lowered her voice at the ugly word – 'in six months...'.[25]

It is not only the egocentric assertiveness and the lowered voice which belie the verisimilitude, if not the commitment and the energy, but her subsequent labelling of the Piccadilly prostitutes as 'poor wretches'. The target here is not simply middle-class philanthropy but the failure of individuals to explore fully their political opinions, the ways in which we are all, to varying degrees, positioned by language, and how engaging with a wider society inevitably means repositioning ourselves, or allowing ourselves to be repositioned, intellectually. Evelyn imagines herself approaching the prostitutes and telling them:

> 'Now, look here, I'm no better than you are, and I don't pretend to be any better, but you're doing what you know to be beastly, and I won't have you doing beastly things, because we're all the same under our skins, and if you do a beastly thing it does matter to me'. (p. 289)

The satire in passages such as this clearly reveals Woolf's own responsiveness to the wider political and cultural critiques to which, according to Zwerdling, the Bloomsbury Group introduced Woolf. Leonard, whom she married in 1912, was an important influence on her as she was on him. He was drawn to the Women's Co-operative Guild – the Women's branch of the Co-operative Society which organised working-class women into regional groups based on the principles of consumer control and consumer co-operation – and she and Leonard visited provincial Guild centres in northern England in 1913. For four years she presided over monthly meetings of the Richmond Branch of the Women's Co-operative Guild where with the stimulus of a guest speaker the group, about 12 women usually, discussed social questions, labour problems or travel. Unfortunately, the group was often not as stimulated or as stimulating as Woolf would have liked and she did eventually question why some of the members attended.

However ambivalent and disappointing some of these experiences, there is no doubt that they testify to a different Woolf from the British-generated caricature of the isolated, upper-middle-class artist confined by the parameters of her upbringing. Indeed, by 1922 she felt that she and Leonard had 'bitten off a large piece of life'.[26] There can be no denying that Leonard was, as Hermione Lee argues, an important part of that bite.[27] Disillusioned with his experiences as a colonial administrator in the Ceylon Civil Service between 1904 and 1911, he joined the Fabian Society in 1916. After the war, he became involved in the League of Nations and increasingly with the Labour Party for which he served for many years as Secretary of its Advisory Committee on International Affairs. The acquaintance of Beatrice and Sidney Webb, whom he met as a result of his writings on the Women's Co-operative Guild, contributed substantially to his conversion to Fabianism and he and Virginia attended their first Fabian conference in 1913. It is easy to understand why Woolf felt in 1920 that, contrary to the caricature of her as an artist out of touch with her times, they had bitten off 'a large piece of life' when we remember that in 1920 he was invited to stand as a parliamentary candidate for the 'Seven Universities Democratic Association', and that between 1920 and 1922 they visited four of the universities he would represent. His manifesto, of which Woolf approved, is an index of her involvement as well as his in the wider social world: it spoke for equality of education, international disarmament, anti-colonialism and co-operation between classes.[28]

It is important, however, not to divorce the wider social world of the early twentieth century in Woolf's fiction from the Victorian period, especially the late century. All of us are inevitably rooted in our parents' generation as much as our own. Woolf's own Victorian childhood together with the way in which, as S. P. Rosenbaum has pointed out, most of the Bloomsbury writings are related in important ways to Victorian beliefs about religion, philosophy, politics and art,[29] means that Woolf's fiction looks back to the Victorian period as much as forward to the present. Indeed, Gary Day complicates the situation further by pointing out that not only are there important continuities between the Victorian and subsequent periods so that many of the issues of the twentieth century are also Victorian dilemmas, but that the Victorian period was not the 'smooth continuum from the ascension of the queen in 1837 to her death in 1901' it is often taken for. These years, he reminds us, 'cover huge changes that make the early Victorian age quite different to the mid-or late-Victorian one'.[30] One of the most important differences between the last twenty years of the nineteenth century, when in the Boer War 'the colonial situation had suddenly and dangerously strayed beyond the control of the British', and the mid-Victorian period for our understanding of Woolf's fiction was, as John Peck observes, a fundamental tension between 'a liberal discourse, that continued to be of importance, and an opposed discourse of empire'. While the mid-Victorian years, as Peck points out, 'manage[d] to conceal the cultivation of extremes', the last twenty years witnessed 'an unavoidable clash of conflicting values'.[31] It is when the 'huge changes' that Victoria's reign witnessed, some of which she would have experienced vicariously through her parents' generation and some she would have witnessed for herself, are taken together with the new technologies, social structures and cultural forms of the twentieth century that we can really appreciate that Woolf lived through an unprecedented period of transition. She believed, albeit cautiously, that real change began in the first decade of the new century – even earlier than 1910, the date that she famously identified as a watershed:

> We were full of experiments and reforms. We were going to do without napkins, we were to have [large supplies of] Bromo instead; we were

going to paint; to write; to have coffee after dinner instead of tea at nine o'clock. Everything was going to be new; everything was going to be different. Everything was on trial.[32]

But even here, as Hermione Lee points out, the tone, combining domestic trivia with high-minded artistic ambitions, suggests that 'the lives of these young upper-middle-class free thinkers, all in their early twenties, were shaped by overlaps and gradual shifts, as well as by startling moments of change'.[33]

The issues for today's reader are how Woolf responded to these changes, how they are incorporated in her works and how Woolf conceived of writing history. Two significant areas of Woolf's work highlighted in post-1970s scholarship are her critique of the material conditions affecting women's lives in the early twentieth century, and the extent of her concern with, and critique of, war. In both these areas Woolf's fiction acknowledges that the dominant attitudes and beliefs were shaped, and often contested, during the Victorian period as much as it explores their survival and reformulation in the twentieth century.

IV

While many readers will be familiar with the radical feminist–pacifist essay *Three Guineas*, and with her representation of shell-shock in *Mrs Dalloway*, it has taken longer, as Mark Hussey points out, for critics to appreciate 'that *all* Woolf's work is deeply concerned with war'.[34] The nature of this concern has not proved easy to define, however. Judith Hattaway has pointed out that Virginia Woolf's view of the war was 'detached and sometimes idiosyncratic'; it 'does not figure in terms of mud or barbed wire but rather through its points of contact with the "ordinary" life left behind, and in its destruction of a secure past'.[35]

Hattaway's point that Woolf represents the war in a way that is 'contemplative' needs consideration. Throughout her work, Woolf is interested in the ontological implications of world events, in their potential to change the ways in which we think about history, social structures, identity, and boundaries, in a more incisive and interventionist way than the word 'contemplate' suggests. These lines of thought were strengthened after the First World War in which the social nexus between war and masculinity, consolidated in the late

Victorian period, fragmented. That war, as Eric J. Leed has reminded us, 'was a nodal point in the history of civilisation because it brought together material realities and "traditional" mentalities in an unexpectantly disillusioning way'.[36] One of the consequences of this was the confounding of 'the logic upon which the moral significance of war and the figure of the warrior had been based'.[37] But that logic was itself under pressure thirty years previously. While, as John Peck points out, the Victorian period saw the disappearance of the military code of the Wellington era, the 1880s saw the re-emergence of a new, strident form of militarism. This new militarism was evident in boys' adventure stories from the 1880s and 1890s, Jingoism, new uniformed organisations, public parades and the cult of empire. But, as Peck goes on to argue, late nineteenth-century culture was being pulled in a number of directions and 'alongside a strain of thinking in which the emphasis was nationalistic and triumphalistic, there existed a sombre stance'.[38]

The influence of the more sombre lines of thought about war in the late century upon Woolf is evident not only in her critique of the social nexus linking war and masculinity but in her refusal to see 'beginnings' and 'endings' as neatly identifiable and definable. One of the primary interests in *Mrs Dalloway* is the way in which the First World War did not end as some people thought with the armistice. As Truti Tate points out, the war actually had 'a number of practical endings: soldiers returning home, demobilisation, a return to a peacetime economy, the expulsion of many women from the labour force', and there were 'other aspects of the war [that] had no conclusion; significant numbers of people were permanently disabled or war neurotic; others were suffering from the deaths of relatives, lovers and friends'.[39] Woolf may not be concerned with 'mud and barbed wire' but, as Tate says, her work is 'a political attack on those who managed the social and economic aspects of the war and kept its victims under control afterwards'.[40]

Indeed, in Woolf's feminist historiography of war the two aspects of her fiction which I said earlier recent scholarship had highlighted – her concern with war and with the material conditions of women's lives – come together. For as James Longenbach has argued, 'the battle for women's suffrage, the battle for modern art, and the battle in the trenches' are all 'inextricably intertwined'.[41] The way they are intertwined in a refiguring of political and social history is very much of the historical moment. As Elaine Showalter points out,

'By the 1920s, women found themselves with little progress besides the vote (which had, in any case, been won by 1914) to show for their brief wartime emancipation'.[42] Although women's employment had skyrocketed during the war, these jobs were returned to men after the war. Consequently, by 1921 the female percentage of the workforce was exactly what it had been in 1911, that is 29 per cent. As Showalter goes on to argue:

> Denied their work and coping with emotional loss, many women felt despair at the prospect of returning to shopworn roles and old routines. For them, too, the war continued to be fought in the psyche, and the period of readjustment precipitated psychological problems.[43]

The Suffragettes undoubtedly had a profound influence on Woolf's life and work. Most of the women involved in politics and social work whom she knew were supporters of the campaign for votes for women. But her own direct involvement with it was more complicated and ambivalent than even she recalled when she boasted in 1940 of working for the vote for women when she was young.[44] As Hermione Lee points out, Woolf's involvement did not last long and in 1910, the year in which the Conciliation Bill was passed giving votes to about a million women, she admitted to Janet Case that she was worried about 'the inhuman side of politics' in which all 'the best feelings are shrivelled'.[45]

That worry is all too evident in Woolf's concern with war. Mark Hussey suggests that 'reading Woolf as a war novelist marks out a new trajectory for her fiction'. The domestic conflict he sees as engendered by the patriarchal family in the first two novels gives way to direct consideration of the effects of war in *Jacob's Room* and to fiction in which the private and the public are inseparable. But in the course of this book I seek to establish a different trajectory for Woolf's fiction to which readings of her as a war novelist have contributed.

The censorship, propaganda and myth-making which are essential elements of war confirmed, if they did not stimulate, Woolf's interest in how modern sensibility is shaped by mass culture. Although she did not feel that she could put the events in Europe into fiction because they were too close, she was both shocked and interested in Siegfried Sassoon's war poems, not simply because of their realism but because they exposed 'the terrible pictures which lie behind the colourless phrases of the newspapers'.[46] I do not wish to suggest that this was the first time that Woolf would have encountered such pictures. She could not have but been familiar with Kipling's representation of the overcrowded dykes in the Boer War, in which not only the glory of war but the Empire itself seemed to collapse. But the impact of Sassoon's work cannot be gainsaid. Nevertheless, while much criticism has emphasised Woolf's reaction to the 'terrible pictures', there is another dimension to Woolf's recognition of the importance of Sassoon's work – the way in which it reveals what is hidden by 'the colourless phrases of the newspapers'. Of particular interest in her fiction, as the passage quoted earlier from *The Voyage Out* suggests, is the way in which the individual life can be formed by language according to a larger system of thought embedded in that language. And that language has both surface and concealed meanings which, as in Evelyn's case, can block out part of the field of perception. During the war, Woolf, no doubt remembering also the scepticism of those strains of late-century thought opposed to Empire and colonialism, found herself doubting 'what some of the phrases we're ruled by mean'.[47]

V

As Kathy Phillips pointed out in 1994, 'it is only in the past fifteen years or so that Woolf has been recognised as a social thinker, let alone someone with a sophisticated grasp of complex ideologies'.[48] Nearly ten years previously, Alex Zwerdling lamented: 'Why has Woolf's strong interest in realism, history, and the social matrix been largely ignored? Why has it taken us so long to understand the importance of these elements in her work?'[49] But I quote from these critics not only to remind us that the notion of Woolf as a socio-political writer has a short and fairly recent history, but also to draw attention to the shift in the language used to describe this aspect of her work. While Zwerdling writes of 'realism', 'history' and the 'social matrix', Phillips thinks in terms of a 'sophisticated grasp of complex ideologies'.

From what Phillips says, the Virginia Woolf whom for years we were encouraged to see as an '*old-fashioned* avant-garde novelist, engaging in purely formal experiment with narrative and time',[50] would seem to have been laid firmly to rest. Or perhaps the enthusiasm for the reclamation of Woolf as a political writer has pushed the claim too far. The caricature of Woolf, wryly observed in Alex Zwerdling's words, as 'the immured priestess in the temple of art' who was 'interested in states of reverie and vision, in mapping the intricate labyrinth of consciousness', is not without its truth, albeit, at best, only a half truth.[51] Paradoxically, for a writer 'deeply engaged by the question of how people are shaped (or deformed) by their social environment',[52] many of the key political events of her day are marginalised or even ignored in Woolf's fiction. And often those events that are acknowledged are treated so cryptically or obliquely as to be scarcely visible. Although *The Years*, for example, is a historical novel covering the period from 1880 to 1937, the major happenings of those years – the Boer War, the death of Queen Victoria, the First World War, the rise of the Labour Party, the demise of the Liberals, the General Strike, the Wall Street Crash and the rise of the British Union of Fascists – are barely touched upon.

More than a decade on from Zwerdling's book, the question to ask is not why Woolf's strong interest in the socio-political matrix was largely ignored for nearly half a century but, given Woolf's interest in domestic and international politics, why do many key events enter into her work only cryptically – that is if they enter it at all? Even those critics who have acknowledged Woolf's cryptic rendering of contemporary history have had difficulty theorising what is happening in her novels. For example, Kathy Phillips argues convincingly that the various fragments of Woolf's fiction do trace a coherent though non-linear pattern, but she theorises this by invoking and taking issue with a tired argument – George Lukács's thesis that modernists jumble 'naturalistic' elements at random.

The pieces of the jig-saw begin to fit together when we realise that Woolf was interested not in historical events *per se* but in those historical forces embedded in organised social life that impinge on an individual life and determine its course. Even in her first novel, *The Voyage Out*, the narrator observes: 'The next few months passed away, as many years can pass away, without definite events, and yet, if suddenly disturbed, it would seem that such months or years had a character unlike others' (p. 103). In the course of her novels she returns to this notion of the 'character' of a milieu, developing an increasingly sophisticated understanding of what she meant by the term.

Any full discussion of Woolf's interrogations of the concept of history must inevitably involve us in modern theoretical explorations of historicism, to which I shall return later, and, because empire is a recurring preoccupation in Woolf's novels, of colonialism and post-colonialism. In several respects her thinking about empire is the product of the Victorian period mediated by the influence of the Bloomsbury group as metropolitan intellectuals and by writers such as Joseph Conrad, who highlighted the discrepancy between the orthodox views of empire and his own based upon lived experience. Throughout her fiction, as I shall demonstrate in the course of this book, it is possible to glean even in Woolf's early novels a number of the Victorian preoccupations with empire that lay behind the public grandiloquence of imperialism: fear of rebellion by subjugated peoples upon whose labour the empire depended; horror and guilt at the brutality involved in empire; distaste of mercantile colonialism which became more intense among Victorian metropolitan intellect-uals after the Great Exhibition of 1851 and was shared by Dickens and Tennyson; anxiety that the domestic economy was being bled dry by competition with other European powers for African territory and that Britain could not afford her rule over India; and disgust at the way Anglo-Indians treated the indigenous population. Woolf also draws on tropes evident in travel narratives, memoirs and letters produced by Victorian women that empire adversely affected the men brought up with its ideologies as well as those who worked for it.

Woolf's critique of empire, then, is liberatory but it is not unique to her, developing arguments against colonialism that were prevalent in the late nineteenth century. But she was also complicit, as was much Left-wing thought of her day about empire, in the disposition and operation of the contemporaneous world order. Highlighting colo-nial discourses as the object of analysis, her fiction displaces the cultures of India and Africa proper. *The Waves* evades cultural nationalism in India from the Indian's perspective and in focusing on reinscribing colonial anxieties about Indian independence risks privileging the cultural authority of the West. Any discussion of Woolf's critique of empire has thus to confront a sometimes blurred boundary in her work between an agency that is individuated, con-scious and active, and an agency that is social, unconscious and passive. In other words, one that can be devastatingly parodic and insightful in its critique of imperialism and one that is insufficiently conscious of its complicity in the disposition of the West's cultural authority. But Woolf goes beyond even radical nineteenth-century discourses in recognising, in *The Years* and *The Waves* for example, that subaltern notions of empire enter the master discourse of Englishness and transform it. In distinguishing itself from the colonised 'Other' and from the de-forming mimic countertext, Englishness in these novels is seen as constantly redefining itself.

VI

One of the key issues in recent critical theory is the extent to which postcolonial literary criticism has over-emphasised actual, historical events. It is now beginning to be recognised that such an emphasis in postcolonial criticism has displaced the importance of what Woolf called the 'character' of a milieu.[53] Obviously, one of the achievements of her fiction in its approach to politics is the way in which, as Zwerdling says, 'she takes up a public issue under discussion in her society, translates its dry abstract language into a particular human situation, finds her way to the heart of the conflict, and gives it intense dramatic life'.[54] But in her novels, Woolf also resists extrapolating from the epoch about which she is writing a history which strings one historical event or moment to another. Anticipating late twentieth-century criticism, Woolf is interested in the deep social structures hidden in the history of any period. As early as 1919, Woolf had become not merely sceptical but contemptuous of what she called 'historians' histories':

> No one who has taken stock of his own impressions since 4 August 1914, can possibly believe that history as it is written closely resembles history as it is lived; but as we are for the most part quiescent, and, if sceptical ourselves, content to believe that the rest of mankind believes, we have no right to complain if we are fobbed off once more with historians' histories.[55]

When Woolf is viewed as a novelist who is interested in the way in which history is turned into narrative and in how people's lives are shaped and deformed by the 'character' of a milieu, her 'sophisticated grasp of ideologies' can be seen as shaping, rather than as contradicted by, her oblique approach to key historical events.

How successfully post-1970s Anglo-American feminist criticism has reclaimed Woolf's interest in the politics, and especially the sexual politics, hidden in conventional histories is evident in recent, ostensibly unlikely, comparisons of Virginia Woolf and Angela

Carter.[56] The linking of Woolf, a celebrated modernist, with Carter, an *enfant terrible* of postmodernism, provocatively rewrites the history of the twentieth-century *avant garde*. It reveals two writers who in their different milieux are seriously engaged not only with the cultural, philosophical, scientific and psychoanalytic issues of their day, but also with how those issues are rendered in different discourses.

This understanding of Woolf's work takes us beyond some of the paradigms in which criticism of Woolf has become stuck; seeing her work as a response to a neo-realism in which 'things are meant to be as convincingly solid and opaque as brick even when they are not',[57] or commending a binarism of text and context that ignores how the latter is rendered, and even coded, in various discourses such as those mentioned above.

Throughout her work, there are suggestions that she sees 'reality' as a 'coded reality' to be deciphered before it can be reinterpreted. Critics have generally noted this in her, often oblique, writings on same-sex relationships. But with the exception of Angela Ingram, few critics have appreciated that Woolf was always a 'reader of culture'.[58] The breadth of her interest in interpreting cultural texts is evident in her review of Kipling's *Letters of Travel, 1892–1913* (1920) where she compares railway advertising posters and Kipling's depiction of the colonies: 'Just as the railway companies have a motive in hanging their stations with seductive pictures of Ilfracombe and Blackpool Bay, so Kipling's pictures of places are painted to display the splendours of empire and to induce young men to lay down their lives on her behalf.'[59] Alex Zwerdling suggests that her cultural critique had its origins in the way she survived the fashionable parties that she was forced to attend by turning them into a spectator sport.[60] An early story, 'Phyllis and Rosamond', suggests that this may have been partly true, but it undoubtedly had wider origins – in her day-to-day experiences as a woman, her observations, her conversations with other intellectuals, Victorian realist fiction, Renaissance literature, and in Victorian history and biography. In 'Phyllis and Rosamond', Woolf observes how

a study of history and biography convinces any right minded person that these obscure figures occupy a place not unlike that of the showman's hand in the dance of the marionettes; and the finger is laid upon the heart. It is true that our simple eyes believed for many

ages that the figures danced of their own accord, and cut what steps
they chose; and the partial light which novelists and historians have
begun to cast upon that dark and crowded place behind the scenes has
done little as yet but show us how many wires there are, held in
obscure hands, upon whose jerk or twist the whole figure of the
dance depends.[61]

Woolf's interest in 'that dark and crowded place behind the scenes'
– that may be interpreted both socio-politically and psychoanalytic-
ally – and in the number of wires upon which the dance depends was
also undoubtedly stimulated by, and in turn stimulated, her interest
in the Renaissance. As Juliet Dusinberre has observed, Woolf
regarded the Renaissance as 'the historic moment of rebirth for
women as readers and writers, and for men ill at ease with their
own inherited masculine culture'.[62] Despite the fact that in Montaigne's work 'women, children, madmen and the common people
jostle each other...in credulity, ignorance and irrationality',[63] it
seems to have offered Woolf a way of thinking which confirmed
her approach to a British, or specifically English, culture, in which
she was a participant but from many aspects of which as a woman
she was excluded. Like Woolf, Montaigne witnessed a society where
a particular codified version of reality was fostered by a reading of
Roman battles and the Roman ideals of heroism. Having found in
Montaigne the argument that 'an artificial, learned and bookish
eloquence is simply a means by which the ruling classes enforce
their authority over the commons, and by which men assert their
ascendancy over women',[64] Woolf became interested in how the
'artificial, learned and bookish eloquence' that had its roots in the
late nineteenth century and in the Renaissance itself reflected a
particular, structured version of 'reality', and in how it, in turn, fed
into a coded reality.

While, as critics have generally acknowledged, Woolf made external description illuminate psychic processes, she also made
external description illuminate the 'character' of a milieu, the
codified nature of reality. Although with less 'sport' and 'high-
kicking' than Carter,[65] Woolf is as impatient with what she perceived
as the distorted and distorting nature of the conventional and emergent social narratives that impinged on, and determined, individual
lives. Her fiction explores how these social narratives, particularly of
gender identity, war, imperialism and Englishness, are embedded in,
and legitimated by, the coded nature of 'reality'.

Woolf, of course, was not the only writer of the time or even of the late century, and certainly not the only woman writer, to question the distorted and distorting nature of how 'reality' was represented and presented, especially from the point of view of gendered expectations. Such a viewpoint was the pivot upon which what came to be regarded as New Woman writing turned. Much late-century, New Woman fiction, exemplified by Mona Caird and George Egerton, as Lyn Pykett argues, 'broke with or modified the representational conventions of realism ... either offered a different view (that of woman-as-outsider) or constructed a new version of reality shaped to a woman's desires'.[66] It rethought some of the basic Victorian assumptions, rewriting, for example, the plots of domestic realist fiction, by questioning whose interests were represented by them. In particular, as Woolf was to go on and do in her own fiction, it exposed the conflict between the fluid and changing nature of (particularly) women's experience and the fixed models of identity imposed by conventional gender roles.

VII

Throughout Woolf's fiction, certain gendered themes and preoccupations recur in her depiction of post-war Britain – for example, the greater preponderance of women in the public sphere, the emergent sexualities, the changing nature of the symbolic order, the relationship between war and masculinity, how national identity is defined, the shifting nature of the family, the politics of the urban environment and the increasingly bourgeois nature of the upper classes. While some of these themes are to be found in the work of other post-war writers, in Woolf's case they reflect her concern not only with the gendered but the codified nature of post-war English social life. Ultimately, the two perspectives are inseparable in her fiction.

If the first important point to bring to the fore in the wake of the demise of Woolf as an '*old-fashioned* avant-garde novelist' is the close interconnection in her work between narrative experiment, political analysis and intellectual debate, then the second is the way in which the 'textuality' or codified nature of her social milieu is consciously incorporated into, challenged and rewritten in her fiction. This requires us to read her work in a way which would be described in modern critical theory as 'cryptanalytical'.[67]

'Cryptanalysis' is a mode of reading which focuses upon what is concealed in the text. Its roots are in the Latin *crypta* – usually referring to any vaulted building partially or entirely below ground level – and *analyéin* meaning to loosen or untie. Woolf's interest in the *crypta* undoubtedly has its roots in her criticism of usually male-oriented histories and biographies. The lives of women, as is demonstrated in her short story 'The Journal of Mistress Joan Martyn', are partially hidden. The story's heroine, Rosamond Merridew, based on Woolf's cousin Rosamund Stephen, is a historian interested in family histories who discovers at Martyn Hall the journal of a fifteenth-century diarist, Mistress Joan Martyn, who prefigures the character of Judith Shakespeare in the later novel, *Orlando*. The diary is handed to her by her host, John Martyn, after a tour of the ancestral portraits from which wives and daughters are absent. The family is one which, as John says, 'deal[s] in grand-fathers' and he recommends the journals of the men rather than of Mistress Martyn.[68] Interestingly, there is a contradiction between what he says are Joan's dates and what is discernible from the diary itself. Since he had earlier prided himself on his knowledge of his (male) ancestors, we can only conclude that the error may not be Rosamond Merridew's mistake but his indifference to the female ancestral line. He has tried to read the journal, however, but it took him 'some time to get used to the writing' and the apparently crypto-graphical element of the text is underscored by 'the old girl's spelling' and by 'some queer things in it' (p. 41). While he means this rather negatively, it may be seen as positive if what John Martyn regards as the norm, his masculine way of looking at things, is rendered odd. The implication from this story is that Woolf's writing which privileges women's lives would appear as cryptographic from the perspective of mainstream biography as Joan's journal to John Martyn. Indeed, the conclusion of the story emphasises the *crypta* – literally as well as metaphorically. The last pages of the diary record Joan hiding what she is writing from her father's gaze. The story ends at a tomb in a church where Joan Martyn's grandfather is buried. She recalls how stone carved figures in crypts frightened her as a child but now she would like to do something that gave them pleasure but 'it must be something secret, and unthought of . . .' (p. 62).

Critics have usually adopted a cryptanalytical approach as part of a psychoanalytical reading of Woolf's work. Clare Hanson points out, for example, that particular passages of her first novel, *The*

Voyage Out, contain sub-textual references to Woolf's childhood abuse.[69] However, not only are historical and political events included in her fiction to be read in ways which we might today describe as cryptanalytical, but Woolf herself read events and the external world cryptanalytically. By describing Woolf's approach to events and the external world as cryptanalytical, then, I am suggesting that she analyses them in order to reveal what is partially hidden in them.

This approach is illustrated by her essay 'The Plumage Bill' (1920)[70] on a parliamentary bill to prohibit the importation of plumage which was the subject of public controversy while Woolf was working on *Jacob's Room*. The significance of the bill for that novel I shall discuss in a later chapter. The bill, after a successful initial passage through both houses and having become the subject of considerable press attention, was repeatedly balked in committee by the failure to secure a quorum. The essay is a reaction to this and more specifically to a comment made by H. W. Massingham, the editor of the *Nation*, directing attention to the fashionable women of Regent Street, declaring that '[the egrets] have to be shot in parenthood for child-bearing women to flaunt the symbols of it...'. The essay unearths and deciphers what is hidden or partially hidden in these events and in this statement, noting the misogynistic conflation of parent birds and child-bearing women. The essay begins with an image of what lies partially hidden, in this case behind the plate glass in the lower half of the houses of Regent Street. Those who 'steal a look and hurry on' are implicitly contrasted with the author who, as spectator, assumes a studied gaze and seeks to fill in 'certain blank spaces'. Woolf decodes Massingham's statement to find that what is hidden in its 'certain blank spaces' is the displacement of male guilt onto women. The women are blamed, concealing the part played by the hunters (who are men) who torture and kill the birds for profit, and also concealing the associated guilt of those (who are also men) who failed to support the bill in parliament.

The cryptographic nature of much of Woolf's writing creates problems for the reader. Why does Woolf apparently choose to complicate the interpretative nature of her work? What does the cryptographic handling of political events in her work suggest about her attitude towards them? Even while working on the fiction of the late 1930s in which the social criticism is more explicit than in some of the earlier 'modernist' writing, Woolf acknowledged the cryptic nature of her work and admitted that it may not be readily understood as a result. She was relieved by the reception of *The Years* because the greater social purpose of the novel 'may not be so entirely muted & obscured as I feared'.[71]

VIII

In the light of Woolf's own fears concerning the ostensible oblique nature of her fiction, and the danger she identifies here of writing cryptically, her sophisticated grasp of the ideologically coded nature of social reality may be usefully approached through ideas developed by the French social philosopher Michel Foucault. In the course of this book, I wish to suggest that Woolf's work should be seen in terms of his concept of 'archaeology' and the related concepts of 'historical *a priori*' and 'archive'. In *The Archaeology of Knowledge* (1969), Foucault argues that meaning can only be understood in relation to the discursive system as a whole. While initially he argued for an objective rather than an interpretative account of discourse, he revised this view out of growing recognition of the interconnectedness of discourse and power. Foucault came to think of the discursive system as consisting of a 'discursive formation', in which certain statements are granted a force and legitimacy denied others that are excluded from it, and 'discursive events' in which an utterance changes the configuration of statements that operates in a 'discursive formation'.

Although discourses in Foucault's view are precarious ensembles, 'conditions of existence' can be elicited from them by the 'archaeologist'. Foucault defines 'archaeology' as a practice that, like much of Woolf's writing, 'questions the already-said at the level of its existence'.[72] While this may sound initially applicable to the work of any writer, Woolf anticipates Foucault in her understanding of 'the already-said' as a discursive formation related to wider systems of power and also as a socio-cultural text. Foucault highlights how discourses like natural history, political economy or clinical medicine – to employ his examples – acquire a unity through time which cannot be attributed to the influence of particular *oeuvres*, books and texts.[73] Woolf's engagement with, for example, Englishness, imperialism, a consumer-oriented society or patriarchy, is with the unity that they have acquired through time. She is, therefore, really engaged by the statements, attitudes and practices that have acquired currency and legitimation over time or by those statements, attitudes and practices that have been excluded over time.

If Woolf's 'reading' of external reality has its origins, as Alex Zwerdling says, in her enforced attendance at fashionable parties she detested, her interest in how attitudes were encoded in cultural statements or texts may also have had its origins in her early life. Pinned over one of the fireplaces in her family home at Hyde Park Gate was the statement: 'What is it to be a gentleman? It is to be tender to women, chivalrous to servants.' Indeed, much of her fiction can be interpreted as a cryptanalytical reading and reinterpretation of this. Woolf is interested in Englishness, patriarchy, empire and masculinity as 'fields' constructed upon, and through, such statements.

These interests were undoubtedly inspired by Leonard Woolf's *Empire and Commerce in Africa*, published in 1920, and discussions of its ideas which she had with Leonard for at least the previous five or six years. Throughout the book, Leonard Woolf insists that historians have tended to discuss the effects of beliefs and ideas about Europe, Britain, France, Germany and Africa upon those countries and continents and have not paid sufficient attention to their effects 'upon the lives of men and women'.[74] Echoing his wife's feelings about history, Leonard is critical of the way in which 'from our schooldays history is represented falsely to us as the logic of events rather than the logic of men's beliefs and desires....'[75]

At about the same time, then, the Woolfs became interested in abstractions and metaphors and the relationship between these and attitudes and behaviours in individual lives. Leonard urges the reader to listen in the speeches of politicians for what contemporary critical theory would call 'discourses' – for how what appear to be statements of facts are statements of ideas and beliefs. For example, he argues that all Chamberlain's speeches during the 1890s were informed by a particular discourse about the State – that the machinery of Government should be directed towards the commercial interests of the nation.

The currency that particular discourses such as nation, masculinity or medicine, and the way of looking at the world that they represent, acquire over time constitute in Foucault's terms the 'historical *a priori*'. By historical *a priori*, Foucault meant not only that certain beliefs, values and attitudes were embodied in discourse but that discourse forced these historically determined beliefs on to others. Two aspects of the historical *a priori*, as defined by Foucault, are pertinent to Woolf's engagement with the key discourses of post-war Britain. First, while Foucault maintains that discourses impose certain ways of looking at the world on to participants, he accepts that the basic statements in which these beliefs are embodied cannot be completely uncovered by the 'archaeologist' and often emerge only in fragments. Second, Foucault does not see the rules that characterise discursive practice about, for example, what constitutes 'Englishness' as 'imposed from the outside on the elements that they relate together' but as 'caught up in the very things they connect...'.[76]

The domain of statements constituting the historical *a priori*, and through which it is articulated, Foucault called an 'archive'. In the way in which it anticipates Foucault's notions of the historical *a priori* and of the 'archive', Woolf's fiction presents us with a particularly sophisticated attempt to understand and explore post-war Britain. Like all modernist fiction, it calls into question the assumptions of classic realism about the certainty and totality of truth, knowledge and perception, offering the reader instead a more fragmented, partial and subjective world. But its fragmentary nature is also a result of the fact that it is written within the space opened up by what is not incorporated within the historical *a priori*. Thus, Woolf's fiction is written both within the historical *a priori*, as no individual can be entirely free of his or her historical context, and in a dialectical relationship to it or to aspects of it. Bearing in mind the difficulty, according to Foucault, of uncovering the statements and discourses that constitute the *a priori*, the fragmentary and oblique nature of Woolf's social criticism is not surprising.

An issue in scholarship pertaining to Woolf's novels has been the perceived shift in the later fiction to a more overt social realism. But, in many respects, criticism which tries to anchor the later fiction in a traditional form of verisimilitude misses the point of Woolf's work. In the course of this book I wish to argue that even in her later work Woolf is nearer Foucault's concept of an 'archaeologist' than of a social realist. Woolf's primary aim is not simply to define the thoughts, representations, images, preoccupations that are concealed and revealed in discourses. The primary purpose in her work seems to be, as Foucault says of the 'archaeologist', with how knowledge about, for example, masculinity, sexuality, Englishness, or a consumer-oriented economy is diffused, gives rise to concepts, and takes form in cultural texts; with how notions and themes migrate from the field (of statements) in which they originated to another; and with how the 'historical *a priori*' relates to institutions, social customs, private and public behaviours, or political discourses.[77]

We can see this in brief if we take up Susan Stanford Friedman's argument that we should pay more attention to the tropes of travel and movement in Woolf's work; that 'we should shift our emphasis from reading Woolf's texts as ethnographies of dwelling – deconstructions of family plots; revisionings of domesticity – to seeing them as ethnographies of travelling'.[78] Within Foucault's framework the recurring significance of movement in Woolf's fiction opens up not only the fluid nature of empire, places, institutions, customs and behaviours but her interest in the migration of ideas from one domain to another, her concern with 'statements' in their dispersion, and with what is not unifiable in the historical *a priori*, something evident even in her first novels.

3

Pent-up Voices:
The Voyage Out (1915),
Night and Day (1919) and
'Kew Gardens' (1919)

> *But it is in the future; and there is a deep gulf to be bridged between the dying world and the world that is struggling to be born.*
> Virginia Woolf, 'The Leaning Tower'[1]

I

Although not as radical as her later fiction, Woolf's first two novels are more innovative than critics have generally recognised. Reflecting perhaps the influence of New Woman writing to which I referred in the previous chapter, they subvert established genres – the male-oriented narrative of voyage and the romance, respectively – resisting the traditional closures associated with them. This rewriting of established genres is evidence not only of Woolf's desire to do something new – which she was to realise fully in the 1920s – but of her awareness, shared by the New Woman writers, of the ideological nature of narrative.

Each of the early novels is highly derivative. The plot of *The Voyage Out*, as Alice Fox has observed, resembles Elizabethan prose narratives, especially Hakluyt's *Voyages, Travels, and Discoveries of the English Nation*,[2] and, in its river journey into the jungle, also recalls Joseph Conrad's *Heart of Darkness*, both authors who are recalled in Woolf's review of Kipling's *Letters of Travel, 1892–1913* (1920). Again, Julia Briggs has pointed out that *Night and Day* is in the British tradition of novels of social comedy, ultimately derived from Jane Austen, which was revived by E. M. Forster: novels focusing on the experiences of a young woman within a particular milieu or social group and culminating in her marriage.[3]

As Clare Hanson observes, Hakluyt and Conrad 'do not seem at first particularly relevant to Woolf's purposes [in *The Voyage Out*], until we recognise that one of the points she wishes to underscore is the world of difference between the possibilities open to men both in the Elizabethan period and the early twentieth-century, and those open to women'.[4] Woolf to my mind, though, seems to be less interested in making that point *per se* than in suggesting how it is embodied in, and legitimated by, a range of texts that in her day were taken too much for granted. Critical discussions of this aspect of Woolf's first novel have tended to focus on her use of the male, imperialist adventure genre in terms of the differences between the genders. But, in different ways, each of the first two novels demonstrates Woolf's wider concern with the dominant political thinking of her day concerning not only gender identity but Englishness and empire, and with what was concealed in or by these discourses, in particular relationships between women and debates concerning colonialism.

The Voyage Out can be seen as a 'voyage out' into womanhood and into empire. Both interpretations of the book's central metaphor reflect Woolf's interest even at this early stage in her writing with the intersection of space, political history and the 'imaginary'. While for men there were 'voyages out', for women there were only 'voyages in' – to marriage and domesticity. However, in this chapter I want to suggest that these interpretations of the novel's metaphor – an exploration of womanhood and empire – are not mutually exclusive, and in fact are interleaved throughout.

The version of *The Voyage Out* with which most readers are probably familiar is the one which Virginia and Leonard Woolf published at the Hogarth Press in 1929, based on the 1915 edition;[5] itself the product of numerous rewritings. There is not the space in this book to discuss the many changes that Woolf made. Throughout all the revisions of the novel, the nuclei of the plot remained the same. Rachel Vinrace takes a voyage to South America on her father's ship, accompanied by her uncle and aunt-by-marriage,

Ridley and Helen Ambrose and an acidic friend of Ridley's from his Cambridge University days, Mr Pepper. At Lisbon, they are joined by Richard and Clarissa Dalloway who disembark on the coast of Africa. At the Ambroses' villa in the imaginary resort of Santa Marina, Rachel meets a varied cohort of tourists including Arthur and Susan. But the Rachel who appears for the first time in the 1912 draft (in which the novel is entitled *Melymbrosia*) suggests that, while working on the book, Woolf became interested in realising an ambition she had first mentioned to her friend Lytton Strachey in 1909, to articulate some of the perplexities in the condition of being a woman. It is important, though, not to allow this intense scrutiny of an individual psychic life in Rachel to distract us from the novel's remaining primary concern with the social discourses embodying the values associated with 'romance', marriage and domesticity. The ideology of romantic love confidently assigned women a place in the social order mediated through relationships with men, suggesting that they might achieve happiness only by undergoing a complex process of self-subversion, and defined love as a state of self-transcendence and self-forgetfulness. By contrast, in each of the first novels, Woolf presented the social discourses of romance and marriage as, in Foucault's terms, 'precarious ensembles'.

In the account of Rachel catching sight of Arthur and Susan making love, for example, the focalisation of Rachel and the narrator merge to undermine conventional assumptions about heterosexual relationships. The passage emphasises Rachel's repulsion – Arthur is described as 'butting [Susan] as a lamb butts a ewe' – and, unable to decipher 'from her expression whether she was happy, or had suffered something' (p. 156), Rachel is positioned both within and outside the dominant discourse of heterosexuality, and within a space in which covert attitudes and feelings are indicated but not fully articulated, as in the following conversation she has with Terence Hewet:

> 'I don't like that,' said Rachel after a moment.
> 'I can remember not liking it either,' said Hewet. 'I can remember –' but he changed his mind and continued in an ordinary tone of voice, 'Well, we may take it for granted that they're engaged. D'you think he'll ever fly, or will she put a stop to that?'
> But Rachel was still agitated; she could not get away from the sight they had just seen. Instead of answering Hewet she persisted:
> 'Love's an odd thing, isn't it, making one's heart beat.'

'It's so enormously important, you see,' Hewet replied. 'Their lives are now changed for ever.'

'And it makes one sorry for them too,' Rachel continued, as though she were tracing the course of her feelings. 'I don't know either of them, but I could almost burst into tears. That's silly, isn't it?'

'Just because they're in love,' said Hewet. 'Yes,' he added after a moment's consideration, 'there's something horribly pathetic about it, I agree'. (p. 156)

Throughout the novel, as here, the social expectations of 'romance', of how women should behave and feel, and of what constitutes gender identity, are alternately affirmed and undermined. Helen Ambrose most obviously represents, perhaps, what is concealed in the dominant ideas of womanhood and how these occluded elements threaten to destabilise them. But through her views and her behaviour she also demonstrates that the dominant discourses are fluid and mutable, engaged in constant dialogue with those elements that challenge them.

From the outset of the novel, Helen is an enigmatic character who invites reading from a cryptographic perspective. We do not discover her reasons for undertaking the voyage with her husband or why it involves separation from her children. Throughout the voyage, she prefers the company of men rather than women, indulging in reading and intellectual conversation, and, most cryptically of all, is the preferred companion of the homosexual St John Hirst. Her behaviour suggests that gender identities as personal spaces are 'performative' and concealing. This duality is mirrored in the representation of the family house as having a public, patriarchal front that belies an alternative, feminine space:

> They were very much afraid of [Rachel's] father. He was a great dim force in the house, by means of which they held on to the great world which is represented every morning in *The Times*. But the real life of the house was something quite different from this. It went on independently of Mr Vinrace, and tended to hide itself from him. (p. 246)

But, if the novel is a 'voyage out' into the nature of womanhood and of love and friendship between women, that does not mean it is simply an exploration of covert lesbian relationships.[6] Rather, it explores the boundaries between friendship and love and between emotional intimacy and homoeroticism, suggesting the fragility of these concepts but also, in anticipation of Foucault, exploring how they are related to concepts of power.

Helen's relationship with Rachel may be a complicated mosaic of sexual and emotional attentiveness and aloofness, but it is also shot through with a number of covert, power scenarios. Helen admits to Rachel that her one true woman friend was her husband's sister, whose place she would seem to want her daughter Rachel to take, thus complicating the position of Helen as a maternal surrogate for Rachel. The inequality in their relationship, however, is brought to the fore when Helen is aroused to jealousy by Clarissa's interest in Rachel and Rachel's involvement with Terence Hewet. At their first disembarkment, Rachel and Terence, who by now have agreed to marry, wander into the wilderness, itself a symbolic space in which the conventional discursive formations have collapsed. There she not only finds herself knocked to the ground by Helen, in what, as Patricia Smith points out, is 'savage and erotic violence',[7] but sees Helen and Terence 'looming' over her kissing. Hence Helen is not only linked with Terence as co-predator in Rachel's rape fantasies but posited as a rival with Terence for Rachel's love.

There is a comparable imbalance of power in Rachel's other two important assignations with women. On both occasions, women who are more confident than Rachel invite or take her into their territorial space – literally and metaphorically – in which she becomes both excited and confused. Evelyn Murgatroyd marches Rachel forcefully to her room, two stairs at a time, while Miss Allan, a schoolmistress, invites Rachel to her room with the sense of authority one feels that she exercised in the classroom. Evelyn, who is motivated to help 'unfortunate women' because her own parents are unmarried, is clearly an important site of illegitimate power in the novel. But she is also specifically seen as a predator: 'she never gave up the pursuit of people she wanted to know, and in the long run generally succeeded in knowing them and even in making them like her' (p. 285). Both women proceed cryptically, employing subterfuge to get close to Rachel. Evelyn tries to enlist Rachel's help in women's rights and social causes, but her real motive seems to be to get physically and emotionally close enough to Rachel to put her hand on her knee. Miss Allan invites Rachel to try ginger during conversation in which ginger is analogous to covert sexual pleasures and in which she provocatively undresses in front of Rachel, even conspicuously seeking her help in undoing the hooks on her clothes. Reading signs and faces is an important part of these encounters: Evelyn 'searched up into [Rachel's] face as if she were trying to read what kind of character was concealed behind the face' (p. 290), while nearly everything Miss Allan says – 'it is your duty to try now' and 'you may add a new pleasure to life' (p. 295) – has to be read cryptanalytically.

II

Too little attention has been paid, though, to how far the social imaginary of women as 'Other' is linked in the novel with patriarchy, and with the 'othering' of what is not English. Ridley Ambrose is called 'Bluebeard' by the small boys on the London Embankment, an insult that conflates the two senses in which the novel may be viewed as a 'voyage out', into womanhood and into empire. Here patriarchy, the 'othering' of the female and empire are interlinked in a single image. Helen Wussow points out that Ambrose resembles Bluebeard, the notorious husband who hid his murdered wives in a closet, in more than his beard. He is a fervent misogynist and on board the *Euphrosyne* he hides away in a secret room.[8] But Bluebeard's castle can also be seen as analogous to the empire; precious tapestries woven of silver and gold – like the spoils of empire and the magnificence of its cities – hid the horrors within, prefiguring Richard Dalloway's admission, in turn echoing Conrad's *Heart of Darkness*, that he knows of 'horrors – unmentionable things done in our very midst!' (p. 67) under colonialism.

The duplicity of patriarchy and the nature of empire are linked in the image of the sphinx which Ridley passes on the London Embankment on his way to comfort Helen who is crying because she is to be separated from her children. While, at one level, Helen is emblematic of the mother country weeping for her lost children, at another level she underscores Ridley's misogynism in that he is unable to show her genuine emotion. In Greek legend, the sphinx devoured everyone who could not answer the question: 'What goes first on four feet, then on two, then on three, and is the weaker the more feet he has?' While referring to the idea of human ageing, that man is weaker the more feet he has, the sphinx might also allude to the fear of many Victorian intellectuals that the empire, once a strength, had overreached itself and become a drain on the country.

There is a pointed irony – of which he is unaware – in Dalloway's remark that the 'English seem, on the whole, whiter than most men, their records cleaner' (p. 67). In *The Voyage Out*, Woolf tries to exploit the parallels between narratives of popular romance and narratives of empire: the dramatisation of conquest and resistance; conflicts over desires and aspirations; the imagination of a different way of life; and journey as a metaphor of physical and emotional transformation. In Pepper's account of the discovery of what became known as Santa Marina, the colonies are seen in terms of the female to be penetrated and conquered – South America is 'a virgin land behind a veil' (p. 96). But Woolf does not draw a reductive analogy between the condition of being a woman under patriarchy and the colonised subject under empire. Pepper's rather simple-minded analogy is only one voice in the novel that as a whole explores not only the irreducible complexities but the shifting notions of class and gender in relation to the myths of empire and Englishness. This is evident in the comparison of the place of the female in Elizabethan family life, where the male is traditionally the head of the household, and with the expectations that men had of women in the colonies.

Pepper's version of the comparison is again rather simple-minded, 'Here a settlement was made; women were imported; children grew' (p. 96). There is some truth in what he says, women were imported into the colonies that men had made as they were imported into the homes that men had made for them and for the purpose of bringing up children. Pepper's stark account highlights the gendered nature of movement in both the Elizabethan and Victorian periods that cannot be gainsaid. In both domestic narratives and the stories of empire, it is usually the men who are able to initiate movement and determine their destinations, while the women are the subjects of travels and destinations that have been chosen for them. But the novel as a whole offers a more sophisticated version of women's position in the domestic sphere and in the empire. Rachel's experiences on her own 'voyage out' are employed to challenge the expectations of patriarchy and the way in which they are represented in Victorian romance narratives. *The Voyage Out* links home and empire as places of unbelonging – as unstable, conflictual and alienating – as well as places of belonging. Women, Woolf points out, are not simply objects of movement as the word 'imported' suggests, but are subjects within that movement, to which they have a critical and dialogical relationship.

In the coupling of the ships of the Mediterranean Fleet with predatory beasts, the interleaving of patriarchy and the empire acquires a particularly sinister edge, for this imagery, suggesting the brutality of colonisation, also invokes Rachel's fear of sexuality and of men. As Helen Wussow observes, 'Within the context of *The Voyage Out*, sexual encounters between men and women in a patriarchal society frequently take on the dynamics of physical violence and international conflict'; Dalloway's kiss is 'a method of attack', and later Rachel's search for a definition of love ends with her returning home 'much as a soldier prepared for battle'.[9] But the ships of the Mediterranean Fleet as predators are linked to women as well as men as co-predators in Rachel's rape fantasies. Evelyn Murgatroyd, whom I pointed out earlier is seen in the novel as a predator, is associated through her language with empire and particularly with the way in which imperialism conceived of its territories as blank spaces – de-scribing them – in order to impose its own interpretations:

> 'If I were you,' said Evelyn, turning to him and drawing her glove vehemently through her fingers, 'I'd raise a troop and conquer some great territory and make it splendid. You'd want women for that. I'd love to start life from the very beginning as it ought to be – nothing squalid – but great halls and gardens and splendid men and women. But you – you only like Law Courts!'   (p. 151)

Here Evelyn unwittingly invokes a particular cartographic practice that has become the subject of much attention in recent postcolonial theory and would have been obvious to Woolf from her husband's work on *Empire and Commerce in Africa*, which reproduces maps of Africa in 1880, where the vast interior is literally blank, in contrast to the crowded map of partitioned Africa circa 1914. As Simon Ryan has observed,

> the cartographic practice of representing the unknown as a blank does not simply or innocently reflect gaps in European knowledge but actively erases (and legitimizes the erasure of) existing social and geo-cultural formations in preparation for the projection and subsequent emplacement of a new order.[10]

III

In scrutinising notions of Englishness and empire, Woolf draws attention in *The Voyage Out*, as in all her work, to the inevitable internal and external exclusions of nationhood. Evelyn's invocation of British military heroes – 'I'd raise a troop and conquer some great territory...'– is a cryptic reference not only to the way in which Victorian history and biography are constructed around the exploits of the great men, but the new militarism emerging in the late century to which John Peck has drawn attention, exemplified by figures such as General Gordon and associated with race, empire and nation.[11] Her identification with them suggests in turn how the privileged position enjoyed by men of the upper class was inextricably linked to empire, a point developed later in Rachel's reading of the entries in *Who's Who*. Not only are women absent from the professions, though conspicuously included as 'actresses', but Sir Roland Beal's biography is constructed around education at one of the best public schools, marriage and distinguished regimental service. Significantly, his wife is not named and only referred to as the daughter of a person whom we may presume is distinguished enough to be recognised by readers of the time. Women, and the female body in its softness and liquidity, represent a threat to the imaginary masculinity, particularly in its psychotic hardness, that drives empire and which in its extreme form is evident in the account of the massacre of the wounded and dying at Santa Marina.

The link between empire and opportunities for upper-class men is reinforced in Richard Dalloway's account of his youth which also suggests that men of his class had the kind of amateurish approach to politics and empire – and all the more English for that – later satirised by Kazuo Ishiguro in his novel *The Remains of the Day*:

> Walking – riding – yachting – I suppose the most momentous conversations of my life took place while perambulating the great court at Trinity. I was at both universities. It was a fad of my father's. He thought it broadening to the mind. I think I agree with him. I can remember – what an age ago it seems! – settling the basis of a future state with the present Secretary for India. We thought ourselves very wise. I'm not sure we weren't.   (p. 66)

While women in Victorian and Edwardian Britain usually had to endure a static domestic situation – although in Woolf's fiction domestic situations are hardly ever entirely static – men's lives are full of movement. In this cryptically written passage, Woolf is criticising the ease of access to education and power for a particular class of males of which Richard Dalloway is a representative. He is able to attend 'both universities' – he feels no need to name them because his class is so closely linked with Oxford and Cambridge – not through hard work but because of a 'fad' of his father's. There is an obvious tension between the word 'momentous' (and the discussion of what could affect the lives of another people) and the casually privileged lifestyle of yachting, walking and riding. The reference to attendance at these universities as broadening the mind of people like Richard is overtly ironic – they confirm him in his attitudes. But, as throughout the novel, there is also a suggestion – 'what an age ago it seems' – of significant movement having occurred, of the milieu having had its day. Not only are women absent in this account of Richard Dalloway's universities, but only his father is mentioned. The absence of the mother is a point that conflates both Rachel's 'voyage out' into the discovery of her own body and sexuality and the novel's 'voyage out' from, but into, the nature of Englishness, masculinity and empire. Symbolically, as the *Euphrosyne* prepares to leave South America, it is said to have 'lifted up her voice and bellowed thrice like a cow separated from its calf' (p. 95).

The 'voyage out' is a 'voyage in' to Englishness in that, as in Conrad's *Heart of Darkness*, the real horror is at the heart of civilisation. *The Voyage Out* takes Rachel not only into her own sexuality but elements of her country of which she is not aware. In explaining his ideal to Rachel, Richard Dalloway confusingly shifts from a discussion of empire – 'the dispersion of the best ideas over the greatest area' – to asking Rachel – who had 'scarcely walked through a poor street' – if she had ever been in a factory (p. 67). This only appears confusing until we realise how the novel, from its opening description of London, 'reads' the social organisation of England according to a model of imperialism. The journey which the Ambroses take from the West End prefigures the journey up the Amazon and seems to view the relationship between the West and the East End as analogous to that between the centre and the colonies. The upper-class areas of London, with their electric lamps, well-finished houses, plate-glass windows and hansom cabs, are supported by the working class who live on the bread line, analogous to the way in which English civilisation is propped up by the colonies. But throughout there is a sense of menace and danger, what Freud called the 'uncanny', that anticipates Rachel's fear of adult sexuality and her eventual death, but also suggests that all is not well with the empire at home or abroad.

The link which Woolf saw between the brutality of empire and male sexuality within a patriarchal system is suggested by the objects that adorn the mantelpiece in the sitting room on the boat: 'Twisted shells with red lips like unicorn's horns ornamented the mantelpiece, which was draped by a pall of purple plush from which depended a certain number of balls' (p. 14). Much of the imagery here suggests a preoccupation in the convex and the concave with male and female genitalia. But what is disturbing is the way in which the images represent the repressed uncanny in both adult sexuality and empire. The reference to the mirror framed with shells is perhaps a pointed allusion to Freud's 'mirror stage' that was supposed to contribute to the formation of a boundary body-ego. But Woolf seems to be suggesting that it does not put an end to a child's concern with its own body. Empire is seen as a grotesque extension of the stage at which a child's attention is arrested by objects that are redolent of the pleasurable satisfaction it obtains from its own body.

IV

Throughout *The Voyage Out*, England is rendered 'foreign' and 'strange'. But this is as true of the radicalists' discourses about England as the official histories. In describing his philanthropic achievements, Richard Dalloway almost sentimentalises the Lancashire mill workers for whom he has won an hour a day in the fresh air. In later novels Woolf engages with the texts of the past from the perspective of occluded histories that have not been as determined by the discourses in which they are located as the official histories. However, this is not the case here. Richard Dalloway's philanthropy is the product of Victorian discourses of the working class rather than his own instincts. Similarly, Helen's account of the Mall with men selling picture postcards, 'wretched little shop-girls' and bank clerks in tall coats, seems to be based on a Victorian picture or picture postcard rather than first-hand observation (p. 108). The England invoked in conversation is the mythical England of pre-war English poetry: 'meadows gleaming with water and set with stolid cows, and clouds dipping low and trailing across the green hills'; 'the flat land rolling away to the sea, and the woods and the long straight roads' (p. 350).

As Jane Wheare has pointed out, Woolf's 'diaries record a sharp awareness of the way in which the unfamiliarity of a foreign country may lead the traveller to cast a critical light on accepted cultural habits and customs'.[12] But in *The Voyage Out* Woolf seems to be doing even more than this. Victoria had bound Britain not only to its colonies but to Europe through age, experience and the marriage of her children and grandchildren. But after her death Britain seems a much smaller place and the influence of the empire appeared to being diminishing quickly,[13] as Woolf suggests in the following passage:

> From a distance the *Euphrosyne* looked very small. Glasses were turned upon her from the decks of great liners, and she was pronounced a tramp, a cargo-boat, or one of those wretched little passenger steamers where people rolled about among the cattle on deck. (p. 94)

The declining nature of the empire is pursued through references to Swift's *Gulliver's Travels* – the boat is compared to a 'recumbent giant' with small boats 'swarming about her' (p. 94) – and, divested of the heroism and glory with which the Victorians imbued it, is revealed for what it always was and became increasingly so within the Victorian period as a result of new technology and improved communications – an empire of trade.

Few details in Virginia Woolf's novels are randomly selected and this is as true of the early work as the mature fiction. The Dalloways board the vessel in a country which had established one of the world's most significant empires, especially in the fifteenth and sixteenth centuries, when Portugal took possession of Brazil, Goa, Moluccas, Senegal, Gambia and Ceylon, and had even set foot on Chinese soil. From Lisbon Vasco da Gama had set sail for India. But Lisbon introduces not only the motifs of empire, global exploration and conquest but also the trope of the vulnerability of the great empires: Portugal was itself conquered by the Spanish and in 1755 Lisbon was destroyed by an earthquake. Indeed, the reference to the waves that 'kept returning and washing against the sides of the ship' while the *Euphrosyne* is anchored at the mouth of the Tagus is more ominous than it might appear, for Lisbon, after the earthquake struck, was nearly wiped out by an almighty tidal wave from the Tagus. The vulnerability of empires is suggested here with reference to Britain as well as Portugal, for it was from Lisbon that the Spanish Armada sailed for Britain in 1588, a fact which anticipates the rivalry between the English and the Spanish in Pepper's account of the conquest of Santa Marina in the Elizabethan period.

Eric Hobsbawm maintains that the era from 1875 to 1914 may be called 'the Age of Empire' because it developed a new kind of imperialism, confirming Leonard Woolf's arguments in *Empire and Commerce in Africa* which, as I pointed out in Chapter 2, although published in 1920 would have been the subject of conversations with Virginia while she was working on *The Voyage Out*. While the economic and military supremacy of the capitalist countries had been established beyond question by the middle of the nineteenth century, there was no systematic attempt to translate that power into formal conquests and annexations, Hobsbawm argues, until after 1880. Then, 'most of the world outside Europe and the Americas was formally partitioned into territories under the formal rule or informal political domination of one or other of a handful of states'.[14] The new imperialism of the late nineteenth century was a product of the emergent international economy. One of the key developments of the nineteenth century was the creation of a European-centred global economy which reached parts of the world remote from Europe.[15]

The references to cargo-boats and merchant vessels in *The Voyage Out*, then, reflect Leonard Woolf's argument that the imperialism of the late nineteenth century was different from that of the seventeenth and eighteenth centuries in its determination 'to exploit commercially uncivilised nations'.[16] He was not arguing that economic exploitation was not always a motive in the development of empire but insisting that previously it was not as important as other motives – primarily, an attitude of superiority over other nations. His point was that, in the later nineteenth century, imperialism was distinguished by 'the singleness and purity of motive for the policy, of the keener consciousness of what the motive was'.[17] Of particular relevance to *The Voyage Out* was his observation that 'the nearer we get to 1914, the more single becomes the economic purpose in this movement, and the more conscious of this economic motive become those who direct'.[18]

Although the travellers' destination, the South American Amazon, signifies both a Conradian journey into empire and, for Rachel, a frightening exploration of her own body, it might have been suggested by the Second Book of Spenser's *The Faerie Queene*, a text to which Woolf alludes frequently in her novels:

But let that man with better sence aduize,
That of the world least part to vs is red:
And dayly how through hardy enterprize,
Many great Regions are discouered,
Which to late age were neuer mentioned.
Who euer heard of th' Indian *Peru*?
Or who in venturous vessell measured
The *Amazons* huge riuer now found trew?
Or fruitfullest *Virginia* who did euer vew?[19]

The Faerie Queene is undoubtedly another important intertext given
the novel's juxtaposition of the twentieth century and the Elizabethan period. Spenser's work, written between 1579 and 1594, is
very closely associated with its milieu, and portrays Spenser's fascination with the achievements of Elizabethan England, rendered as a
land of fairy and romance. Woolf might well have had this depiction
in mind in the account of Rachel's room where she could 'defy the
world, a fortress as well as a sanctuary' for, as well as being described
in these military terms, it is 'an enchanted place, where the poets
sang and things fell into their right proportions' (p. 136). Spenser's
poem also anticipates *The Voyage Out* in its focus upon the navy,
celebrated through the inclusion of prominent figures such as Lords
Howard, Essex and Hudson.

In *The Voyage Out*, the link between Englishness, patriarchy and
imperialism is cast in a particularly sinister light by the appearance of
the British navy, the Mediterranean Fleet, and the effect that it has on
the observers on board the *Euphrosyne*. The fleet itself signifies, as
Leonard Woolf pointed out, how the axiom that 'the power of the
State can be and should be used upon the world outside the State for
the economic purposes of the world within the State' had 'turned
whole nations into armies, and industry and commerce into weapons
of war'.[20] Described as 'sinister grey vessels', the ships are 'eyeless
beasts seeking their prey' (p. 72). 'Low in the water, and bald
as bone', their description suggests pirate ships with their skull and
crossbones, rather than a British naval fleet. But it also foreshadows
the account of the Elizabethan English sailors' behaviour in South
America where they are said to have 'despatched the wounded, drove
the dying into the sea, and soon reduced the natives to a state of
superstitious wonderment' (p. 96). Again, the picture of the Elizabethan sailors having 'fangs greedy for flesh' (p. 96) conflates the
predatory nature of imperialism, prefigured in the description of the

Mediterranean Fleet, and, from Rachel's point of view, male sexuality.

There is, however, no hint of an association between colonialism and male sexuality in Clarissa Dalloway's response to the Mediterranean Fleet, even though the reader cannot help but notice how her sense of awe at the appearance of the British warships anticipates the 'superstitious wonderment' of the natives at Santa Marina, prior to their massacre. For Clarissa Dalloway, the Mediterranean Fleet is an element within a particular version of British history which is, to use Hayden White's term, 'poetic', as she demonstrates in remembering England in a conversation with her husband:

> Being on this ship seems to make it so much more vivid – what it really means to be English. One thinks of all we've done, and our navies, and the people in India and Africa, and how we've gone on century after century, sending out boys from little country villages – and of men like you, Dick, and it makes one feel as if one couldn't bear *not* to be English! Think of the light burning over the House [The Houses of Parliament]. (p. 51)

Her response is not simply to a warship but to a larger codified 'reality' of which it is a part. The Mediterranean Fleet makes Clarissa proud to be English. Not until the ships are out of sight are the British able to talk to each other 'naturally', and then the talk is of 'valour' and 'death', the heroic ideals of empire (undermined by the reality of an empire of trade routes) which lead to talk of the magnificent quality of British admirals. However, to many readers at the time, the Mediterranean Fleet would have signified Britain's vulnerability as well as her greatness. For between 1905 when Woolf began to conceive the novel and 1913 Britain was locked in a naval race with Germany which for much of the time she appeared to be losing – and Germany knew it, repeatedly refusing to agree to the limitations which Britain sought to impose. In 1912 Lord Haldane, and in 1913 Churchill, were rebuffed by Germany in their attempts to negotiate a limit to German naval activity.

If Woolf derived her location of South America from *The Faerie Queene*, it may be that she also borrowed Spenser's technique of intertwining the narrative with topical allusions. As de Selincourt maintains, these are 'not coincident throughout with the main plot, but fitful and elusive, appearing and disappearing according as the characters and situations suggest a parallel to the actual world'.[21]

Throughout *The Voyage Out*, Woolf's allusions to contemporary events are similarly 'fitful and elusive' and occur according to characters and situations. As in many of her novels, there are cryptic references to parliamentary events of the years during which the novel was written. For example, the novel alludes to Lloyd George's abortive attempt to introduce Women's Suffrage (women over 30 received the vote eventually in 1918; women over 21 in 1928). Miss Allan's sister, Emily, writes to her in a letter that the political prospects for women in England are not good and that although Lloyd George has taken up the Bill she is doubtful that he will be any more successful in getting it adopted than those before him. The difficulties are seen, however, as yet another challenge to be overcome. An allusion to Arthur Balfour's involvement with the Irish Question as Chief Secretary for Ireland in 1887 and his recommending the partition of Ireland in 1911 is also introduced. But *The Voyage Out* reflects its times more broadly, too. Woolf began work in earnest on the novel shortly after the Conservatives in 1906 suffered one of the most overwhelming and spectacular defeats in the history of the party to which the increasing sense of disillusionment had contributed. Criticism of politicians and especially of the growing gap between the rich and the poor were very much a sign of the times after Edward VII assumed the throne in 1901. Indeed, as L. C. B. Seaman points out, Edward was the only monarch since Charles II to identify himself with 'smart' society and the 'much increased display of affluence by the rich' contributed to the 'increasing hostility of the poor towards the wealthy which Lloyd George was to exploit so high-spiritedly between 1909 and 1911'.[22] In taking the upper-class English out of their supporting social structures, therefore, the novel mirrors the kind of critique which was occurring in Britain itself in the period 1905–12.

Ostensibly, though, Rachel's death appears to contradict the subversive nature of the novel. It might be seen as a punishment for her transgressive character and even as a symbolic restoration of order. However, her suicide could also be seen as the only option open to her and an attempt on Woolf's part to resist the traditional closure of the novel in which the heroine falls in love with and marries the hero. It has also to be considered in context with other elements of the novel's ending. The storm at the end would seem to symbolise the reconfiguration within the novel of the discourses of romance and womanhood. The guests who cannot but be aware of social and cultural change gather in the hall, secure because they are able to retreat from the windows – so as to avoid looking out – but still hearing the thunder outside. The lightning almost lifts the skylight from its joints. These images of traditional structures being threatened are juxtaposed with that of a moth whizzing over their heads, dashing in a confused state like Rachel herself from lamp to lamp. Significantly, given what happens to Rachel, one young woman suggests that it would be kinder to kill it, anticipating the decision to which Woolf seems to have come.

V

Many of the discourses questioned in *The Voyage Out* – Englishness, empire, the social structure, love and marriage – Woolf was to regard as part of the rationale for fighting the First World War and, not surprisingly, they are subject to further scrutiny in her second novel conceived in 1916 and published in 1919. While recent scholars such as Julia Briggs have argued that although *Night and Day* does not specifically mention the war it is 'shaped by it and the sense of crisis it induced',[23] not all its reviewers recognised this. Katherine Mansfield famously criticised it in a letter to J. M. Murray for (in her opinion) ignoring the war: 'The war never has been: that is what [the novel's] message is'.[24] In fact, the subversive content of the novel, belied by its conventional format, passed most critics by. In her review, Mansfield summarised the case against the book, arguing that it had been written as if modernist and experimental fiction had never been: 'We had thought that this world was vanished for ever, that it was impossible to find on the great ocean of literature a ship that was unaware of what has been happening'.[25]

The criticism that the novel depicted 'an untroubled Edwardian tea-party world' took Woolf herself by surprise because she was writing similar criticism of other novels. Hermione Lee observes that, in her journalism, Woolf was carving out her own version of modernism:

> The war drastically confirmed that there had to be 'new forms for our new sensations'. Novels which realistically described pre-war families, like Galsworthy's *Beyond* or Hugh Walpole's *The Green Mirror*, were reflecting a world which 'the war had done nothing to change'; but those mirrors had been 'smashed to splinters'. By 1920 she felt that

there was a case to be made against anyone who read like 'a pre-war writer'.[26]

Lee asks us to accept that Woolf was preaching one thing and doing another. In her essay 'Modern Novels', Woolf, alluding to *Night and Day*, admitted that she was writing 'thirty-two chapters after a design which more and more ceases to resemble the vision in our minds'.[27] But, this admission notwithstanding, her surprise at the novel's reception, and the vehemence with which she otherwise argued for a 'new writing', suggest that, despite her misgivings, she believed while she was writing it that it was more radical than reviewers found, and that even she considered it so, with hindsight. Ironically, the debate over the traditional and modernist nature of fiction enters the novel, albeit cryptically, when Cassandra challenges William Rodney for not having read Dostoevsky's *The Idiot* – which Woolf read herself in 1915 while she was working on *Night and Day* – prompting William to respond that he has at least read (the traditional) *War and Peace*.

While recent criticism has been kinder to the novel, it has generally sought to excuse rather than refute the allegation that it is set in 'an untroubled Edwardian tea-party world' that was inappropriate to post-war Britain. John Mepham, for example, suggests that Woolf, having 'withdrawn into her own terrible, dark night of the soul . . . was in no mood to respond to the broader historical catastrophe that had been going on all around'.[28] One of the reasons why its subversive nature has not been fully recognised is that it is such a cryptic text for which its heroine, Katharine Hilbery, acts as an anchor and point of focus.

It is now generally accepted that Katharine is based on Woolf's sister Vanessa Bell to whom the novel is dedicated and with whom Woolf stayed, together with the pacifist Duncan Grant, while working on it. But there are similarities between Katharine and Woolf herself. Not only was she born, like Virginia and Vanessa, into an upper-middle-class literary family but also, like Woolf, reacts vehemently against her family's obsession with the works of great men. Like Mistress Joan Martyn's house in Woolf's earlier short story, this is a residence that seems to 'deal in grandfathers', or at least one in particular, for the household is dominated by the worship of her grandfather, Richard Alardyce, buried in Westminster Abbey at Poet's Corner. Both her parents live 'cryptic' lives in both the literal and metaphorical sense of *crypta* – they are preoccupied with the trivial minutiae of the lives of the dead poets Byron and Shelley. (This may be itself a cryptic criticism of Woolf's own father's work as the editor of the *Dictionary of National Biography*.) Since Katharine's role is to help her mother with the biography she is writing, and to show visitors the relics of empire which the Hilberys keep in the house, her life, too, is virtually identified with a crypt, for 'The smaller room was something like a chapel in a cathedral, or a grotto in a cave. . . . But the comparison to a religious temple of some kind was the more apt of the two, for the little room was crowded with relics'.[29] The connection between Katharine and a crypt is developed later in the novel when we learn that every time she enters her mother's room, the atmosphere reawakens 'early memories of the cavernous glooms and sonorous echoes of the Abbey where her grandfather lay buried' (p. 114). Invoking the ancestors buried at the Abbey, Woolf conflates the two meanings of *crypta* – the literal meaning of 'vault' and the metaphorical meaning of 'secret'. Such is Katharine's identification with them that she feels that 'she knew their secrets and possessed a divine foreknowledge of their destiny' (p. 115).

VI

Night and Day, then, is a novel that has to be read with secrets and a hidden sense of destiny in mind. Katharine's identification with the room in which the relics are kept is evident in her extensive knowledge of its contents. But the identification, imposed upon her by her mother, is not what she would wish for herself. Her mechanical explanations of the relics signify her alienation but are also acts of subversion. She challenges many of the narratives of empire, simultaneously deconstructing (in the sense of 'undo') her family's close association with British imperial history.

A number of the items reveal how the family's distinguished ancestral line is inextricably bound up with the British empire in India, in particular. The walking-stick belonging to her uncle, Richard Warburton, for example, is significant because he rode with Havelock to the relief of Lucknow during the Indian Mutiny. However, their importance is dependent upon a particular interpretation of the Indian mutiny and of Lucknow, for example, as a historical event. The novel, thus, exploits a tension between the relics

viewed synchronically as heirlooms and objects of historical significance and perceived diachronically within an interpretative narrative
that is subject to change. In her presentation of the sword belonging
to Clive of India, who is generally regarded as responsible for laying
the foundations of the British empire in India, Katharine refers to him
as 'Clive' as if to suggest that not only the sword but Sir Robert Clive
himself has been appropriated by the family. In other words, she
relocates Sir Robert Clive, a remote historical figure, to a place of
familiarity within the family. This proximity is entirely imagined but
dependent again upon a shared cultural acknowledgement of Sir
Robert Clive's place in the foundation of the British empire. In fact,
the obvious respect accorded Clive within the family and within the
culture to which the Hilberys belong is not commensurate with the
facts about Sir Clive with which Woolf could expect her readers to be
familiar. As Kathy Phillips reminds us, 'in contrast to his idealised
reputation...Clive's career was rife with disobedience to company
orders, swashbuckling, and bribery'.[30] The way in which the Hilberys have turned objects associated with the British in India into
family relics parallels the imaginary figuration of events such as the
siege of Lucknow in British history in order to create an hegemonic
understanding of empire. But, ironically, as a rebel who obviously
does not share her family's obsession with these relics, Katharine
would seem to identify with the Indians rather than with those who
crushed the rebellion and with the maverick, rather than the idealised, Clive of India.

The books in the relic room are red and gold while behind the glass
there is a long skirt in blue and white colours associated, as in the
previous novel, with the British empire. We are informed that
Katharine's 'background was made up equally of lustrous blue-and-
white paint, and crimson books with gilt lines on them' (p. 14). This
sentence epitomises the cryptic nature of the novel. While it appears
to reinforce Katharine's association with the ancestral line and its
involvement with empire, she is being observed at this point by Ralph
Denham who disapproves of the family's involvement in India. The
word 'gilt' is thus double-edged and might also be interpreted as lines
of family guilt.

Indeed, when we first encounter Katharine, it is clear that her
subversively cryptic ways of speaking and behaving have become
an important part of her personality even though her irony is lost
on Denham. For example, in picking up a pair of the poet's slippers

she comments, 'I think my grandfather must have been at least twice as large as anyone is nowadays' (p. 10), allowing such mundane remarks to express her secret sense of rebellion. But, paradoxically, Katharine is also notable for her silence (her rebellion is expressed through gestures and what is not said rather than what is said). Visitors are puzzled by Katharine's silence, which they can only seem to explain in terms of what it is not, rather than what it is: 'the only other remark her mother's friends were in the habit of making about it was that it was neither a stupid silence nor an indifferent silence' (p. 41). Despite her own silences, though, Katharine sometimes finds silence difficult to cope with in others:

> Here she stopped for a moment, wondering why it was that Mr Denham said nothing. Her feeling that he was antagonistic to her, which had lapsed while she thought of her family possessions, returned so keenly that she stopped in the middle of her catalogue and looked at him. (p. 11)

Its preoccupation with silence (particularly silence as itself cryptic and difficult to decode) reinforces the cryptic nature of the novel as a whole, which in many respects is the 'novel about Silence...the things people don't say' (p. 249) that Terence Hewet talked of writing in *The Voyage Out*. Indeed, the closing scenes of the novel are structured on the articulation of silence: Mrs Hilbery 'seemed to draw her conclusions rather by looking at her daughter than by listening to her' (p. 507); Mr Hilbery is alerted to his daughter's feelings by 'the ominous silence with which his words were received' (p. 500); Ralph Denham's sense of Katharine causes him to lapse into silence; Denham and Katharine sit 'depressed to silence at the dining-room table' (p. 498), and at the end of the novel they bring themselves 'acting on a mood of profound happiness, to a state of clear-sightedness where the lifting of a finger had effect, and one word spoke more than a sentence' (p. 532).

VII

Although the whole of *Night and Day* is based around apparently static situations such as those that close the novel, their significance depends upon movement rather than stasis. The novel begins with Katharine imagining someone bursting in upon the tea-party when that is precisely what happens. As a stranger, Ralph Denham is an agent of disruption. Katharine lives in Cheyne Walk, an exclusive street in Chelsea, while he lives in Highgate, merely an up-and-coming middle-class district. In their initial conversation, Denham makes Katharine defensive – 'We don't live at Highgate, but we're middle-class too, I suppose' (p. 13) – suggesting that the relative status of the upper middle and lower middle class was changing. Within this context, Denham's entry into the house is important because he brings with him the movement of the world outside, for his body is 'still tingling with his quick walk along the streets' and the omnibuses and cabs of the street are still 'running in his head' (p. 4). He represents the space of travel and of the larger social world to which Katharine has limited access. However, it would be too simple to argue that Denham brings change into a static environment. He may criticise Katharine implicitly (in asking her what she does) and her family explicitly (in railing against the nineteenth-century worship of great men), but if he had been more alert to her he would have realised that Katharine had already begun to criticise herself and her family. Importantly, this is a novel where most of the significant movement occurs beneath the surface. As Julia Briggs points out, 'Katharine's desire for power and independence remains largely unrecognised, operating at a subliminal level...'.[31]

In *Night and Day*, Katharine can be seen as embarking, albeit less dramatically than Rachel, on a 'voyage out'. Like Woolf herself, she is the product of an upper-class literary family and rejects 'conventional' suitors for a man from a lower class with passionate convictions. But *Night and Day*, mainly located in peacetime Chelsea, is a less exotic novel than *The Voyage Out*. South America, the other side of the world literally and metaphorically, functions in *The Voyage Out* as an imaginary, symbolic and linguistic space through which Woolf is able to render Englishness as 'foreign'. If the novel had been set in England it would have been difficult to imagine Woolf being able to attempt such a critique and employing such sensational imagery as that used to describe the Mediterranean Fleet, for example.

Some of the differences between the mood of *Night and Day* and *The Voyage Out* are evident in the different ways in which space, cultural politics and the imaginary intersect in the descriptions of the London Strand in each novel. In *Night and Day*, what Michel de Certeau calls the 'believable' – the material organisation of space – seems to be privileged:

> Late one afternoon Ralph stepped along the Strand to an interview
> with a lawyer upon business. The afternoon light was almost over, and
> already streams of greenish and yellowish artificial light were being
> poured into an atmosphere which, in country lanes, would now have
> been soft with the smoke of wood fires; and on both sides of the road
> the shop windows were full of sparkling chains and highly polished
> leather cases, which stood upon shelves made of thick plate-glass.
>
> (p. 132)

However, Woolf emphasises objects in the shops – 'sparkling chains',
'highly polished leather cases' and 'thick plate glass' – not for themselves but for the total atmosphere that they create. In other words,
the material 'reality' of the Strand is transfigured by an imaginary
'reality' that is not imposed from outside but created, like discourse,
by the interconnection of the various elements of which it is composed. In the account of the Strand in *The Voyage Out*, as I suggested
earlier, the imaginary 'reality' is based on what de Certeau calls the
'memorable' (comparable to Freud's the 'uncanny'):

> As the streets that lead from the Strand to the Embankment are very
> narrow, it is better not to walk down them arm-in-arm.... One after-
> noon in the beginning of October when the traffic was becoming brisk
> a tall man strode along the edge of the pavement with a lady on his
> arm. Angry glances struck upon their backs. The small, agitated
> figures – for in comparison with this couple most people looked
> small – decorated with fountain pens, and burdened with despatch
> boxes, had appointments to keep, and drew a weekly salary, so that
> there was some reason for the unfriendly stare which was bestowed
> upon Mr Ambrose's height and upon Mrs Ambrose's cloak. But some
> enchantment had put both man and woman beyond the reach of
> malice and unpopularity. (p. 3)

Here the intersection of a material space – for example, the narrow
streets – and an imaginary space of guilt, anxiety and anger creates
an environment that is oppressive, oppressed and threatening. While
in *Night and Day*, Ralph is able to step out into the Strand, the
Ambroses feel that they have to stride. In *Night and Day*, the Strand
is a place of 'belonging', suggested by the reference to the smoke of
wood fires. But in *The Voyage Out*, the Strand is an imaginary and
linguistic place of 'unbelonging' as the language – 'angry', 'agitated',
'burdened', 'unfriendly', 'malice' and 'unpopularity' – suggests, and
from which the Ambroses are saved by the 'enchantment' of their
wealth and position.

Recognition in *Night and Day* of the need to disrupt traditional notions of place for a more symbiotic relationship between the imagination and its surroundings is commensurate with the way in which the novel challenges conventional linguistic structures (although it is only later that Woolf developed techniques based on this principle). When Ralph Denham first enters the novel as an agent of disruption, he interrupts people who are already 'launched upon sentences' (p. 4), and although he speaks fluently and spasmodically at the end of the book, he 'persuades' Katharine into

> a broken statement, beautiful to him, charged with extreme excitement as she spoke of the dark red fire, and the smoke twined round it, making him feel that he had stepped over the threshold into the faintly lit vastness of another mind, stirring with shapes   (p. 531)

This is paralleled in the way in which the novel severs the taken-for-granted affinity between the rational self and the accepted social order, positing a new imaginary, 'stirring with shapes, so large, so dim, unveiling themselves only in flashes, and moving away again into the darkness, engulfed by it' (p. 531). As Ralph and Katharine walk together at the end of the novel, the street becomes a site of impulse (they suddenly mount an omnibus), of darkness and, in the exaggerated shadows that are too close to their faces, a site for the return of what Freud called the 'uncanny'. The darkness is interrupted by 'great knots of activity', and stirs with shapes, as lights are drawn close together and then separate. The street is also a site of fantasy as they imagine themselves 'victors in the forefront of some triumphal car' and 'spectators of a pageant enacted for them' (p. 529). But there is also something primal about this new imaginary. The city has the capacity to bring its walkers into confrontation with what is beyond the semblance of its daytime configuration. They enter a non-verbal, pre-logical space that is elusive, enigmatic and beyond the orderly, believable world, and is only partly translatable into language. Donatella Mazzoleni, in an essay on the city and the imaginary, maintains that elementary pulsations emerge sensationally where the habitat has 'lost its ancient organic characteristics', its similarity to the body and where 'the modality of continuity between body and space has been replaced by the modality of "difference"'.[32] At one level, this account of Ralph's and Katharine's experience of space anticipates Mazzoleni's argument that space cannot be adequately theorised only in terms of semiology but within a framework that acknowledges the origin of space in our bodies. But it also demonstrates how the city by the beginning of the twentieth century had lost what Mazzoleni calls its 'ancient organic characteristics' and how continuity of body and space had been replaced by 'difference'.

At the end of the novel, Ralph Denham and Katharine find themselves for reasons that they do not understand at the bottom of the stairs leading to Mary Datchet's flat: 'a thin, yellow blind caused them to stop without exactly knowing why they did so' (p. 532). Despite her relationship with Ralph, Katharine's eyes rest 'satisfied' on Mary's window. Exactly what is the nature of the relationship between Katharine and Mary and the satisfaction that she finds in thinking of Mary remains enigmatic, but it also belies the conclusion of the novel as a traditional romance or as a novel of social manners. The cryptic and elusive last few pages resist a traditional sense of closure. Ralph is left 'trying to piece together in a laborious and elementary fashion fragments of belief, unsoldered and separate, lacking the unity of phrases fashioned by the old believers' (p. 534). He and Katharine are in the midst of a discursive event in which the old configurations are being realigned: 'Together they groped in this different region, where the unfinished, the unfulfilled, the unwritten, the unreturned, came together in their ghostly way and wore the semblance of the complete and the satisfactory' (p. 534). But there is more than realignment being proposed here. The references to the 'unwritten', the incomplete and the 'different region' draw attention to the *crypta* in the dominant discourses of gender identity and gender relationships. When Ralph thinks of Rodney, Cassandra and Old Joan, he finds that it is not possible 'to link them together in any way that should explain the queer combination which he could perceive in them' (p. 533).

VIII

Whereas *The Voyage Out* challenges the traditional discourses of Englishness, empire, love and romance, exposing their fluid and precarious nature, *Night and Day* is more concerned with dramatising what is occluded by them and is often incomplete and difficult to articulate. The central protagonist of the first novel of the 1920s similarly finds himself confronted by what the discourses of Englishness, empire and masculinity with which he has grown up suppress, but the bridge between Woolf's first two novels and *Jacob's Room* is provided by the short story 'Kew Gardens', published in the same year as *Night and Day*. The Gardens, providing an image of fecundity, are the setting in *Night and Day* for the initial attraction of Ralph and Katharine. But in the short story, the Gardens provide a vehicle for suggesting the fragmentariness of English life and of the influence of the war on the public mood. The latter is not revealed until the end of the story and even then obliquely in, for example, the drone of the aeroplane through which 'the voice of the summer sky murmured its fierce soul' and the reference to how 'all gross and heavy bodies had sunk down in the heat motionless and lay huddled upon the ground'.[33] The horror of war is suggested even more cryptically in the references to 'wrought steel turning ceaselessly', the 'yellow and green atmosphere' which in colour is redolent of mustard gas, and in the image of the 'shattered marble column' (p. 95).

The effect of this ending is to cause us to rethink the suggestiveness with which the story presents 'reality'. In the light of the concluding paragraph, the story would seem to present us with the 'raised and symbolic' quality of the language that characterises the writing in *Between the Acts*, Woolf's last novel written at the outset of the Second World War. In the opening description of the oval flower bed, the red, yellow and blue flowers cast intricate colours on the brown earth, echoing how empire has coloured the earth at Santa Marina in *The Voyage Out*. The attention to the 'surfaces of things' in what E. M. Forster called the 'queer world of Vision' of 'Kew Gardens'[34] is not simply a reaction against the style of Arnold Bennett. Details are observed with an attention that is unusual and an imagination that is reluctant to impose coherence on the fragmentariness of life around the narrator. What seems to be important is interruption – in the snail's progress, in the interplay of light and shade, in conversations, in relationships. The writing is located not at the surface of things as Forster suggests, but in the *crypta* beneath the surface signified by 'the vast green spaces beneath the dome of the heart-shaped and tongue-shaped leaves' (p. 90). The shapes that the leaves suggest – 'heart' and 'tongue' – are not coincidental. For the story enters the space beneath the heart in Eleanor's secret memory of a kiss by a grey-haired old woman when she was a child – 'the mother of all my kisses all my life' (p. 91) – that has remained for Eleanor a symbol of the bond between daughters and mothers that exists beneath but outside the predatory heterosexuality in the space beneath Simon's words. Insensitively recalling a previous love of his to Eleanor, he projects his desire into a circling dragonfly.

It is difficult to read this story without recalling the interest in silence in *Night and Day*. The more ponderous of the two women walking together ceases to listen to her partner's conversation, looking 'through the pattern of falling words at the flowers standing cool, firm and upright' (p. 93). Trissie's male partner obviously feels distanced by the *crypta* in what she says – 'but who knows... what precipices aren't concealed... he felt something loomed up behind her words, and stood vast and solid behind them' (p. 94). Their relationship is expressed in the pauses between what they say and through silent actions. The story is situated at the cusp of the articulated and unarticulated, the visible and the concealed. An interest in the 'in-between' pervades the entire story. Again, one of the two women walking together sees 'as a sleeper waking from a heavy sleep' (p. 93), the young couple are 'in that season which precedes the prime of youth' (p. 94) and the mad gentleman positions his thoughts between heaven and earth. The combination in this story of a sense of the fragmentariness of modern life, of the importance of what is unspoken, of a 'reality' encoded beneath the surface of things and of the sense of something looming up behind words is developed, as we will see in the next chapter, as an important dimension of *Jacob's Room*.

4

Pre-war England:
Jacob's Room (1922)

> *How essential it is that we should realize that unity the dead bodies, the ruined houses prove. For such will be our ruin if you, in the immensity of your public abstractions, forget the private figure, or if we in the intensity of our private emotions forget the public world.*
>
> Virginia Woolf, *Three Guineas*[1]

I

Jacob Flanders' name predicts his death in the First World War, itself frequently anticipated throughout *Jacob's Room* in its imagery and cryptic connotations. Thus, for the astute reader, the experience of reading this novel is one in which the future, which we usually read to discover, is known virtually from the outset. By the time the novel was published, of course, Flanders had become synonymous with death in battle. It was common knowledge that nearly a third of the million Britons who went to war were killed in Flanders, a loss commemorated in John McCrae's then popular poem 'In Flanders Fields'. However, while we are clearly meant to read Woolf's first post-war novel in relation to a particular historical context, its relationship to that context is a complex one.

The war enters *Jacob's Room* only indirectly. The novel is concerned with a pre-war England, viewed from a post-war perspective, in which a particular generation of men were brought to death, and with a society that in its cultural and psychological make-up seemed drawn to war. As Alex Zwerdling has said, 'we may be reading about

[Joseph's] intellectual and amorous adventures, but we are also witnessing the preparation of cannon fodder'.[2] In this respect, *Jacob's Room* can be seen as a rejoinder to McCrae's poem:

> In Flanders fields, the poppies blow
> Between the crosses, row on row...
> We are the Dead. Short days ago
> We lived, felt dawn, saw sunset glow.
>> Loved and were loved, and now we lie
>> In Flanders fields.[3]

The subject of the novel is what is absent from these lines: the real lives of the soldiers, their characters and their motivations that are denied in their idealisation. Zwerdling sees the novel as a response to obituaries which sentimentalised death in battle, arguing that Woolf's intention is to show that many of those who died were not heroic but 'confused and immature'.[4] Woolf herself was under no illusion as to the nature of some of the war heroes. In 1915, she commented in a letter: 'one might have thought in peace time that [our compatriots] were harmless, if stupid: but now that they have been roused they seem full of the most filthy passions'.[5]

The crude public image of the Great War, as Elaine Showalter has observed, was one of 'strong unreflective masculinity, embodied in the square, solid untroubled figure of Douglas Haig, the British commander-in-chief'.[6] *Jacob's Room* by contrast places Jacob in the middle of a complex web of shifting, imagined, half-imagined, imposed and semi-imposed 'realities'. Although Betty Flanders is not herself upper class, through her association with wealthy and well-connected men her son Jacob is able to attend Cambridge while her brother Archer enters the Royal Navy. He can thus be seen, like Richard Dalloway in *The Voyage Out*, to be privileged by his gender and class. But he is also a prisoner of them, as is apparent when he finds himself alone in his rooms at Cambridge University:

> The stroke of the clock [in the swaddlings and blanketings of the Cambridge night] even was muffled; as if generations of men heard the last hour go rolling through their ranks and issued it, already smooth and time-worn, with their blessing, for the use of the living.
>
> Was it to receive this gift from the past that the young man came to the window and stood there, looking out across the court? It was Jacob. He stood smoking his pipe while the last stroke of the clock purred softly round him. Perhaps there had been an argument. He

looked satisfied; indeed masterly; which expression changed slightly as
he stood there, the sound of the clock conveying to him (it may be) a
sense of old buildings and time; and himself the inheritor.[7]

The problematic nature of Jacob's 'inheritance' is underscored by the
allusions to the biblical Jacob who stole his brother's blessing and
birthright. The privileged life which Jacob inherits is similarly a
'blessing' and 'a gift from the past'. But it is also a curse not only in
that it condemns him to die at Flanders but because of the alienated
and alienating nature of his life as described in the novel.

Jacob's Room is unusual for its time, even though some reviewers
welcomed it as a typically modern work, because of the opaque way
in which pre-war English culture is represented. But the novel is more
than a modernist experiment. Woolf's purpose was to present a
critique of pre-war England without sacrificing the subtlety of its
discursive formations on the altar of polemic. As one reviewer
observed: 'It is not Jacob's history simply, nor anyone else's, but the
queer simultaneousness of life, with all those incongruous threads
which now run parallel, now intersect, and then part as unaccountably'.[8]

Jacob's Room does not conform to the structure and characteristics of the *bildungsroman*, the narrative of a character's social and
personal development. As one reviewer noted: 'In *Jacob's Room*
there is not only no story, but there is no perceptible development
of any kind. We get an outline of the kind of young man that Jacob
was and of the kind of woman that his mother was, and very subtly
and admirably are some of the features touched in.'[9] Like *Orlando*,
the novel reflects Woolf's long-standing interest in debunking traditional biography. Here we must remember that, educated at home,
she was given the nineteenth-century classics of history and biography to read but that she responded to them in more critical
ways than her father probably intended. *Jacob's Room* is a novel
which in many respects is the product of that radical, intelligent
reading. Jacob's life is presented in the barest detail and in short
sections that do not have clear chronological links. There is not
the in-depth discussion of the conventional turning points in the
character's life – childhood, education, obtaining a profession and
making one's way in the world. Relationships between essential
characters are outlined in episodes that seem to have been chosen
at random while Jacob's romantic encounters – with Florinda, Fanny

Elmer, Clara Durrant and the older married woman Sandra Wentworth Williams – do not lead to any important growth in self-knowledge.

II

Jacob's Room should also be seen as a response to Edward Marsh's *Memoir* of Woolf's friend Rupert Brooke, written to accompany the *Collected Poems* (1918). Several critics have stressed the obvious connections between Jacob and Brooke who died during the Great War.[10] While there are parallels between Jacob Flanders and Woolf's brother Thoby, whose silence and awkwardness Jacob shares, Brooke was the primary influence on Jacob even though he did not die in Flanders, but of blood poisoning in April 1915, in the Aegean while serving in the British Navy. As Judith Hattaway notes, Jacob Flanders and Rupert Brooke 'inhabit[ed] the same world – Cambridge, travel, living in London, philosophy, poetry, studying Elizabethan poetry and drama'.[11] Woolf knew Rupert when they were both children and the opening sequence of the novel may owe something to the holiday he spent with the Stephen family at St Ives, Cornwall. She met Brooke again when he was a student at Cambridge, visiting him at Grantchester in 1911. Such was the closeness of their relationship for a time that they swam naked together and she knew details of his life – that he had an affair with Ka Cox and that he had a nervous breakdown – that were not commonly known. However, critics have been reluctant to consider fully how Woolf was disturbed by the mythologising of Brooke in Marsh's *Memoir* which she found 'disgraceful soppy sentimental'.[12]

Although Woolf initially found the *Memoir* 'repulsive', her attitude towards it was more complicated than Hermione Lee implies in her biography of Woolf. In August 1981 she wrote to Mrs Brooke:

> I had rather hoped that you would *not* see my review, as I felt that I had not been able to say what I wanted to say about Rupert. Also I am afraid that I gave the impression that I disliked Mr Marsh's [M]emoir much more than I meant to. If I was at all disappointed it was that he gave of course rather his impression of Rupert than the impression which one had always had of him partly from the Stracheys and other friends of his own age. But then Mr Marsh could not have done otherwise, and one is very glad to have the Memoir as it is.[13]

While critics have generally stressed the differences between *Jacob's Room* and the conventional *bildungsroman*, the similarities between Woolf's novel and Marsh's *Memoir* have not received the same attention even though the style and format of the novel – 'an imaginative portrait from scraps of memory, fragmentary reports of friends, books fingered, scenes visited by Jacob'[14] – suggests someone writing a memoir rather than a full-blown biography. There are a number of parallels between the two works. Marsh's *Memoir*, albeit within a tighter chronological structure, similarly sketches Brooke's background, the periods spent in Cambridge and London and in travel. One of the earliest symbols that anticipates Jacob's death and contributes to the dark, brooding side of the novel is the black rock, emerging from the sand 'like something primitive' (p. 6) beside which the reader first encounters the child Jacob. It echoes, and may well have been suggested by, the image of 'Rupert's island' with which Marsh closes his *Memoir*: ' . . . it stood out in the West, black and immense, with a crimson glowing halo round it'.[15] Woolf, however, removes the halo, intent to demythologise Brooke, the war and the generation of 'doomed youth'. The rock is covered with 'crinkled limpet shells' – the noun 'shells' is ominously double-edged – and, significantly, the small boy is able 'to feel rather heroic, before he gets to the top' (p. 63). The scene in which Jacob sits naked in the sun looking at (the) Land's End may well have been inspired by Rupert Brooke's letter cited by Marsh in his *Memoir* in which he describes himself 'lying quite naked on a beach of golden sand' at Lake George.[16] Certainly the image of Jacob sitting naked would have a particular resonance for readers of Woolf's own generation. For Jacob is soon to be a soldier and much war writing drew upon a pre-war tradition of homoerotic poetry that ran from Whitman to Hopkins and Housman. As Paul Fussell maintains,

> One of the pre-existing motifs available for 'translation' and 'purification' by Great War writers was provided by the tradition in Victorian homoeroticism that soldiers are especially attractive.[17]

Images of naked young men and boys bathing from Victorian homosexual writing and photography bequeathed to war writing a trope of youth unscathed. Here nakedness liberates the male subject as Jacob is momentarily liberated. But post-war, the trope acquired new associations, of soldiers bathing and of vulnerable flesh soon to be destroyed by machines.[18]

There are, though, a number of differences between the account of
Jacob at Land's End and Brooke at Lake George. Not only the
geographical but the emotional context has been changed. Challenging Marsh's eulogy for a generation 'willing to die for the dear
England whose beauty and majesty he knew', Woolf introduces a
profound melancholy that is encapsulated subsequently in the waves
that 'slapped the boat, and crashed, with regular and appalling
solemnity, against the rocks' (p. 67). However, she borrows the
suddenness with which Marsh transports Brooke back to society
with one line – 'But he was quite able to cope with civilisation
when he got back to it.' Jacob is also returned to 'civilisation' in
one sentence: 'After six days of salt wind, rain and sun, Jacob
Flanders had put on a dinner jacket' (p. 74). The dinner jacket
suggests Woolf's interest in how English society is 'framed'. Here
again the novel may be a response to Marsh's *Memoir*, or at least to a
quotation within it from Rupert Brooke about the *a priori*. Brooke's
understanding of it, however, was less subtle than Foucault's when he
wrote of the 'historical *a priori*' and Woolf's own appreciation that in
its complexity anticipates Foucault. Brooke offers Ben Keeling advice
about art: 'I charge you, be kind to life; and do not bruise her with
the bludgeon of the *a priori*'.[19] Woolf, with more subtlety than
Brooke or Keeling might have imagined, is concerned to expose the
a priori while suggesting the importance of breaking free of it.

III

Recognising *Jacob's Room* as a response to Edward Marsh's
Memoir reclaims the novel's historical context and sense of political
purpose. It is rescued from the misleadingly pure literary context in
which, as Alex Zwerdling has pointed out, it has been so often
placed:

> *Jacob's Room* appeared in 1922, the *annus mirabilis* of modern literat-
> ure that also produced *Ulysses* and *The Waste Land*. Perhaps because
> it was associated with these works, and because the novel was the first
> of Woolf's longer fictions to break with conventional narrative techni-
> que, it is often interpreted as a quintessential modernist text rather
> than as a unique work. Its peculiarities are treated as illustrative of the
> revolution in twentieth-century literature, though in fact some of them
> are idiosyncratic.[20]

When we realise that the novel is a response to Marsh's *Memoir*, it becomes clear that Woolf is not interested in making 'real' the character of those who died, but in the cultural *archive*, to employ Foucault's term, that shaped their world-views, their modes of behaviour and their attitudes as men.

The *Memoir* of Rupert Brooke that is being rewritten, as it were, in *Jacob's Room* is seen by Woolf as an extension of the Edwardian culture which created Jacob. The way in which he treats women, and expects them to behave towards him, for example, is the result of the *a priori* into which men of his class and generation grew. The sense which we have in the early part of the book of a young man with so much before him is not intended to emphasise the tragedy of Flanders *per se* but the privileged centrism of Jacob's social and moral position. It is also important to realise that Jacob is born into a generation of males within his particular class which, unlike the previous generation that had conducted itself (however hypocritically at times) according to a mannered morality, was characterised by a more blatant arrogance and a craving of new experiences.

Central to the novel, and anticipating her later work – particularly *The Years* – is how masculinity, albeit within a particular class, is constructed in pre-war England in ways which resulted in the First World War. It was an argument that Woolf had developed during the course of the war in her reading of newspaper accounts. In 1915, for example, she complained that: 'I become steadily more feminist, owing to the Times, which I read at breakfast and wonder how this preposterous masculine fiction [the war] keeps going a day longer – without some vigorous young woman pulling us together and marching through'.[21] This 'masculine fiction' was one that the nation's leaders identified with Rupert Brooke's poetry, as Winston Churchill's eulogy in *The Times* cited in Marsh's *Memoir* testifies: 'A voice had become audible, a note had been struck, more true, more thrilling, more able to do justice to the nobility of our youth in arms engaged in this present war, than any other – more able to express their thoughts of self-surrender...'.[22] But it was also one of a number of fictions that this particular class of young men had about themselves and about the West. England, as the cradle of civilisation, was located in an historical narrative linking Athens with London and Cambridge. As John Mepham has pointed out,

In 1914, as the young men marched to the trenches they had no idea of what they were doing, and the copies of Homer which they carried in their pockets helped to blind them to the fact that in the mud of Flanders they would be transformed not into heroic Greek sculptures but into corpses.[23]

The rise of Hellenism in Oxford and Cambridge, and in the public schools which prepared their students for entry to these universities, was an important curriculum development in the latter half of the nineteenth century that corresponded with major social and political changes in England. Science, technology, utilitarianism and positivism changed the intellectual temper of the country while the growth of industrialism, Empire and population seemed to threaten the position of the ruling class. Hellenism was part of the need to confirm the superiority and position of the ruling class within this changing climate through a traditional classic education. In 1850, Oxford divided the *Literae humaniores* into two parts, the second of which – the *Literae humaniores* proper – stressed poets and orators drawn from the Greek philosophical and historical context.[24] No wonder, then, that Jacob, contemplating the presence of women at the King's College Chapel service, draws attention to the Latin and Greek knowledge of their husbands, for through this knowledge they maintained, in Jacob's opinion, a patina of physical and intellectual superiority.

Several critics have argued that the repeated references to Greece and Greek culture are employed to underscore the patriarchal culture in which Jacob has been educated.[25] Others have noted that Greek statues and art are employed to suggest a monolithic and one-dimensional culture.[26] But the novel is more subtle than this. Woolf's text draws attention not to Greek culture as monolithic but to an interpretation of Greek art and culture as monolithic. Jacob's reading of the Greek statues – 'And the Greeks, like sensible men, never bothered to finish the backs of their statues' (p. 206) – is about the way in which Greek culture has been presented to him so as to suggest a particular type of masculinity rather than the logocentricity of Greek culture *per se*. Similarly, Fanny's idea of Jacob from the statues in the British Museum as 'more statuesque, noble, and eyeless than ever' (p. 238) has been influenced by the postcards she has received from him over the previous two months. Woolf's argument in the novel is that it is the logocentrism in the interpretation of

Greek culture and not necessarily in Greek culture itself which has been appropriated in support of a masculinist hegemony. In this respect, the novel may have been a response to the work of Jane Harrison, an anthropologist and classicist who was a friend of Woolf's, who argued that warlike patriarchal culture began with the Greeks when they conquered peaceful indigenous goddess cults.[27] Woolf's library contained an autographed copy of Harrison's *Ancient Art and Ritual* and the Hogarth Press published her *Reminiscences of a Student's Life* in 1925.

Woolf, then, was as interested in the way in which Greek culture had been appropriated as in Greek culture itself. Acknowledging that her 'Greekness' may be an illusion, she was interested, as Hermione Lee argues, in how the English, literary upper classes idealised the Greek spirit.[28] In emphasising the link between Greek culture and monolithic masculine culture in the upper-class education system in *Jacob's Room*, critics have failed to give sufficient weight to the fact that what Woolf stresses is the ignorance of Greek history and culture among Jacob and his friends: 'Durrant quoted Aeschylus – Jacob Sophocles.... Durrant never listened to Sophocles, nor Jacob to Aeschylus' (p. 101) and 'Jacob knew no more Greek than served him to stumble through a play. Of ancient history he knew nothing' (p. 102). It is when Jacob maintains that 'we are the only people in the world who know what the Greeks meant' that he is ironically taken for 'a military gentleman' (p.102). The association in the novel is not between Greek culture and militarism but between a privileged kind of militarism and a supposed knowledge of Greek which actually masks real ignorance.

The unreality informing the upper-class usurpation of Greek culture within their own limited frame is treated most sardonically in the novel in the account of the romantic encounter between Jacob and the promiscuous Florinda:

> Jacob took her word for it that she was chaste. She prattled, sitting by the fireside, of famous painters. The tomb of her father was mentioned. Wild and frail and beautiful she looked, and thus the women of the Greeks were, Jacob thought; and this was life; and himself a man and Florinda chaste. (p. 105)

There are a number of subjects here to which, under the influence of Defoe's *Moll Flanders*, Woolf was to return in a different way in the mock biography *Orlando*: the intermingling of confession and deceit around half-hidden sexual assumptions; the confusion of an individual woman with Woman; a sense of masquerade; and a particular masculine centrism that through codified notions such as chastity and frailty inferiorises what it desires and pretends to elevate. There is also an allusion to the way in which the notion of the Greek hero is posited, which Woolf would certainly have derived from Jane Harrison, on the death of the goddess.

The satiric preoccupation with the interpretation of Greek culture in *Jacob's Room* may have been stimulated, once again, by her quarrel with Marsh's *Memoir*. Rupert Brooke was buried in an olive grove on the island of Skyros where Achilles hid. In the *Memoir*, Marsh describes how an interpreter wrote in Greek on the back of the white marble cross, 'Here lies the servant of God, Sub-Lieutenant in the English Navy, who died for the deliverance of Constantinople from the Turks'.[29] This Greek inscription is juxtaposed with a valorisation of Brooke's life, unwittingly reminding us of the idealisation of Greek culture among the English literary upper classes:

> To his friends Rupert stood for something so much purer, greater, and nobler than ordinary men that his loss seems more explicable than theirs. He has gone to where he came from; but if anyone left the world richer by passing through it, it was he.[30]

To the English literary upper classes, Greek culture stood for an idealised notion of beauty in art and truth in philosophy to which they believed they aspired. In the account of Jacob on the beach, to which I referred earlier, Woolf caustically observes: 'No doubt, if this were Italy, Greece, or even the shores of Spain, sadness would be routed by strangeness and excitement and the nudge of a classical education' (p. 63).

IV

Given the obvious parallels between Jacob and Rupert Brooke, Brooke's letter to Woolf in 1912, in which he describes the repeated buggery of a child by two fourteen-year-old choir boys while there was a service for 'men only' in progress, assumes particular significance. It emphasises the apparent contradiction between the signs and symbols of an affective national identity and the lived experiences of some of the males within it. But Woolf suggests that the

whole letter should have been marked 'men only' and Brooke himself
emphasises the connection between the choir boys' behaviour and a
segregated male society. The implication is that male-only societies
create this kind of bestial behaviour. Significantly, Woolf wrote
Jacob's Room at a time when it would have been difficult for her
not to be aware of what went on, if only through rumour, among
men within the war zone.

William R. Handley has argued that Woolf's modernist novel form
in *Jacob's Room* is an attempt to resist 'the epic closedness and the
kind of militaristic authority in this world that will eventually
destroy [Jacob]'.[31] But its form is also an attempt to resist the
solipsism of the particular kind of masculinity, nurtured within the
officer class in Edwardian England, to which Brooke's letter alludes.

Jacob's Room begins with Betty Flanders writing on and ignoring a
full stop. In a sense the novel refuses to accept Flanders as a full stop.
Flanders in the novel can be seen, in Foucault's terms, as a 'discursive
event' in which the key ideologies of pre-war England are reconfi-
gured. The period from the beginning of the Great War to that in
which *Jacob's Room* was written was characterised, as Paul Fussell
has said, by the size of the shift from innocence to disillusionment.[32]
Over-emphasis upon the fatalism implicit in Woolf's choice of
'Flanders' as Jacob's surname thus detracts from its disruptive function in social and political historiography.

The subversive nature of Flanders as an ideological sign is reinforced by the choice of Jacob's first name. There is little doubt that
Brooke, 'with his long golden hair, sensual energy and powerful,
unsettled personality',[33] contributed to Woolf's mental picture of
Jacob. Jacob, like Rupert Brooke, is more akin to the smooth-skinned
Biblical Jacob than to Esau, the Biblical Jacob's brother. That Woolf
had the Biblical Jacob in mind is reinforced by the choice of the name
Rebecca – Jacob's conspiratorial mother in the Bible – for Betty's
maid and the fact that Rebecca is described at one point as a fellow
conspirator. Significantly, Woolf herself thought of Brooke as an
unsettling and destabilising figure:

> He was living at Grantchester, his feet were permanently bare; he
> disdained all tobacco and butcher's meat; and he lived all day, and
> perhaps slept all night, in the open air.... Under his influence the
> country near Cambridge was full of young men and women walking
> barefoot, sharing his passion for bathing and fish diet, disdaining book

learning, and proclaiming that there was something deep and wonderful in the man who brought the milk and in the woman who watched the cows.[34]

Jacob fulfils a disruptive function in Genesis, for, as I suggested earlier, he twice subverts the law of primogeniture – obtaining his brother's birthright from him and deceiving his father to give him the blessing intended for Esau. What Woolf's Jacob steals, through a modern version of primogeniture in which all men of his class are apparently implicated, is women's birthright. Patriarchy in the novel cripples women, leaving them at the mercy of men – Mrs Dickens, the wife of Captain Barfoot's manservant, is trapped within a rheumatic body and Mrs Barfoot is confined to a wheel chair – as the war crippled men.[35]

The way in which *Jacob's Room* ruptures what at the time were conventional modes of behaviour and traditional attitudes for men, particularly of the class about which she is writing, has been received approvingly by Clare Hanson for whom Jacob is 'connected with a disturbing violence which seems to come "naturally" to him',[36] but with some anxiety by Alex Zwerdling for whom 'Woolf's elegiac novel is persistently small-scaled, mischievous, and ironic'.[37] But Zwerdling forgets that there were Victorian precedents for the kind of 'mischief' in which Woolf is engaged. For example, *Punch* ran satirical engagements with Victorian popular fiction posited on their excessive imperialist zeal. William Gordon Staples, author of a host of classic imperialist adventure yarns in *The Boys' Own Paper*, found himself lampooned in *Punch* as 'Our Boys' Novelist' in a spoof entitled, 'Wet Bob; or The Adventures of a Little Eton Boy amongst the Hotwhata Cannibals'.

V

The elegiac mood of *Jacob's Room* – established from the outset by the presence of the widow, Betty Flanders – and the way in which it is so critical of Jacob and his generation, are not, I would suggest, incompatible. Central to the novel is the experience of mourning. But the mourning which is at the heart of the book is different from that which informs Marsh's *Memoir* with which Woolf specifically quarrelled. The most significant aspect of her complaint was that Brooke's friends had not been willing 'to tell the public the informal things by which they remember him best'.[38] In this quarrel with Marsh's *Memoir*, Woolf is clearly reformulating what memory and mourning involves. Although this aspect of the novel has been generally overlooked by critics, Lyndall Gordon has drawn attention to it, pointing out that while the elegiac poem is consolatory, covering 'the dead with verbal extravagance', *Jacob's Room* 'demonstrates how to be inconsolable'.[39]

In so far as the novel is concerned with a 'doomed generation', the entire narrative can be said to be posited on the mourning into which post-war Britain was plunged. In her work, perhaps based on her response to her mother's death, Woolf became increasingly interested in the complex, ambivalent and indeterminate emotions generated by mourning, particularly in the way in which it revealed a love–hate relationship with the deceased. Mourning makes us realise, what Jacob's various women friends discover in their relationships with him, that we can never know a person entirely and even those we allow a most intimate presence in our lives are still to some extent absent from us.

In his relationships with his friends, Jacob is often aloof, authoritative and severe. Sometimes his women friends begin talking of him sympathetically but then break off in an unspoken critique of his behaviour. Clara Durrant writes in her diary that she likes him because he is unworldly but also admits that he is 'frightening because . . . ' (p. 94). The narrator's account of him walking Florinda home concludes with his silence and Florinda's ominous remark, 'I don't like you when you look like that' (p. 110). This disturbing aspect of his character is linked to his particular upbringing and class as well as to his gender. For example, in the concluding sentence of a passage from the novel quoted earlier, he is described as 'satisfied' and 'masterly', indifferent to what is excluded by his privileged, social centrism. Jacob is separated from the world around him, as some of his 'friends' such as Florinda half-realise, not by anything unique in himself but what he has in common with the other members of the social élite to which he belongs.

The extent to which Jacob is observed by women, not only those with whom he is romantically involved, is a key feature of the narrative method. Here Woolf anticipates French theorists such as Hélène Cixous and Luce Irigaray in undermining notions of the unitary self that they attribute directly to Western humanism and which they see as unreservedly male in origin and values. However,

Jacob is not only viewed from multiple female perspectives but placed in the context of feminine language which for Woolf, as for Irigaray, is inherently multiple and thereby renders the notion of self which Jacob represents in the novel absurd. The perspectives of the women who observe him are generally relational rather than alienated and objectifying. Their views, since they are marginal to the masculine world he inhabits, provide the basis for an off-centre critique of the pre-war English culture which he represents. Two aspects of this culture are particularly disturbing: the unquestioned authority enjoyed by the male subject and the passivity with which Jacob and other males of his generation and class accept their position. As Jacob and Florinda walk home, the narrative describes what they pass on the streets and what they observe in the various windows: a boarding house whose occupants are dressed like ladies and gentlemen; wives of coal merchants who retort that their fathers kept coachmen; servants bringing coffee and having to move crochet baskets; a prostitute; an old woman selling matches; the crowd from the tube; a solitary policeman. While this presents us with a modernist writer's appreciation of the fragmentariness of pre-war London, there is more to the description than merely broken images. Jacob is both excluded from the scene and a part of it. Its marginality confirms the centrism of his gender and class evident also in the way others such as Captain Barfoot and even Barfoot's manservant occupy more privileged positions than many of the women. However, Woolf is alert to how women's identities are complicated across a number of different types of 'disablement'. All the women in the novel are disabled by their gender, but not equally. Unlike Betty, the upper-class widow Mrs Durrant is able to be driven about in a carriage and enjoy an independent life style. And Betty, of course, is better off than Mrs Barfoot and Mrs Dickens.

VI

The way in which the men of Jacob's class accept the authority of their position and the concomitant inferiorisation of women anticipates the link between Fascism and patriarchy in Woolf's pamphlet *Three Guineas*, (1938), and also reflects the line of thought in Woolf's essay on the Plumage Bill which she not only wrote at the time of working on *Jacob's Room* but which she complained prevented her from getting on with the novel. The bill in question, which caused much controversy in the Press, was introduced to prohibit the importation of plumage. As I noted in Chapter 2, after a successful passage through both Houses of Parliament, it was balked in committee by a failure to secure a quorum. While the bill and the practice of obtaining plumage from exotic overseas birds are the ostensible subjects of her essay, it is really an attack on the complacency of men, that many of them could not be bothered to turn up for the reading of the bill, and on those men who shift the responsibility for the import of plumage on to the women who wear feathered hats while ignoring the fact that it is men who are directly involved in torturing birds for their feathers. The subjects of the essay, then, are the violence of men, their complacent arrogance and the way in which they inferiorise and treat women:

> The Plumage Bill supporters say that the hunters 'are the very scum of mankind'. We may assume that the newspapers would have let us know if any of the other sex had been concerned in it. We may fairly suppose then that the birds are killed by men, starved by men, and tortured by men – not vicariously, but with their own hands. A small band of East End profiteers supports the trade; and the East End profiteers are apt also to be of the male sex.[40]

The critical views of Jacob held by his different female friends, echoing the ideas expressed in the Plumage Bill essay, challenge the uncritical opinion that men of Jacob's class, the young officer class, have of themselves and the opinions of them assumed by authors of memoirs. In other words, the critical stance of *Jacob's Room* is closer to the real experience of mourning than the ideal portraits painted in obituaries. And because we can think of post-war Britain as a country plunged into mourning for its war dead, Woolf's novel appears to suggest that it would be healthier for post-war Britain to adopt a more realistic appraisal of them. For the kind of questions which Woolf appears to feel needs to be asked about masculinity, identity and class are excluded by the kind of framework assumed, for example, in Edward Marsh's *Memoir* of Rupert Brooke.

Notwithstanding what was said above, Jacob's women friends are themselves problematic constructions, as reviewers at the time noticed. For example, Rebecca West observed:

> Only the long drive of the human will can be fitly commemorated in the long drive of the novel form. Now from that point of view *Jacob's*

Room is a failure. The fault of it is not that it is about commonplace people – that, indeed, is never a fault – but that it is not about individuals at all but about types as seen through the refractions of commonplace observers' eyes. Jacob's mother, Betty Flanders, is based on the conventional exclamations that such a figure of bluff maternity would evoke from a commonplace observer; so, too, Florinda the whore, so, too, Mother Stuart, her *entrepreneuse*; so, too, Clara Durrant, the nice girl; and Sandra Wentworth Williams, humorous but wholly a reported thing, dredged up from the talk of some cosmopolitan tea-party.[41]

West's comments may seem harsh, but she does raise the issue that, at least to some extent, these women are types. A number of reviewers shared her reservations about the novel's characterisation, as is evident in the debate between Virginia Woolf and Arnold Bennett. Bennett admitted that *Jacob's Room* was 'packed and bursting with originality' but also felt that the 'characters do not vitally survive in the mind because the author has been obsessed by details of originality and cleverness'.[42] How far characters in novels should be as fleshed out as Bennett would like is not the issue here in my opinion. Despite echoing Rebecca West's criticisms of *Jacob's Room*, Bennett recognises that the characters in the novel are 'busy with states of society'. But while Bennett sees this as a weakness of the book, it can be seen as a strength within the novel's intellectual framework.

Critics have tended to focus on the characters as individuals and have ignored the fact that Woolf's primary concern is with the social discourses of womanhood and how they entrapped different types of women in different socio-political situations. The point that Bennett, and most reviewers of the time, overlooked is that the relationships with which Jacob becomes involved are not the kind in which the idealised young men of the officer class, as remembered (or constructed out of memory) in war memoirs, would be said to be involved. Woolf is interested in the way in which women are located – socially, economically and sexually – within male discourses of which they then become the victims. The upper-class Mrs Durrant's daughter Clara might be a stereotypically 'nice girl' but Florinda is regarded as a prostitute. In fact, they are both the victims of discourse, in this instance the Victorian distinction between the angel – all sexuality has been refined out of Clara – and the whore. Captain Barfoot's Wednesday night visits to Betty Flanders are well known in Scarborough. But the issue they raise is not simply that of Betty's dependence on well-connected men like himself but that there is an unchallenged public discourse surrounding the social and sexual status of widows. The novel points out that these discourses inferiorise women, but also asks in whose interests have they been constructed. Permitting men of a higher social status to abuse women sexually (as Captain Barfoot uses Betty Flanders) and politically (as he exploits his wife's connections) while preserving their own place within the social order, these discourses demonstrate Woolf's larger concerns in this novel with the interconnections between sociocultural discourse and the gendered nature of power relationships.

Jacob's Room is open to criticism for the way in which it comes close to essentialism in presenting 'masculinity as the norm of a culture in which maleness automatically guarantees the authenticity and authority of the subject'.[43] But Jacob is also presented as a man who is unhappy with the position in which he finds himself, although ultimately he is unable to break free of it:

> In spite of defending indecency, Jacob doubted whether he liked it in the raw. He had a violent reversion towards male society, cloistered rooms, and the works of the classics; and he was ready to turn with wrath upon whoever it was who had fashioned life thus.   (p. 110)

Here we are reminded of Jacob as the troubled child on the beach confronted with his own isolation. What Jacob glimpses, but does not fully comprehend here, is the gap between the world to which he is symbiotically connected and the culturally determined desires and aspirations constructing a relationship with a different, imagined world. Thus he is alienated from and rendered 'strange' by pre-war England.

The depiction of the maternal at the beginning of the novel is closely involved with the dark forces troubling the young male child. At one level, of course, Woolf tries to untangle what is universal in the mother concept, aware that the protective, nurturing mother is a phantasm of discourse as well as a 'reality'. It is Betty who proffers the notion that 'every woman is nicer than any man' and whimsically associates women with 'mother wit, old wives' tales, haphazard ways, moments of astonishing daring, humour, and sentimentality' (p. 9). But all this has to be read within the context of the coming war and the fact that Betty is still grieving for her husband. The 'yellow and black mutability' (p. 9) against the sun that makes Betty think of danger and responsibility cryptically suggests the war and Jacob's death in it. With a mother's wit, Betty knows that her son's generation is doomed. Her protectiveness, gathering up the children, is ironic in the context of the First World War recruiting posters that were to exhort women to let their sons go to the Front. Betty's idealisation of the mother is interrupted by thoughts of meat – into which the war will turn her sons – and by the appearance of Rebecca at the window.

Betty's warmth is contrasted with the bareness of Mrs Pearce's front room – she is another type of woman – and the harsh light that falls on the garden. There is a sense, too, of Betty Flanders as an older type of mother figure summarised by what she has left in her room – 'her large reels of white cotton and her steel spectacles; her needle-case; her brown wool wound round an old postcard' (p. 10). Bending over Archer who cannot sleep, she tells him to think of the birds settling to sleep and of 'the old mother bird with a worm in her beak' (pp. 10–11). The plumbing of the house is analogous to the maternal body 'gurgling', 'rushing', 'bubbling', 'squeaking', 'stream-ing' – to which Arthur (and Jacob) must return as an imaginary – and which is displaced in the description of the lovely nests that enclose, womblike, the young birds. But Arthur, kept awake by the storm, associates the plumbing with water rushing into a ship. The large world of danger which he will enter as a male in the war stands in contradistinction to the maternal. The baby asleep but frowning is already caught between the two worlds.

It is the alienating effects of Edwardian England with which we are presented in the novel. While Jacob has absorbed many of its values and perspectives – for example, the way in which the women with whom he comes into contact are rendered as objects – he is not at home in it. There are many characters who are introduced – such as the couple sunbathing on the beach, and Rebecca – who do not play any significant part in the novel. They provide, like the view which Jacob has of the London streets as he walks home with Florinda, a sense of a fragmentary world. But most of all their cursory presences in the novel reinforce what from his perspective is an alienating and alienated environment.

Jacob glimpses early in life the dreary predictability that lies before men of his class and generation. This is itself a product of how the norm of masculinity and the conventions of male biography colluded in pre-war England to eschew inner, emotional development. Throughout the novel, Woolf distinguishes between the complex feelings one person may have of another that are of the kind which are revealed in the attitudes of some of Jacob's women friends towards him and the real experience of mourning, and those 'unreal loyalties' which fill male biographies, obituaries and memoirs. If there is an essentialist element in *Jacob's Room*, it is because masculinity within men of Jacob's particular class and social upbringing is essentialised by the culture into which they grow. The novel suggests that the 'unreal loyalties', on which this constructed and essential masculinity is posited, facilitates war:

> Look, as they pass into service, how airily the gowns blow out, as though nothing dense and corporeal were within. What sculptured faces, what certainty, authority controlled by piety, although great boots march under gowns. In what orderly procession they advance. Thick wax candles stand upright; young men rise in white gowns; while the subservient eagle bears up for inspection the great white book. (p. 38)

This passage ostensibly describes a service in King's College Chapel, Cambridge. The location is important for a number of reasons. The chapel, located in the golden triangle of England, epitomises Englishness, or rather that fusion of God, Monarch and country which came to represent Englishness for a particular cultural élite. It also delineates the way in which, within this particular cultural framework, religion (love of God) and war (sacrifice for one's country) had become linked. In this respect, *Jacob's Room* anticipates a line of thought that can be traced through the principal works of non-fiction, *A Room of One's Own* (1929), *Three Guineas* (1938) and the biography of Roger Fry (1940). The association between public buildings and the dominant discursive formations of society is a recurring trope in Woolf's writings. As Angela Ingram has pointed out, 'there seems never to have been a time when she didn't see public edifices as "symbolic" – of the crampings of the mind, or of the freeing of the spirits of people to whom such buildings were "appropriate"'.[44] In *Mrs Dalloway*, as I shall argue later, public buildings and monuments reflect dominant discursive formations that are also the sites of tension between emergent, competing attitudes and priorities in post-war Britain. In *Jacob's Room* the emphasis is not on the way in which a 'congregation of buildings' may become a site of conflict between competing discourses as in *Mrs Dalloway* or be seen differently by men and women as Woolf argues in *Three Guineas*, although both of these positions are reflected in the novel, but on how 'the semi-monastic look' of the old universities and the public schools encapsulate and forge a particular pattern of male development.

The passage describing the King's College service quoted above begins with the narrator making an appeal to the reader: 'Look'. 'Look' here means 'see, do not just look'. And this passage is almost impossible to glance over. The members of the chapel are said to 'pass into service'. The word 'service' is ambiguous, suggesting both religious and military service. But the ambiguity begs the question of how does the one lead to the other. Already we are being alerted to the historical *a priori*; the 'archive' of formulable cultural assumptions into which the young males of this particular class and generation have been/are being inducted. The description of the faces as 'sculptured' anticipates the Greek statues associated later in the novel with this class and generation.

The war, and the ultimate destiny for these men of the young officer class, is predicted in the reference to 'the great boots' in which they 'march', by the use of the word 'advance' and in the reference to the 'eagle'. The connection between the two forms of service reflects the authority and certainty which is not only in the young men's faces but the 'archive' of cultural assumptions upon which Englishness within this particular corner of England is posited. This unshakeable authority and its associated cultural assumptions are actually epitomised in what surrounds these young men: the thickness of the wax candles, the greatness of the boots, and the solidity of the great Bible. The passage makes clear that they are introduced to the historical *a priori* through objects and symbols as much as through verbal language. They are metonymic of a larger hegemony.

In the passage, the men are passing into what is ostensibly a religious service, but what is really an *archive of* statements about an essentialised English masculine norm that will lead them eventually to their deaths in Flanders. The passage also suggests that they are marching from knowledge of their own bodies and, because that is where their bodies have their roots, the maternal body. Jacob's musing on the absence of women reflects the anti-feminine discourses that are part of the public male ideologies epitomised in the Chapel's architecture and the content of the service. The subtlety of the passage lies in the way it suggests how for men of this class and generation, with this kind of upbringing, where God, monarch and country are fused in a confusion of patriotism and belonging, the very ambience of their lives are informed by the historical *a priori*.

Jacob's Room, then, anticipates Woolf's concern with the revisioning of historiography in the later non-fiction. The Great War, as Fussell has said, 'was perhaps the last to be conceived as taking place within a seamless, purposeful "history" involving a coherent stream of time running from past through present to future'.[45] Recruiting posters, such as one in which a worried father is asked by his children what he did in the war, reflected the confidence of the time that social and moral values would remain the same in the future. Woolf's concern with the historical *a priori* of pre-war Britain similarly implies that Jacob's education took place in a world which for men of his class and generation was more stable than that which followed the war. But while Fussell's concern is with the shift from stability to instability, Woolf, as a modernist and experimenter, is interested in the nature of what at the time seemed permanent and reliable abstractions. It is this which makes *Jacob's Room* more than a simple experiment.

5

'National Conservatism' and 'Conservative Nationalism': *Mrs Dalloway* (1925)

> *The little twisted sign that comes at the end of a question has a way of making the rich writhe; power and prestige come down upon it with all their weight. Questions, therefore, being sensitive, impulsive and often foolish, have a way of picking their asking place with care. They shrivel up in an atmosphere of power, prosperity and time-worn stone.*
>
> Virginia Woolf, *A Woman's Essays*[1]

I

Mrs Dalloway, written between 1922 and 1924, is generally regarded as the first important novel resulting from the techniques and approaches to fiction that Woolf discovered in writing *Jacob's Room*. In this novel, too, Woolf dispenses with the usual conventions of plot and, in passages employing a stream-of-consciousness technique, seeks to narrate the inner worlds of characters. But what distinguishes *Mrs Dalloway* from the previous novel is that the narration of the inner worlds of characters is much more sustained. The immediate stimulus for the novel was undoubtedly James Joyce's *Ulysses*, published in Paris in 1922, which Woolf read before she started work on the draft of *Mrs Dalloway* as we now know it – it was originally conceived as a series of short stories, to be called 'At

Home: or The Party'. Like *Ulysses* which records life on a single day in Dublin on 16 June 1904, *Mrs Dalloway* takes place on a specific day but in London on Wednesday, 13 June 1923.

One of the most puzzling aspects of *Mrs Dalloway* for readers and for some critics has been the apparent unconnected nature of the two narratives. The novel follows the central character Clarissa Dalloway, a different personality from Mrs Dalloway in *The Voyage Out*, from early morning through to night on a day on which she gives a formal party. The narration jumps between her story and the more sensational narrative of a shell-shocked war veteran, Septimus Warren Smith, and his eventual suicide. Ostensibly, the two stories are not linked and appear to merge only when Clarissa overhears a guest at her party talking of Septimus' death. Moreover, *Mrs Dalloway*, through Clarissa's memories of her adolescent home Bourton, is actually structured around two locations, again with no immediately obvious narrative connections between them; there is no account of Clarissa's marriage, of Elizabeth's birth, or of the move and adjustment to London. On reflection, the novel appears to have been deliberately organised as to invite the reader to compare these two chronotopes as regards their respective significances within different characters' subjective, temporal experiences and the ways in which they relate to various ideological conventions. However, it is almost impossible to read the text only in terms of the contrast between Bourton and London and only focusing on the narratives of Clarissa and Septimus. Firstly, Bakhtin reminds us that chronotopes are interwoven in a narrative and may 'replace or oppose one another, contradict one another or find themselves in even more complex interrelationships'.[2] The more obvious relationships between the two key chronotopes – a female-centred natural world contrasted with the patriarchal social world of London or a comparison of two locations concerned with female loss – are complicated by the way in which, as Bakhtin suggests, different meanings are assigned to each chronotope in the course of the novel. Secondly, the stories of Clarissa and Septimus are expanded through the introduction of a host of minor characters, some fleetingly introduced and others the subject of more sustained attention, through which Woolf delineates and explores London 'Society' and the nature of the wider milieu that followed the First World War. While critics have tended to stress Joyce's influence on the narration of the inner minds of characters, they have overlooked Woolf's indebtedness to other aspects of

Ulysses. The subject of both novels, which their different narrative threads intersect and probe from a variety of perspectives, is the dominant fictions of a particular milieu and what is hidden within or by these fictions.

The narrative technique of *Mrs Dalloway*, in which an omniscient narrator conveys the thoughts and impressions of a number of characters and the focalisation moves between their different perspectives, has frequently been associated with the novel's emphasis on the fragile nature of 'reality' and the problematic concept of an 'autonomous "full" subject'.[3] However, its multivalent narrative point of view is also central to the novel's engagement with the difficulties of writing history. In *Mrs Dalloway*, the narrator speaks from some indeterminate later point in time. Hence an issue for Woolf is similar to the one raised by Hans-Georg Gadamer, to whom I referred in Chapter 1, that of how to ensure that the dialogue with the past is not over-weighted in the direction of the present. In other words, how to ensure that the present is in a dialogue with the past and not with itself. The narrator of *Mrs Dalloway*, seeking to preserve the evanescent thoughts, sensations, mental images and interior speech of the characters, is dependent on the characters' minds. As Gadamer argued, a critique of the past should be dependent on being addressed by the past, its evanescent thoughts, sensations and mental images. In *Mrs Dalloway*, Woolf has sought to create a narrator who is addressed by, and is not simply a ventriloquist of, the characters' pasts.

For J. Hillis Miller one of the achievements of the novel is the way in which Woolf justifies 'the power she ascribes to her characters of immediate access to their pasts'.[4] This aspect of the novel belies the myth that Woolf's fiction is a response only to the early twentieth century when it is in fact often rooted, as I suggested in Chapter 2, in the continuum of social change and development from the mid-Victorian period onwards. The extent to which the narrator is addressed by these pasts has its corollary in the way in which the characters in the novel are addressed by further pasts which they in turn revivify. For example, since Mrs Dalloway is fifty-two years of age, her affair with Sally Seton when she was eighteen years of age must have occurred a few years after the criminalising of male homosexual relationships. Her memory of Sally Seton reading William Morris is also convincingly located in the 1880s, for Morris founded the Socialist League in 1884. Aunt Helena Parry, on the other hand, is addressed by the mid-nineteenth century – her memories are of India in the 1860s and

Burma in the 1870s. India at a later date enters the novel in Peter Walsh's memories, as does the rise of socialism among intellectuals in the 1890s which resulted in him being sent down from university.

However, although the multivalence of the novel pluralises the concept of history as well as the notion of 'reality' and extends its imaginative reach back to the mid-Victorian period, an important dimension of the text is a dialogue between post-war and pre-war England, the latter having its roots as in *Jacob's Room* in the nineteenth century. The period with which it is primarily concerned, despite engaging through the characters' memories with a longer span of time, is identified by Peter Walsh, one of the more important secondary characters, as a period of significant social change: 'Those five years – 1918 to 1923 – had been, he suspected, somehow very important'.[5] Recalling the England he knew before, Peter observes how people dress and behave differently; how newspapers tackle previously taboo subjects and demonstrate a less constrained sense of their public function; and how women, in particular, enjoy greater independence and a freer sexual identity.

While there are many differences between Woolf's and James Joyce's work, as between the two modernists themselves, Woolf shared Joyce's realisation that neither the fluidity of the mind's activity – the jostling of memory, stimulus, projection and perception – nor the fragmentary codes of culture exist independently of the other.[6] Her concern to explore the interrelationship between them is evident in Peter Walsh's notion of an imagined, conservative, upper-class England despite his own reservations about what he is invoking: 'A splendid achievement in its own way, after all, London; the season; civilisation' (p. 71). Whereas Joyce stretched realism to its limits by addressing the products of modern life, Woolf is interested in her novel in how an imaginary, communal identity can preserve itself in the face of an intelligent scepticism that subjects it to scrutiny. The highly fragmentary nature of Peter's imagined realisation of England confirms that the mother country is more obviously located in, and is the product of, cultural iconography than geography. The 'London' Peter recalls is not the diverse, sprawling city of the 1920s, but an imagined ideal of a particular class. Observing Septimus Smith and his wife, Rezia, together in the park, Peter contemplates:

> The amusing thing about coming back to England, after five years, was the way it made, anyhow the first days, things stand out as if one

had never seen them before; lovers squabbling under a tree; the domestic family life of the parks. Never had he seen London look so enchanting – the softness of the distances; the richness; the green-ness, the civilization, after India, he thought, strolling across the grass. (p. 92)

Although Peter admits that the imaginary England of 'butlers; chow dogs; girls in their security' is 'ridiculous', it reassures him as to his own sense of identity. He himself is not English but the product of an Anglo-Indian family that has served the administration of the British empire for three generations. The precariousness of his 'English' identity is compounded by his own dislike of India, empire and the army. On his return, he avoids the Oriental Club 'biliously summing up the ruin of the world' (p. 212). What Peter invokes is an imagined national identity; imagoes – the butlers, the dogs, the girls – invested with memories of his own childhood.

II

Significantly, it is through Peter Walsh's focalisation that the reader observes how London's geography is laced with British history. He passes down Victoria Street, opened in 1851, which keeps alive the Victorian past in the present, past St Margaret's church restored by Gilbert Scott in 1838 and, walking along Whitehall, passes the statue of the Duke of Cambridge, Commander-in-Chief of the British Army from 1856 to 1895. While critics have observed that London land-marks such as these acquire symbolic significance within *Mrs Dallo-way*, they have often overlooked the fact that Woolf incorporates them into the novel not for their significance in their original context but for how they have acquired new meanings in the period after the war. The aim of Britain and the Dominions at the Paris Peace Conference in 1919 was to reverse the trend of British foreign policy since 1904 and return to the days of splendid isolation. Indeed, the only ceremonial spectacle mounted for the British public in the 1920s was the British Empire Exhibition held at Wembley in 1924 and 1925. What seems to have interested Woolf is the contradiction in post-war British life between withdrawal from imperialist expansion and anxiety about the war and the empire, on the one hand, and a perceived need to preserve the ideologies that informed empire, Englishness and masculinity, on the other.

Like North Pargiter in *The Years*, Peter is implicated in the *crypta* of empire and this enables Woolf to return to the way in which the empire had become a site of anxiety in the post-war years reflected in Walsh's neurotic behaviour with his penknife and Whitbread's obsessive drawing of rings around his capital letters. When Walsh wonders what the 'conservative duffers' are doing in India, he reflects the concern of the period about the agitation for independence in India and Egypt where the British position was becoming increasingly untenable. While the Indian National Congress emerged in 1885, by the 1920s there were two more sites of Indian popular agitation – the young Gujerati lawyer, Gandhi, who returned to India in 1915 and was mobilising the Indian masses in the cause of national independence, and the Bengali nationalist movement based on the sophisticated, educated middle classes of Bengal who stood to the left of Congress. It is significant that when Peter Walsh thinks of India he compares it to Ireland. Irish semi-independence won in 1921–2, together with the granting of semi-autonomy to Egypt, marked the first partial retreat from empire.

Contemporaneous readers of the novel would know that Walsh was in India in 1919 when Brigadier-General Dyer ordered his troops to fire on an unarmed assembly following a Briton being mauled by a crowd. Dyer was able to do so because of the negative and reductive way in which he perceived Indians, forcing those who had to use the street on which Miss Marcia Sherwood was assaulted to crawl on all fours. It is, then, somewhat ironic that Clarissa, in remembering Peter interrupting herself and Sally when they were alone together, describes how 'she felt only how Sally was being mauled' and 'maltreated' (p. 46). And equally ironic, it is Peter's own observation that 'after India of course one fell in love with every woman one met' (p. 93). Notwithstanding his dislike of empire, Walsh is so much the product of one strain of Victorian thought about British India that his implied view of the Indians is no less negative than Dyer's. Having brought wheelbarrows to India, he offers no explanation of the fact that the Indians chose not to use them other than implying that that was no more than one would expect from their lack of intelligence.

At one level, the multifocalisation of Woolf's fiction reflects the different late nineteenth-century perspectives and debates on colonialism to which I referred in Chapter 2. But the discovery of techniques for narrating the inner minds of her characters enabled

Woolf to explore the importance of fantasy in the principal discursive formations of Englishness, empire, masculinity and sexuality. For example, we soon learn that the wife of a young army officer in India with whom Peter Walsh is having an affair has become part of his fantasy of himself as an Anglo-Indian representative of the empire. When he empties his pockets in his London hotel, his pen-knife – a phallic object and signifier of his general neuroses – and a picture of Daisy are brought out together. Ironically, given the British reaction to what happened to Miss Marcia Sherwood in India, Walsh enacts his fantasies of himself in pursuit of young women on the streets of London – thus associating him with the figure of the male predator that stalks *The Voyage Out*:

> He pursued; she changed. There was colour in her cheeks; mockery in her eyes; he was an adventurer, reckless, he thought, swift, daring, indeed (landed as he was last night from India) a romantic buccaneer, careless of all these damned proprieties.... He was a buc-caneer. (p. 69)

III

Fantasy is a very different but equally important aspect of Clarissa's relationship with Sally Seton in the 1880s, where Woolf incorporates into the novel not only an allusion to the radical feminist ideas of that decade but the way in which ostensibly radical female behaviour was eroticised in the 1920s. The phrase 'she sat on the floor', significantly repeated, suggests that Sally not only departs from upper-class etiquette which dictated how young ladies were sup-posed to sit but that she takes control of her own body. Her non-conformist behaviour is linked to her intellectual dissent – she engages Clarissa in talk of reforming the world and abolishing private property. Her daringly transgressive actions compound her eroticism. But her attractiveness to Clarissa is also enhanced by a further erotic fantasy stimulated by her 'unEnglish' appearance: 'It was an extraordinary beauty of the kind she most admired...a sort of abandonment, as if she could say anything, do anything; a quality much commoner in foreigners than in English women' (pp. 42–3). And there could be no better illustration for Clarissa of Sally's erotically unEnglish, devil-may-care abandonment than her running naked from the bathroom. The way in which the prose halts after, indeed seems to hesitate over, the word 'admired' suggests that perhaps it ought to read, 'desired', which as we learn is closer to Clarissa's true feelings for Sally. Sally introduces into the novel what Jean Braudillard calls an 'erotic nakedness', that characteristically 'inaugurates a state of communication, loss of identity and fusion'.[7] But she is also introducing the eroticism and excitement that was so much a part of the 'Roaring Twenties' myth of itself, especially for those of the middle and upper classes.

The positive depiction of Clarissa's and Sally's relationship thus challenges the way in which same-sex relationships were perceived by some contemporaneous sex psychologists such as Havelock Ellis and Stella Browne. Through her association with Edward Carpenter and John Symonds, who were part of the Bloomsbury group, Woolf would have been familiar with the debates around same-sex relationships, especially the controversial psychoanalytic view of them as the result of either congenital sexual inversion or sexual inversion caused by temporary emotional or cultural influences. Doris Kilman's name and her German origins – a reference to the German sex psychologists of the 1890s – suggest that she is not simply a character but an illustration of how hostile discourses about same-sex relationships can affect an individual's emotional and psychic development. Whereas Clarissa accepts her attitudes towards other women as something private and hidden within herself, Doris is more candid about her sexuality. It would be too simple, though, to regard Doris as Clarissa's alter ego. Despite her name, Doris Kilman retains in her relationship with Sally many of the features of heterosexual relationships that Woolf found unpalatable – she expects Elizabeth to be subordinate to her will and it is her interests that are highlighted in the relationship. Clarissa and Doris enable Woolf to locate different discourses about same-sex relationships and to permit different attitudes and perspectives to circulate in the novel. Thus Clarissa's view of Doris' relationship with her daughter Elizabeth as a 'degrading passion' (p. 166) reflects her own jealousy of Doris, her regrets over her relationship with Sally and her own frustrations in her marriage to Richard, but equally importantly the way in which same-sex relationships were a site of anxiety in post-war Britain, evident also in the way in which Doris turns for a while to the church to try to assuage 'the hot and turbulent feelings which boiled and surged in her' (p. 162) before learning to trust her desires.

The relationship between Clarissa and Sally can also be seen as an intervention in the heated debates taking place in London over the respective importance attached to the roles of the mother and the father in the formation of gender identity. London became the centre of debate between the patriarchalists such as Sigmund Freud, who argued that the relationship to the father is the most important determining factor in gender identity, and the matriarchalists, such as Melanie Klein who moved to London in 1926, who argued for the importance of the relationship with the mother. In 1924, Ernest Jones, President of the British Psycho-Analytical Society, suggested that 'few themes, if any... arouse more emotional prejudice than the comparison of male and female, particularly if it includes the question of the respective parts played in life by the father and the mother'.[8] As Elizabeth Abel has pointed out, Sally replaces both Clarissa's dead mother and her sister, Sylvia, whose name hers echoes.[9] The relationship between Sally and Clarissa is disrupted by the appearance of Peter, echoing the way in which in the Freudian narrative of gender identity formation the girl-child's relationship with her mother is disrupted by the father. Recognising that her mother is a 'castrated' version of the father, the girl-child suppresses her active sexual orientation towards her mother and accepts a passive orientation towards her father. As Abel points out, 'Woolf organises the developmental plot so that Clarissa's love for Sally precedes her alliances with men'.[10] The scene that Clarissa always remembers is the one in which Peter interrupted Sally's kiss. Indeed, her version of what happened reconfigures the Freudian Oedipal narrative – Peter is cast as the jealous male attempting to rupture the female bond.[11]

The disruption of the female love between Clarissa and Sally by the appearance of Peter parallels the death of Clarissa's sister from a fallen tree for which her father is to blame. But the death of Sylvia and her separation from Sally have even larger significances. Critics have generally argued that the loss of intimate female relationships in Clarissa's life mirrors the loss – through oppression – of the female in the country as a whole, in turn symbolised by the shattering of the plaster cast of Ceres, goddess of fertility and mother love, in the war. It is evident, too, in that Clarissa Dalloway and Lady Bradshaw have both had to sacrifice their own aspirations for the careers of their husbands. The stern maiden aunt's habit of pressing flowers suggests a general oppression of women which is also part of the general condition into which post-war Britain seems cast. As Abel observes, the novel, in which 'the youngest generation... is almost exclusively, and boastfully, male', indicates 'the masculine tenor of post-war society'.[12] But the novel is more complicated than this would suggest because post-1918 British society had developed a feminine tenor of which *Mrs Dalloway* is a sophisticated exploration.

IV

Following the armistice, Britain sought to stabilise its cultural codes and social practices against a shift in its cultural centre of gravity that Alison Light has described as

> a move away from formerly heroic and officially masculine public rhetorics of national destiny and from a dynamic and missionary view of the Victorian and Edwardian middle classes in 'Great Britain' to an Englishness at once less imperial and more inward-looking, more domestic and more private – and, in terms of pre-war standards, more 'feminine'.[13]

'Englishness' was reformed in the period between the wars to meet, as John Taylor (drawing on Light's work) says, 'middle-class aspirations for a more domestic and dependable way of life than had been fostered in the preparations for and propaganda of war'.[14] The transformation in the nature of Englishness described by Light and Taylor gave rise to what Light calls a 'conservative modernism'[15] but what Taylor calls a 'conservative nationalism'.[16] This 'conservative modernism' or 'conservative nationalism' became embedded in codified texts characterised by nostalgia for pre-war landscapes, country villages, country houses and mythical, stable relationships between the classes.

However, in Virginia Woolf's fiction, the emergent, 'national' text of a conservative, middle-class and 'feminine' England, in which the domestic and the private constitute the privileged codes, is complicated in a number of ways, not least because of the changing nature of class references themselves. The 'conservative nationalism' that Taylor identifies was under pressure from some of the very forces that helped create it, such as increased social mobility, the emancipation of women, the growth of an urban population that destabilised the traditional urban/rural binarism and the rise of a demanding tourist industry. Indeed, this tension was only too evident in the tourist guides of the 1930s, to which Woolf alludes in *Between the Acts*,[17] conspicuously focused, as Taylor says, on the legacy of 'Olde England' – on history, topography and antiquarian interest.[18]

Woolf's fiction also distinguishes between a post-war 'feminine England' and an England in which the preponderance of women over men was at its height as a result not only of the war but, as A. J. P. Taylor points out, of the rate of infant mortality among male babies.[19] The emphasis upon the greater preponderance of women on the shopping streets of London in Woolf's fiction is not only a social fact but an acknowledgement that this had become itself a cultural 'text' in post-war England. But an important question posed by *Mrs Dalloway* is whether this new freedom really amounts to anything. Mrs Dalloway steps out at the beginning of the novel, but she may be stepping out only to participate in the spectacle of early twentieth-century modernity – a subject to which Woolf returns in *The Years*:

> Was everybody dining out, then? Doors were being opened here by a footman to let issue a high-stepping old dame, in buckled shoes, with three purple ostrich feathers in her hair. Doors were being opened for ladies wrapped like mummies in shawls with bright flowers on them, ladies with bare heads...women came; men waited for them, with their coats blowing open, and the motor started.   (pp. 214–15)

By the beginning of the twentieth century the Capital had become the location of department stores that Woolf described in her diary as 'fairies' palaces',[20] such as Liberty's (1875), Bon Marché (1877), the Junior Army and Navy at Waterloo Place (1879) and Selfridges (1909).[21] But although shopping, as Reginald Abbott points out, is the primary activity in *Mrs Dalloway* [22] – the Dalloways, Rezia, Miss Kilman and Hugh Whitbread all go shopping – Woolf's concern again is with the 1920s at the cusp of two political economies. In one, individuals are bound to particular circumstances originating in accidents of birth and fortune, epitomised in the way in which Clarissa's fondness for flowers keeps alive her connections with Bourton, while the other offers a commodity universe, as in the florist's shop Clarissa visits, in which the spectacle lifts consumption above mundane exchange.[23]

V

The spatial geography of the novel reflects Britain's position *vis-à-vis* these two economic orders symbolised in the contrast between Big Ben, the solemn and majestic icon of old England – the bell was tolled at the funeral of Edward VII in 1910 – and the 'other clock' which blends with the world of commerce, of vans, 'flaunting women', and the domes and spires of offices and hospitals (p. 167). While there is mention of streets such as Victoria Street associated with the zenith of Imperial Britain there is also reference to Leaden-hall Street, the business centre of London. Within this framework the Army and Navy store that Doris Kilman and Elizabeth visit becomes important. Founded in 1871 to supply the military, it became an omnipresent symbol of the empire. But the department store that opened in 1920 placed it at the cusp of the two orders, the one rooted in the old imperialist ideologies and the other in a shifting, consumer-oriented society.

Previously, the large department stores had assumed an 'aristo-cratic' style of shopping, known as 'through shopping', in which women were met at the door by a shop walker and led from counter to counter, symbolic of the servant–mistress relationship but also of the way in which women in most spheres of their lives were osten-sibly controlled by men. Incorporating Bond Street in *Mrs Dalloway*, Woolf was actually including a controversial 'text' that would have required little further explication in the 1920s. After the war, Old Bond Street, the centre for aristocratic shopping where not even buses were allowed in case they splashed the carriages, was amalgamated with New Bond Street, the centre for modern-style shopping. The amalgamation can be seen as the signifier of a wider social embourgeoisment. The entire economic sphere was becoming diffuse so that the idea of England, around which a sense of national identity was cohering, seemed posited on consumption and the polit-ical economy. The 1920s was increasingly changing into an age of display advertising; hitherto shops had advertised almost entirely in the classified columns of newspapers and magazines. The point is well made in *Mrs Dalloway* in the appearance of the sky writer who mesmerises the crowd with loops that spell a brand name they may recognise even before he has finished. Depending on one's point of view, the aeroplane is either associated with the mendacity of advertising or with the fairy-tale spectacle of modern consumerism, the discourses of which associate it mainly with women.

The attitude adopted towards modernity in the 1920s in *Mrs Dallo-way* is, in this sense, ambiguous. At one level it appears to offer women opportunities but, at another level, it either defines them as consumers or as participants whose roles are defined by its continual patriarchal control. There are important differences between Elizabeth Dalloway and Maisie Johnson whom critics have hardly ever compared. Nineteen-year-old Maisie, who has come to London from Scotland to take up a post at her uncle's business in Leadenhall Street, represents women for whom in the 1920s there were apparently new economic possibilities. Although the kind of post which she is entering is probably clerical or secretarial work, her arrival in London is real. But in Elizabeth's case, mounting an omnibus (one of the recurring metonyms of post-war modernity in Woolf's fiction), her opportunities are still the product of fantasy. For her, modernity is much more of a spectacle:

> The impetuous creature – a pirate – started forward, sprang away; she had to hold the rail to steady herself, for a pirate it was, reckless, unscrupulous, bearing down ruthlessly.... And she liked the feeling of people working.... It was quite different here from Westminster, she thought, getting off at Chancery Lane. It was so serious; it was so busy. In short, she would like to have a profession. She would become a doctor, a farmer, possibly go into Parliament if she found it necessary, all because of the Strand.   (pp. 177–9)

Of course, unlike Maisie, Elizabeth can fantasise in this way because of her class and because her father is an MP. Maisie, too, is privileged but not to the same extent – she has a relative who has a business in London and her family in Edinburgh can spare her. But it is at the end of the novel that the difference between them becomes important. Richard Dalloway's declaration that Elizabeth is a 'lovely girl' reduces her to the ideal female in the male gaze and suggests that she will follow her mother's role rather than Maisie's.

While it is true to say that post-1918 England acquired an increasingly significant middle class, Woolf's fiction acknowledges the complicated relationship between the emergent, conservative middle class and the more overtly political high Toryism. As A. J. P. Taylor reminds us, after the war 'there was still an unmistakable upper class' and although the war had been expected to threaten their power and income, the governing class was still largely drawn from a few hereditary families.[24] Many who had been officers in the war, refusing to return to a life of leisure, set themselves, like some of their contemporaries before the war, to earn a living in business, finance and industry. The effect of this was to bring about a qualified

embourgeoisment of the upper class that in *Mrs Dalloway* underpins
Peter Walsh's observations of Lady Bruton: 'She had her t··¹·
minor officials in Government offices who ran ab····
little jobs on her behalf, in return for which she
(p. 227). Indeed, the two upper-class world-vie
Mrs Dalloway when Richard Dalloway, who m
believes in work, meets Hugh Whitbread, whose   ·egards
as worthless, in the appropriately named Condu·   ·· while contrary winds buffet the street corner.

In post-war England there was a discernible tension between the
national images of 'conservative nationalism' described by John
Taylor and the lived experience of modern England for the majority
of people in which business, finance and industry, technical and
industrial development figured significantly. It is evident in *The
Years* in Eleanor's attitude towards the House Agent, Mr Grice.
Just as Estella in *Great Expectations* notices Pip's working boots,
so Eleanor observes Grice's 'business man's buttoned boots' and that
he is 'hauling himself up into the class above him . . . by means of long
words' (p. 205). When Mrs Manresa invites herself to lunch at Pointz
Hall in *Between the Acts*, demanding literally and symbolically 'a
seat at the table', the focalisation of the novel shifts to that of the
beleaguered upper class: 'There must be society. Coming out of the
library it was painful, but pleasant, to run slap into Mrs Manresa. . . . No escape was possible; meeting was inevitable' (p. 34). Her
voice, with rounded vowels that the consonants can hardly contain,
expresses an energy which is suddenly invigorating at this point in the
novel but threatens the decorum of the dining room in which she
finds herself: 'A seat at the table – that's all we want. We have our
grub. We have our glasses' (p. 35).

VI

Woolf recognises that 'foreignness' is something that exists within
ourselves as well as others. Becoming aware of foreignness
within ourselves involves recognising not only our plurality but the
excitement of reclaiming our innate sense of strangeness. By contrast,
the national images of England in circulation after the war were
located, inevitably, at the public face of national identity, the boundary between Englishness and the implied 'Other' against which it is
defined. Julia Kristeva has argued:

[Freud] teaches us how to detect foreignness in ourselves. That is perhaps the only way not to hound it outside of us. After Stoic cosmopolitanism, after religious universalist integration, Freud brings us the courage to call ourselves disintegrated in order not to integrate foreigners and even less so to hunt them down.[25]

In anticipation of Kristeva, Woolf sees England as 'disintegrated' while the emergent public idea of England was one in which 'disintegration' had been exchanged for 'universalist integration'. Frequently in her work, Woolf uses foreignness, the perception of foreigners, or those who have been out of the country for some time, to challenge the myths of homogeneity and of origins which underpinned post-war notions of Englishness – a strategy deployed most extensively in her final novel, set on the eve of the Second World War. A recurring feature of her critique of Englishness is the notion that it is posited on rigidity in both behaviour and thought. To replace the 'stiff little vases' they always had at Bourton, redolent of the rigid statues of London, Sally Seton picks 'all sorts of flowers that had never been seen together' (p. 43). While elsewhere in this novel, and in Woolf's fiction generally, binarisms are generally confounded, masculinity here is associated with rigidity but flexibility of thought with femininity. Instead of displaying her flowers in a phallic vase, Sally cuts their heads from their (phallic) stems and arranges them in the vulval image of a bowl of water.

One of the reasons why Woolf at times entertains an essentialist masculine/female binarism and uses foreignness to render Englishness as 'foreign' is her apparent distrust of the 'conservative nationalism' that emerged after the war. While Woolf's work certainly acknowledges what Alison Light has described as 'a revolt against, embarrassment about, and distaste for the romantic languages of national pride',[26] it recognises that this was far from a universally held position and embraces a fear that the former heroic, masculinist version of national identity might be resurrected as part of the emergent 'national conservatism'. In the year in which the novel is set the Victoria Memorial was still under construction. Woolf seems to argue that while post-war conservatism might be founded upon a private, everyday kind of middle-class and middle-brow Englishness, it is locked into what is at the heart of national and public life. At that centre of national life, signified in the rigid statues and the formal squares of London, are the homophobic and militaristic ideologies criticised in *Jacob's Room*.

Talk of 'conservative nationalism' in relation to Woolf's fiction, then, is complicated because it is distinguished in her work from what might be called 'national conservatism' which appears to cause Woolf much concern. Her focus is not usually upon the rise of the new Englishness as such but upon the social and ideological pressures equating Englishness with an imagined consensus politics in which its assumptions were taken for granted and the limits of its obligations not sufficiently questioned. It was, as Alison Light has described, 'a politics which eschews politicking; a system of beliefs and values without systematisation; an organic and inevitable way to be'.[27] If 'conservative nationalism' was a product of the retailing of national images, it was also true of 'national conservatism' for, as Light points out, 'the English began to see images of themselves and their cultural behaviour... at "the pictures" and in magazine photography as never before'.[28]

The figure of the Prime Minister at the Dalloway party signifies the restoration of a wholly Conservative Government after two periods of sharing power with the Liberals – during the war and in the period of Lloyd George's Coalition Cabinet (1919–22).[29] The Prime Minister is Stanley Baldwin who in May had succeeded Bonar Law (who had resigned because of ill-health) and who was widely perceived at the time to be leading a dull administration when a more proactive government was needed. Although for a short while Ramsay MacDonald became the first Labour Prime Minister (January–November 1924), *Mrs Dalloway* can only be fully understood against the background of newly emergent conservative forces in England in the early 1920s, forces that brought the Conservatives to power for the periods 1922–42 and 1924–29. These conservative forces reflected the desperate desire of middle-class suburban Britain for tranquillity and social peace after the consensus of the armistice period collapsed. Although the post-war coalition Government had been elected to promote national solidarity and social unity, it found itself faced with new international conflicts, many of which were to shape the first half of the twentieth century, and flux and upheaval on the domestic front. The period between 1919 and 1922 witnessed an unrestrained policy of retaliation and bloody atrocities in the war with the IRA; the use of tough measures, including the deployment of troops as strike breakers, in disputes with miners, railwaymen and other workers; and Britain brought to the verge of war with Turkey.

In *Mrs Dalloway* in particular, Woolf is critical of the new English politics because what may be identified as a 'national conservatism' appears to be posited not only on eschewing 'politicking' but on cultural solipsism. At the outset of *Mrs Dalloway* we are told that the war is over. This is Mrs Dalloway's opinion (not the narrator's) which the novel challenges through the introduction of the shell-shocked Septimus and the Armenian crisis. To believe that the war was over, one had to ignore the presence of those still suffering at home through bereavement or physical and/or mental injury and what was going on in other parts of the world. In the course of the novel, the phrase 'the war is over' comes to summarise the complacency of the period from the armistice to June 1923. Indeed, the Armenian crisis of the summer of 1923 is seen as confirmation of the complacency of post-war England.

The Armenian people, who were Christians in a largely Muslim area, had been colonised and expelled by various Imperial powers. By 1914 the original area of Armenia lay partly within Russian and partly within Turkish territory. The Treaty of San Stefano agreed between these two powers placed Armenia within the Russian sphere of influence. But Britain, fearing a threat to its interests in the area, forced a revision to the Treaty in order to keep the Armenians within the Ottoman empire. This led inevitably to the massacres of 1895–97, 1909 and the holocaust of 1915.[30] Although Woolf could not have but been aware of the atrocities she does not reiterate their details. The crisis is employed more subtly in the novel than that – as a signifier within a wider sign system.

The novel is set a month before Britain signed the Lausanne Treaty which was the final act of betrayal; the idea of an Armenian national home in the Anatolia region was dropped and the non-Soviet Armenians abandoned to Turkey. The narrator is situated in a post-Lausanne Treaty England and is engaged in a dialogue with pre-Lausanne Treaty England, satirising the complacency of a group of powerful people who were responsible for the betrayal of the Armenians. The public coverage of, and interest in, the Armenian crisis, seen as raising 'vital issues about human rights and Britain's quasi-imperial responsibilities',[31] is the 'absent presence' in the following account, when Richard Dalloway is on his way to the House of Commons to sit on the Committee negotiating the Lausanne Treaty:

[Richard] was already half-way to the House of Commons, to his Armenians, his Albanians, having settled [Clarissa] on the sofa, looking at his roses. And people would say 'Clarissa Dalloway is spoilt'. She cared much more for her roses than for the Armenians. Hunted out of existence, maimed, frozen, the victims of cruelty and injustice (she had heard Richard say so over and over again) – no, she could feel nothing for the Albanians, or was it the Armenians? but she loved her roses (didn't that help the Armenians?) – the only roses she could bear to see cut.   (p. 157)

Whatever feminist ideas Mrs Dalloway might have in the novel about refusing to live her life vicariously through Richard are here undermined by the way in which she allows herself to be infantilised and the way in which the passage slips from 'his' roses to 'her' roses. Her complacency in allowing herself to be laid on the sofa, a symbol of comfort and inactivity, mirrors her complacency towards the Armenians – she does not appreciate the differences between the Armenians and the Albanians – encapsulated in the outrageous proposition 'didn't that help the Armenians?'.

VII

The 'internal insularity' of conservative England, the upper and upper-middle classes, is linked, then, to international insularity. But Clarissa Dalloway's failure to appreciate the significance of the treaty, for which the Parliamentary Committee on which her husband serves is responsible, is part of the novel's larger concern with a lack of enquiry in the English intellectual constitution. It is evident in Lady Bruton's scheme to solve the problems of unemployment by sending the unemployed to Canada and it is within this context that Sally's intellectual assault on Hugh – or rather Peter Walsh's version of it – must be seen. Hugh is criticised by Sally according to Peter because 'he's read nothing, thought nothing, felt nothing' (p. 95). In other words, he demonstrates the lack of intellectual enquiry and the monocular thinking that Sally associates with the English upper class. 'No country but England', she declares, 'could have produced him' (p. 95). This is also Peter's view of Richard Dalloway, despite the differences between the two men, evident in his assertion that Clarissa has inherited 'a great deal of Dalloway, of course; a great deal of the public-spirited, British empire, tariff-reform, governing-class spirit' (p. 100). The phrase 'public-spirited' is ambiguous, for

apart from the most obvious meaning, it suggests how Richard
Dalloway is the product of the public sphere, a criticism reinforced
by the suggestion that he is the mouth-piece of the *Morning Post*, a
conservative national paper, and has no thoughts of his own.

The translation of Habermas' concept of Öffentlichkeit – 'a
sphere of private people coming together as a public'[32] – as a 'bourgeois public sphere' can help us to understand how *Mrs Dalloway*
engages with the discourses of its day. Like many of the historical,
political and scientific debates at the time, the novel addresses the
bourgeois ideal of Öffentlichkeit – 'that the personal opinions of
private individuals could evolve into a public opinion through
rational–critical debate of a public of citizens which was open to all
and free from domination'.[33] The notion developed in the eighteenth
century among the bourgeoisie who were otherwise excluded from
the dominant political institutions. Much of *Mrs Dalloway* addresses
this ideal from the perspective of those, largely women, who were
excluded from the official national, public sphere. However, Habermas' concept of a public sphere provides an especially pertinent
framework in which to discuss the novel because it agrees with
Habermas in at least one important respect. While addressing the
ideal of the public sphere, *Mrs Dalloway* suggests that it is also, as
Habermas described it, 'a socially necessary...falsity':[34]

> But Aunt Helena never liked discussion of anything (when Sally
> [Seton] gave her William Morris, it had to be wrapped in brown
> paper). There [Clarissa and Sally] sat, hour after hour, talking in her
> bedroom at the top of the house, about life, how they were to reform
> the world. They meant to found a society to abolish private property,
> and actually had a letter written, though not sent out. The ideas were
> Sally's, of course, – but very soon she was just as excited – read Plato in
> bed before breakfast; read Morris; read Shelley by the hour. (p. 43)

Here the irony points to the fact that even those debates which are
constructed outside the official political sphere are veiled and disin-
genuous expressions of particular interests.

In distinguishing a domain of institutionalised political power
associated with a sovereign state from private concerns of a market
economy and personal or familial relationships, Habermas tended to
confuse and obscure the different senses of private and public.
Martin Phillips suggests that in order to prevent this problem we
should think in terms of a distinction of the official sphere (state,

administration and mass media), the intermediate sphere (interpersonal communication) and the unofficial sphere (nurturing of selves).[35] Woolf's novel does in fact explore the fluidity of the relationships between these different spheres with regard to how particular practices and associated relations operate through institutionalised power and are made visible and accessible to others. The two most obvious, and most important examples, in *Mrs Dalloway* are the connection between notions of Englishness, masculinity and empire, and attitudes towards shell-shocked war veterans.

VIII

Peter Walsh's encounter with the young marching soldiers is framed between two statues – the Duke of Cambridge who, like Walsh, had been sent down from Oxford for his Socialism, and of General Gordon who died heroically at Khartoum, which can be seen as symbolic of the new late-century militarism to which I referred in Chapter 2. At one level the description of the marching soldiers suggests, as Elizabeth Abel points out, that 'military discipline intended both to manifest and cultivate manliness in fact instils rigor mortis in the living as well as the dead'.[36] But it is not just the manliness which military discipline is meant to cultivate that produces 'the stiff yet staring corpse'. Equally significant is the association with the inscription around the base of a statue 'praising duty, gratitude, fidelity, love of England' (p. 66). The inscription reflects the jingoism of the late nineteenth century and the concomitant English nationalism that Iain Chambers has identified:

> But from its sturdy assurance in the market-place this Victorian gentleman gradually succumbed to a neo-Romantic, increasingly anti-market and anti-industrial ethos. Moral certitude, and an individual and pragmatic rationale, gave way to the collective mystique of the nation and its past.... To be 'British' was no longer to demonstrate Christian virtues and the pragmatic pursuits of *homo economicus*, but to pledge allegiance to the imagined state of grace which was the nation.[37]

The elements of the inscription – duty, fidelity, patriotism – suggest what Michel Foucault has called 'that ideal neuvre that reappears totally or in part'.[38] But for Woolf, as for Foucault, the 'ideal neuvre' is an illusion because objects only exist in a complex group of relations – 'relations established between institutions, economic and social processes, behavioural patterns, systems of norms, techniques, types of classification, modes of characterisation'.[39] Duty, fidelity and patriotism were key elements in one Victorian perspective on colonialism, itself reflecting particular concepts of nation, nationality and of race out of which they emanated, but which were the subject of debate at the time and even more so in post-war Britain.

Peter Walsh's reaction to the soldiers, then, is different from that of the narrator. While the narrator, who of course moves through and between a number of focalisations, associates the men with corpses, Peter marvels, albeit sceptically, at the influence that the public sphere has been able to exert on private individuals to create this marching machine: 'One had to respect it; one might laugh; but one had to respect it' (p. 66). Peter's response here can only really be understood within the rather crudely formulated, national ideologies of the day, according to which, as Eric Leed has pointed out, 'the civilian exchanged his private self and his individual self-interest for a public and communal identity represented in the uniform'.[40] But the ceremony Peter is witnessing, as a later version of the original event, is removed from what originally surrounded and supported it. Only an aspect of what gave the initial ceremony its cultural importance has been preserved. The social and cultural norms surrounding the event have changed. In other words, the ceremony has to be placed not only in what Foucault called 'a field of exteriority'[41] but a changing 'field of exteriority'. Viewed synchronically, the marching soldiers signify the value of discipline and self-sacrifice. The Tomb of the Unknown Warrior to which they carry the wreath, created so that parents of the missing dead might feel that their son was buried in Westminster Abbey, allows the nation as a whole to participate in war as a symbolic exchange. But a diachronic approach confronts the fluid nature of the 'field of exteriority' in which the ceremony is located. Although Peter Walsh claims to admire the 'very fine training', he reflects on the changed attitude towards war, and to such public ceremonies, in the 1920s, brought about by the presence of shell-shocked and disabled war veterans in post-armistice Britain.

IX

Although after the war a number of women novelists appropriated the theme of shell-shock, the originality of Woolf's approach, as

Elaine Showalter points out, lies in the connection of 'the shell-shocked veteran with the repressed woman of the man-governed world'.[42] The name Septimus Smith, 'S. S.', was probably suggested by Siegfried Sassoon whom Woolf knew and the impact of whose poems (which she reviewed for *The Times Literary Supplement*) upon her I mentioned in Chapter 2. In fact, as Showalter points out, he visited her in 1924 while she was working on *Mrs Dalloway*. Septimus' middle name 'Warren' suggests the impact of war on his mind and the labyrinthine nature of the medical condition in which it has resulted. But the etymology of 'warren' also suggests 'feminine' qualities of protection and nurturing which are opposed to the traditional qualities associated with manliness while reinforcing how men who had become unstable and emotional as a result of their war experiences were seen as feminine. Ironically, Septimus has separated himself from his mother, and, like Jacob Flanders, denies both the maternal and his own body in the cultivation of 'manliness'. In many respects Septimus, a tragic figure of the class system, is a projection of what would have happened to Jacob Flanders if he had not been killed in the war. The suggestion from some critics that his madness is the product of his repressed homosexuality misunderstands how he has been psychologically and emotionally displaced, like Jacob Flanders, by the system in which he was brought up and educated. Septimus' feelings for men and for women, as his overt fantasies about his teacher at Morley College testify, have been affected by the suppression of his sexuality and by his subsequent guilt over normal attitudes and behaviours.

Septimus is situated at the social margins of the novel. As Eric Leed has pointed out, the veteran was a liminal figure, having crossed the boundaries of disjunctive worlds, in this case war and peace.[43] According to Leed, 'the "liminal type" has always provided the ground upon which those at home could project their own ambivalence toward the social order they inhabited: their fear of disorder and their fear of petrifaction'.[44] Jacques Derrida, however, reminds us that 'the borderline is never a secure place, it never forms an indivisible line, and it is always on the border that the most disconcerting problems of topology get posed'.[45] This leaves us with the question of how Septimus functions as a narrative strategy within the borderland in which the narrative locates him. Septimus' introduction appears to divide the novel, as if he and Clarissa Dalloway exist in different narratives. But, as I suggested earlier, the novel's different narrative threads interconnect in their exploration of the dominant fictions of post-war Britain. Septimus can be seen, I would suggest, as what Derrida has described as a 'charnière' or 'hinge'.[46]

There are several dimensions to Derrida's concept, each of which is applicable to Septimus' role in the novel and the way in which he fuses the different threads of the text. As a hinge in the technical sense, opening and closing, he ushers in a new epoch while an older epoch is brought to a close. The narrator then assumes the role of gatekeeper of the today; the holder of the keys that open as well as close the door. In the anatomical sense of a hinge pin or pivot, Septimus is the axial point which allows the tropes of the novel to circulate. But there is a third meaning of 'charnière' derived from falconry, the place where the hunter lures the bird. In that sense Septimus attracts the main concerns and debates which the novel is obviously meant to raise. In this respect the different meanings of the word 'charnière' are brought together. Where a character functions as a hinge, as Derrida says, there will always be 'an interminable alternating movement that successively opens and closes, draws near and distances, rejects and accepts, excludes and includes, disqualifies and legitimates, masters and liberates'.[47]

Septimus, though, is only one of many liminal figures in the novel who play an important part in connecting the different narrative threads in an analysis of public discourses. One of the most significant is the shawled old Irish woman, Moll Pratt. It is important to acknowledge that the response of the constable to such a figure would have had a strong resonance for readers in 1925 when the novel was first published. Lloyd George's peace treaty with the IRA had been signed, and the Irish Free State brought into being less than three years previously after several years of bloody conflict, reprisals and atrocities. Moll Pratt would have tossed roses into the street as supposedly the Prince of Wales passes had she not felt the policeman's eye on her. It would be impossible in 1925 not to read the suppression of this private gesture as metonymic of the attempt to suppress the Irish within the wider public sphere. As an Irish figure under a policeman's eye, Moll reminds us that if Ireland did not exist, the English nation, as Duncan Kiberd says, would have had to have invented it.[48] As a liminal figure who has crossed from Ireland to England, on the edge of English society on account of her Irishness, her occupation as a pavement seller, her age and her gender, Moll represents what official masculinised Englishness represses or tries to deny.

While critics have focused on the comparisons which may be drawn between Clarissa and Rezia, the relationship between Rezia and Dr Holmes has not received as much attention. However, Rezia – again a liminal figure cut off from her female past – is important to the novel's exploration of how antipathetic social structures can be internalised. The narrative of how she sits with her husband in Regent's Park trying to interest him in an aeroplane overhead elides the omniscient narrator's voice with that of Dr Holmes, '[her husband] had nothing whatever seriously the matter with him but was a little out of sorts' (p. 27). The frustration of her love for him turns to anger, particularly at how he seems to be happy in his solipsism. The way in which she regards him seems to be a product of how shell-shock has not been properly recognised in the collective public discourse. The novel blurs the boundaries between Rezia's despair at her husband's condition, Holmes' failure to recognise that he is ill, her loneliness as an Italian in a foreign country, and public discourses about masculinity, heroism and death.

The interconnection of different private and public spheres in *Mrs Dalloway* is evident in Rezia's response to Septimus' discussion of suicide: 'And it was cowardly for a man to say he would kill himself, but Septimus had fought; he was brave; he was not Septimus now' (p. 29). Here it is difficult to separate her feelings for him from the influence of the public discourse about suicide in which it was seen as a final admission of a shameful and unmanly weakness. When Septimus leaps to his death, Holmes cries out, 'The Coward!' The text alerts the reader to what Rezia cannot see – that her attitudes towards suicide and men going to battle reflect, and are determined by, collective attitudes towards them which are beyond herself and them. As the social theorist Jean Baudrillard points out, the death of millions in war is justified within a larger system of symbolic exchange: 'Millions of war dead are exchanged as values in accordance with a general equivalence: "dying for the fatherland"; we might say they can be converted into gold, the world has not lost them altogether'.[49] Indeed, Eric Leed has decribed this as the very 'paradigm of exchange'.[50] But if 'the citizen-soldier has always been a central figure in what might be called an "economy of social guilt" and public sacrifice', he was also a threat, for he 'can demand restitution for his "sacrifice of himself" as well as for that of his comrades who have died'.[51] In declaring suicide cowardly, Rezia unconsciously reiterates capitalist Britain's perspective on suicide to which Baudrillard draws attention: suicide reverses society's norms and inverts society's law that ' "no-one has the right to remove any capital or value". Yet each individual is a parcel of capital...and therefore has no right to destroy himself. It is against this orthodoxy of value that the suicide revolts by destroying the parcel of capital he has at his disposal'.[52]

The view of war as part of a larger system of symbolic exchange through which the deaths of hundreds is justified is an outsider's critique. It is not the way in which war is made accessible to those, particularly the men, who participate. But war in the novel is associated, like the post-war period as a whole, with corpses on the battlefield, shell-shocked ex-soldiers and bodies in bath chairs. Indeed, Septimus threatens the notion of war as a masculine rite-of-passage because as a veteran he would have been seen as 'primitivized, barbarized, and infantilized; demoted on the scales that measure and define civilized adulthood'.[53] Peter Walsh on his return to London from India, which like the war is a rite-of-passage chronotope, is caught between these two perspectives: between the glamour of traditional masculine heroism represented in the statues of Nelson, Gordon and Havelock – each of whom died in military action – and a burgeoning awareness of the limitations of this stereotype of masculinity, an awareness that shapes the complex structure of *Mrs Dalloway*. It is this same awareness of limitations that informs the thinking of Woolf's next novel, *To the Lighthouse*.

6

Womanhood and Discourse:
To the Lighthouse (1927)

> *It seemed so fitting – one of nature's masterpieces – that old Miss Parry should turn to glass. She would die like some bird in a frost gripping her perch. She belonged to a different age, but being so entire, so complete would always stand up on the horizon, stone-white, eminent, like a lighthouse marking some past stage on this adventurous, long, long voyage, this interminable ... this interminable life.*
>
> <div align="right">Virginia Woolf, <i>Mrs Dalloway</i>[1]</div>

I

To the Lighthouse is generally regarded, along with *Jacob's Room*, *Mrs Dalloway* and *The Waves*, as one of Woolf's formally experimental novels. Thus, the majority of critics prior to the 1960s have approached it principally as an exemplary, high modernist, aesthetic work, largely in terms of its neoplatonism and Post-Impressionism. While in the last thirty years it has been the subject of psychoanalytic and deconstructionist criticism as a feminist text, its wider concerns with history and discourse have been generally neglected.[2]

Woolf began *To the Lighthouse* in August 1925, completed it in January 1927 and revised it at the last minute before its publication in March.[3] In the course of writing the novel, Woolf shifted the centre of the text from Mr Ramsay to Mrs Ramsay and brought into sharp focus the hitherto marginal figure of Lily Briscoe. The novel is clearly indebted to, and most often read in conjunction with, Marcel Proust's *A la recherche du temps perdu*, both texts being concerned with Time Lost and Time Regained. In the third section of the novel, the Ramsay family visit the lighthouse ten years on, after Mrs Ramsay's death, accompanied once again by their guest Lily Briscoe. But despite the similarities between these works, to which I referred in Chapter 2, and their common Post-Impressionist style, I believe that *To the Lighthouse* was written as an 'interruption' of *Jacob's Room* and its narrative of how a young male of a particular class is socialised into a particular masculinity and code of values. Like *Jacob's Room*, *To the Lighthouse*, at least the first section, is set on the eve of the First World War. But in order to explore the nature of pre-war English society, Woolf re-employs the technique of her first novel of taking a group of upper-middle-class English people out of their usual social context. In this case, Mr and Mrs Ramsay, their children and their guests are on holiday on an island in the Hebrides about which we know very little apart from the fact that their house is within walking distance of the town and situated by a bay.

I use the word 'interruption' to mean the way in which Woolf breaks into some of the subjects of *Jacob's Room* in order to develop them or to pursue alternatives to them, for example, the way the upper-class male is socialised to deny the mother and the nature of the mother figure herself. *To the Lighthouse* is an interruption of *Jacob's Room* that has been made possible by the space opened up for Woolf not only through reading *A la recherche du temps perdu* but through writing *Mrs Dalloway* where she returned to relationships between women, a trope in her first novel, and to alternatives to dominant, masculine discourses, a mode of thought that impelled her to subvert traditional narrative formulations in her first two books. Although *To the Lighthouse* retains the method of *Mrs Dalloway* – mingling inward thought with outward action – as Louis Kronenberger acknowledged in his review, 'the method [is] applied to somewhat different aims'. The more radical nature of *To the Lighthouse* was also recognised by the reviewer in the *Times Literary Supplement* who found it 'still more different from most other stories [than *Mrs Dalloway*]'.[4]

There are thus two aspects to this chapter, the way Woolf returns to *Jacob's Room*, pursuing alternative perspectives to that novel and developing some of its understated motifs, and the way writing *Mrs Dalloway* made that possible. In *Mrs Dalloway*, Miss Parry is the lighthouse, symbolic of her eminent monologism and that of her

milieu. But *To the Lighthouse* disrupts such completeness. The journey undertaken to the lighthouse at the end of the novel is really a
journey to Mrs Ramsay, a development of the mother figure in
Jacob's Room, who is perceived differently by each of the characters
in the novel and is herself more than the sum of all of these perspectives. Moreover, *To the Lighthouse* interrupts the concern with
mourning in *Jacob's Room*, Woolf having thought of the novel
herself, when it was a work-in-progress, as an 'elegy'. As I explained
in Chapter 3, *Jacob's Room* can be seen as a response to, if not a
reaction against, the idealisation of war heroes in memoirs such as
Edward Marsh's eulogy of Robert Brooke. The delineation of Jacob
in the novel is closer to the real experience of mourning than the
traditional idealisation of the war dead. In *To the Lighthouse*, Woolf
returns to the subject of mourning, but this time to a middle-aged
woman's mourning of her surrogate mother.

In mourning Mrs Ramsay, Lily Briscoe comes to realise that they
are separate people. She experiences the difficulty of ever knowing
another person, a subject raised but not pursued as rigorously in
Jacob's Room, and begins to appreciate that the people whom we
admit into the most intimate recesses of our consciousness will
always be strangers to us. Indeed, an obvious difference between *To
the Lighthouse* and *Jacob's Room* is that while the latter consists of
many brief sections or slices of Jacob's life, *To the Lighthouse* is a
more integrated work. What is an object of analysis in *Jacob's Room*
becomes the analysing subject in *To the Lighthouse* – all the characters turn their attitudes, experiences and their affections over and
over. Importantly, the soul-searching that occurs at the level of
individuals mirrors the way in which private and public life in the
1920s was being interrogated, challenged and revised.

Interruption is a recurring trope in *To the Lighthouse* on a number
of levels and, indeed, the circumstances surrounding the composition
of the novel can be configured as a series of interruptions. Embedded
in post-war England, it has its origins in a myriad of interruptions –
political, economic, technological and artistic – to English social and
cultural life, not least in the apparent break with the Victorian era
and its class and family structures after the First World War. The
writing of the novel itself was interrupted by the General Strike of
May 1926 that influenced the mood of the section 'Time Passes'.[5]
Interruptions to Woolf's health also threatened the book's completion; she had to break from the work in 1925 and after she had

resumed writing in the following year not only suffered a nervous breakdown but was brought by the first draft nearer to suicide than at any other time. Of course, in 1925 Woolf's life was seriously interrupted by a love affair with Vita Sackville-West that inspired *Orlando* and she also allowed, and probably needed to let, her relationship with her mother interrupt her sense of self, even permitting herself to be photographed wearing her mother's dress. In May of that year photographs of her mother, taken by her great-aunt Julia Cameron (published by the Hogarth Press as *Victorian Photographs of Famous Men and Women*), brought her relationship with her mother to the forefront of her mind. But Mrs Ramsay, whose forenames are never revealed, should not be seen, as Virginia's older sister Vanessa Bell acknowledged in a letter dated May 1927, as a convincing portrait of their mother, but rather as an interruption of the mental portrait that they had always had of her.

As often with Woolf, revisions meant serious interruptions to the existing text. Having produced one draft by September 1926 she interrupted that narrative by the introduction of Lily Briscoe who began as a minor character, Miss Sophie Briscoe, a kindly fifty-five-year-old who painted thatched cottages and hedgerows. Although the first section is set in pre-war England, these were the kind of images which in post-war Britain reflected nostalgia for a pre-war sense of Englishness. But as I suggested in the chapter on *Mrs Dalloway*, these images also reflected a post-war 'conservative nationalism', of which Woolf herself became not only sceptical but suspicious.

To the Lighthouse can also be seen as an interruption of Woolf's process of writing up to this point, allowing space for an analysis of her methods of composition, for the ruminations on Briscoe's art in *To the Lighthouse* are undoubtedly Woolf's own self-conscious reflections on the experience of writing fiction. It is impossible not to read the following account without thinking of the way in which the first drafts of *To the Lighthouse* brought Woolf almost to suicide:

> It was in that moment's flight between the picture and her canvas that the demons set on her who often brought her to the verge of tears and made this passage from conception to work as dreadful as any down a dark passage for a child. Such she often felt herself – struggling against terrific odds to maintain her courage; to say: 'But this is what I see; this is what I see', and so to clasp some miserable remnant of her vision to her breast, which a thousand forces did their best to pluck from her. (p. 28)

Thus, Lily's difficulties in realising her ideas in paint mirror the struggles that Woolf has had in writing. Ironically, Lily's painting is finally realised after four moments of illumination over many years that may themselves be seen as moments interrupting long periods in which she feels blocked in her creativity. The process of the composition of *To the Lighthouse* itself can also be seen as a series of interruptions. Reflecting in 1927 on how the book came to be written, she remembered the 'unexpected way in which these things suddenly create themselves – one thing on top of another in about an hour'.[6] While this entry in her diary has often been noticed by critics, the sense of endless interruptions to her thinking, albeit positive, has been overlooked. Yet notes for a book of stories she was planning in 1925 that became *To the Lighthouse*, about the people attending Mrs Dalloway's party, suggest that she conceived of creativity as interruptions to a stream of thought, as the following entry indicates:

> Topics that may come in:
>   How her beauty is to be conveyed by the
> impression that she makes on all these
> people. One after another feeling it without
> knowing exactly what she does to them,
> to charge her words.
> Episode of taking Tansley to call on the poor.
> How they see her.
> The great cleavages in to which the human
> race is split, through the Ramsays not
> liking Mr Tansley.
> But they liked Mr Carmichael.
> Her reverence for learning and painting.
> Inhibited, not very personal.
> The look of the room – [fiddle?] and sand [shoes?] –
> Great photographs covering bare patches.
> The beauty is to be revealed the 2nd time
> Mr R stops
> discourse on sentimentality.[7]

Gayatiri Spivak argues that the structure of the book may be seen as a grammatical allegory: Subject (Mrs Ramsay) – copula – Predicate (painting). Although describing the second part of the book as the 'copula' is intriguingly appropriate – it is not only the pivot of grammar and logic but has a sexual charge – Spivak is concerned by the second section where the search for language seems strangely unattached to a character.[8] It is possible to see what Spivak describes as a 'copula' as an interruption. In fact, the novel itself, like *Jacob's Room*, is riddled with interruption. Landings at the lighthouse are threatened with interruption by poor weather, Mrs Ramsay's search through the Army and Navy Stores catalogue is interrupted by the frightening roar of the waves she had not previously noticed, and Lily Briscoe is frightened (literally) of being interrupted by Mr Ramsay 'coming down upon her with his hands waving, shouting out "Boldly we rode and well"' (p. 25) – a quotation from Tennyson's 'The Charge of the Light Brigade'. Lily, of course, interrupts the match-making activities of Mrs Ramsay by desiring to identify with her – thus disrupting the dominant discursive narrative of hetero-sexuality with the possibilities of same-sex relationships – while her relationship with Mrs Ramsay is interrupted by death. The most damaging interruptions in the novel, however, are caused by war and death. The war interrupts the family's visits to the island and in the second section, rendering the change and decay their house undergoes, we learn that Mrs Ramsay dies, that their son Andrew is killed in action, and that their daughter dies in childbirth.

The use of brackets and other forms of parentheses is an important aspect of the novel's style, in which, as Hermione Lee has pointed out, a great deal happens.[9] But while much that is in parentheses – silent gestures, alternative perspectives, different points of view, comments and qualifications – suggests, as Lee says, how more than one thing happens at once and more than one time co-exists, it can also be seen as an endless series of interruptions. Of the many interruptions that permeate the text, the most important is the way in which the past apparently interrupts the present. Thus, Lee observes, 'as "Time Passes" comes to a close, its last section bulges with bracketed phrases about the return of life to the house'.[10] The significance of this is that Woolf has become interested not in the way in which the past constantly interrupts or disrupts the present but the way in which the present, contrary to our common-sense under-standing of time, interrupts the past.

II

Although Woolf did not read Freud extensively for herself until 1939, she was familiar with his work that, according to Rosenbaum, was much discussed in the Bloomsbury group and for which their knowledge of continental philosophy had prepared them.[11] The ideas about memory in *To the Lighthouse* are similar to the Freudian concept of *nachträglichkeit* or 'deferred action' from his case-history of the so-called 'Wolf Man' (1914) which challenged conventional notions of the recovery of lost memories. According to Freud, later events inscribe past experiences with their meaning. One way of thinking about this in practice is to imagine that events, particularly those that are traumatic, remain latent in the subject until working over the present endows them with significance. Thus, Woolf's creation of Mrs Ramsay can be seen as releasing the pathogenic force of her mother's death. But another way of thinking about *nachträglichkeit*, which is especially relevant to this novel, is to conceive of us as always in more than one place at any time. While Lily in 'The Lighthouse' completes her painting, she is simultaneously with Paul and Minta picking flowers and playing ball before dinner and with Mr Ramsay throwing his plate on to the terrace at breakfast when he found a earwig in his milk. Such is the significance of what she thinks of as the past in the present, but which I am arguing here is the present in the past, that Hermione Lee calls *To the Lighthouse* a 'ghost story', pointing out that ghosts frequently break into modernist texts such as Leopold Bloom's son in Joyce's *Ulysses* and the ghost of the blind Tiresias in Eliot's *The Wasteland*.[12] Freud's concept of *nachträglichkeit*, however, enables us to think of the present as interrupting their deaths or absences. Mrs Ramsay appears at the end of *To the Lighthouse* as 'part of her perfect goodness to Lily' (p. 272). This does not mean that she appears after death out of 'her perfect goodness to Lily'. While thinking about her present, Lily restructures her past, particularly her relationship with Mrs Ramsay, endowing it with a new significance that she is able to realise in her painting. Her new-found appreciation of Mrs Ramsay releases the force of past events that have remained latent within her. Thus, her projection onto the late Mrs Ramsay of what she now thinks of as the dead woman's 'perfect goodness' to her interrupts her absence from Lily's life and she appears once again before her as a 'ghost'.

Freud's concept of 'deferred action' or 'retroaction' helps us not only to understand how memory in *To the Lighthouse* disrupts our conventional understanding of time, but the way in which *Jacob's Room* functions as an intertext in the novel. In other words, *To the Lighthouse* is not simply an exploration of Freud's concept of *nachträglichkeit* but, in its relationship to *Jacob's Room*, a product of it.

Thus, one way of conceiving of the link between the two novels is to think of *Jacob's Room* as a latent presence in Woolf's consciousness while she was working on *Mrs Dalloway*, but endowed with further meaning in the process of writing and revising *To the Lighthouse*. *Jacob's Room* is not simply recalled in the writing of *To the Lighthouse* or allowed to interrupt her work on it, which would be the conventional way of linking the two works temporally, rather *To the Lighthouse* interrupts the earlier novel, endowing much of its subject matter with new meaning.

Leapfrogging over Clarissa Dalloway and Doris Kilman in her previous novel, Woolf returns in *To the Lighthouse* to Betty Flanders whom she reconfigures in a further kind of interruption. In *Jacob's Room*, Betty's brown wool is 'wound round an old postcard' (p.10), but Mrs Ramsay's wool is unfurled as she impatiently knits reddish-brown stockings for the lighthouse-keeper's child. Through Mrs Ramsay, Woolf seems to break into and unfurl the character of the Mother. But it would be too reductive to suggest that Mrs Ramsay is a summary of nineteenth-century ideologies of motherhood.[13] In the first section of the novel, the longest, we see Mrs Ramsay in a number of roles as mother – knitting a stocking, reading a story to James, comforting the younger children at bedtime – and as wife, negotiating her difficult relationship with her husband (sometimes to her advantage) and acting as a hostess. Like Betty Flanders, Mrs Ramsay is both an individual and a type, for, unwittingly, she is the product of discourse as well as of instinct and spontaneity.

III

As in *The Voyage Out* and *Mrs Dalloway*, the *crypta* within family and heterosexual society in *To the Lighthouse* is same-sex relationships that like mother–son relationships are occluded by the patriarchal culture deconstructed in *Jacob's Room*. An interesting issue in relation to the text is how far it is concerned with the exploration of the ambivalence of the girl-child's relationship to her mother and how far it is concerned with the way that relationship is codified in Freudian psychoanalysis in the Oedipal complex. A point that has not been made often enough in psychoanalytic criticism of *To the Lighthouse* is that it seeks to interrupt not only the Freudian narrative which privileged relationships with the father in the formation of gender identity but the Kleinian narratives of mother–daughter relationships that sought to redress the balance in Freudian discourse.

An important figure in this respect is Mrs Ramsay's daughter Cam even though she is a marginal character – having a sketchy presence in the first section, 'The Window', and reappearing in the final section in the boat journey to the lighthouse where, locked in her own thoughts, she is a much more passive figure. Here, sitting in the bow behind her father and brother, she looks not forward to the lighthouse but back to the island which she associates with her mother. Compared by Margaret Homans both to Cathy in *Wuthering Heights* and to Virgil's Camilla,[14] in 'The Window' she is also comparable to the young lawless female – the imp figure – exemplified in Sir Walter Scott's Peveril in *Peveril of the Peak* or Nathaniel Hawthorne's Pearl from *The Scarlet Letter*:

> She was picking Sweet Alice on the bank. She was wild and fierce. She would not 'give a flower to the gentleman' as the nursemaid told her. No! no! no! she would not. She clenched her fist. She stamped. (p. 31)

Another intertext here may well be *The Winter's Tale* where Perdita accedes to Florizel's request to welcome Polixenes and Camillo and hands them flowers – rosemary, rue and grace. Cam's actions immediately make Bankes feel 'put into the wrong' about his friendship with the family, as is Polixenes in Shakespeare's play.

Cam's attitude as a child towards her mother is ambivalent. This is evident in the reluctance with which on one occasion she returns to her mother having rushed ahead of the adults – 'off like a bird, bullet, or arrow, impelled by what desire, shot by whom, at what directed, who could say?' (p. 74). The change in her demeanour and attitude here anticipates her solipsism in the boat ten years later – she comes 'lagging back, pulling a leaf by the way, to her mother' (p. 75). The reluctance suggests that she is wary of her mother's apparent complicity in the patriarchal system that insists that she gives flowers to men. But it also represents the conflict between the emergence of new desires and fantasies and the limitations of male-dominated social institutions. Ten years on she is more sympathetic towards Mrs Ramsay. The rebellious daughter now empathises with her mother as female. While in 'The Window' Cam responds reluctantly to her mother's voice, in 'The Lighthouse' she remembers her mother's words at her bedside when she was frightened of the boar's skull: 'It was a valley, full of birds and flowers, and antelopes... she was falling asleep' (p. 275). What she remembers are not referential objects but a sequence of non-representational sounds suggesting the link between her own and her mother's body.[15] Nevertheless, the images conjure up the pastoral tranquillity associated in Victorian writing – and Mrs Ramsay is a product of the Victorian era – with romanticised, passive and delicate notions of femininity. In other words, the female world is aesthetically the 'Other' of the male environment determining a particular type of masculinity in *Jacob's Room*.

According to Elizabeth Abel, however, although 'The Lighthouse' replaces the father–mother–son triad of 'The Window' with a father–son–daughter triad, the feminine position has not fundamentally changed. Cam is caught between the Godlike brother and suppliant father – two manifestations of a patriarchal God and two incarnations of Oedipus.[16] But while an allegorical reading of the novel at this point offers one interpretation, the quotidian particulars offer another. Thinking herself back through her mother interrupts Cam's narrative of resistance and creates a 'third' space. But this third space is complex, for while it is anti-patriarchal – reflected in its anti-patriarchal use of language – it is also in danger of repeating the mother's submissiveness. Having lifted herself out of one discourse, Cam cannot be certain that she is not entering another.

Her mother's words interrupt Cam's debate with herself about her father – caught between her attraction to him – 'his voice, and his words, and [even] his hate, and his temper, and his oddity, and his passion' – and her memories of that 'crass blindness and tyranny of his which had poisoned her childhood and raised bitter storms... his dominance: his "Submit to me"' (p. 229). Again, Cam is placed in a complex situation. At one level she is positioned as the object of male discourses of the female which she has hitherto resisted. But, at another level, maturity involves recognising that the position males occupy in those discourses is complicated and often uncomfortable for them, too, as is demonstrated in *Jacob's Room*. At the end of the novel, she sees both the strengths and the weaknesses, the blessing and the curse, in the male situation.

Not surprisingly, then, Cam has been the focus of debate among critics taking psychoanalytic approaches to the novel. Elizabeth Abel argues that Cam represents the loss of the mother and of the mother–daughter language of babyhood whereas Margaret Homans argues that Cam stands for its perpetuation. Homans distinguishes what she describes as the literal maternal language from the French psychoanalytic critic Julia Kristeva's disruptive 'semiotic' language of sounds and rhythms. She argues that the mother–daughter language – the literal maternal – is suppressed but is not repressed, as Kristeva argues of semiotic language.[17] It is perhaps the ambivalence surrounding Cam that gives the novel its distinctive uncertainty.

IV

In making Lily's painting the centre of the novel, and its completion the conclusion of the book, Woolf would appear to privilege painting – specifically Lily's attempt to express herself in terms of colour and form – over language. It is Lily's painting that unites sections 1 and 3 of the novel. In section 3 she obtains the vision that enables her to complete the picture that she began on her first visit. The novel itself extends the colour symbolism of the earlier works. While the masculine is associated with red and browns, the changing colours associated with the female characters suggest the transformation of the view of the mother and the female within the novel. Initially Mrs Ramsay is associated with purple and the lighthouse with bright violet and staring white, but at the end of the novel, when Lily has a better appreciation of Lily's fluid identity, the lighthouse is seen in a blue haze.

On a cursory reading, the text would seem to suggest that Lily's representation of the relationship between mother and child, Mrs Ramsay and James, transcends mother–child discourses, including Freud's Oedipal triangle. In the kind of painting Lily undertakes, Woolf is clearly indebted to the enthusiasm of the Bloomsbury group for Post-Impressionism. Her friendship with Roger Fry, whose lectures on Post-Impressionism she attended, was obviously important, especially his disassociation of art from the aesthetic of verisimilitude. Indeed, Lily's explanation of her work to William Bankes echoes Fry's insistence that responses to art are a matter of the formal relations of masses, of lights and shadows – 'if there, in that corner, it was bright, here in this, she felt the need of darkness' (p. 72). The novel focuses, however, not on Lily's explanations of her aesthetics but Bankes' reaction to her work. He does not simply bring a 'male' response to a female art but an eye used to seeing art in terms of representation. Thinking about art as a relation of 'masses, lights and shadows' (p. 73) is a new experience for him. However, his interrogation of the painting is dependent upon him being able to hold a penknife (redolent of Peter Walsh's penknife) close to it. Its bone handle immediately identifies it with the boar's skull in this novel and the sheep's skull in *Jacob's Room*.

Bankes is attracted to Lily's representation of Mrs Ramsay reading to James as a purple triangle. The only explanation that she offers for her choice of a triangle to represent them is a formal one. In the spatial relations within her painting, she might also have represented them by shadow or light. The novel, like Lily's painting, makes increasing use of shapes including, of course, the lighthouse and the island. But all these shapes are not only opposed to language but are multivalent. What Lily fails to recognise is that triangles are not 'innocent' shapes devoid of cultural significances. Like language, shapes are open to a number of competing interpretations. Woolf warns us not to see language and shape in terms of a simple binarism in one of the most memorable shapes with which Mr Ramsay is associated, the keyboard-alphabet. Thus, the triangle may be interpreted in different ways. At one level it represents father, mother and child which Freud interpreted as the Oedipal triangle. While Lily wishes to think of a dyad of mother and child, she is obviously less able than she thinks to free her thought from the dominant discourse represented in the triangle. Painting Mrs Ramsay and James as a triangle also introduces herself into the relationship, while the shape of the triangle introduces further possibilities that challenge what the triangle is normally taken to represent.

The spire of a triangle is generally taken to represent the masculine while the female principle is represented in mythological symbolism by a triangle turned upside down. The key binarism in the novel, which is eventually undermined, Mr and Mrs Ramsay, could be represented in these terms. His rationalism, brusqueness and dominance might be associated with the upright triangle, while her conventional female qualities, intuition, emotion and sensuality, might be linked to the upside down triangle. But his loneliness and need for affection, echoing *Jacob's Room*, turns his triangle upside down, while Mrs Ramsay's understanding of what is going on turns the triangle with which she is associated upright. A triangle of equal sides suggests that the three partners enjoy equal power or status. One triangle is one part of two interlocking triangles that are generally taken to represent union, and on many levels the novel is a search for this kind of unity, as is Lily's painting. Thus, the triangle not only has specific cultural meanings but some of those meanings in western culture are privileged over other possibilities; the triangle in Lily's painting can represent what is absent as well as what is present on her canvas.

Not only are we made aware of the difficulty of working outside of discourses even when we are dealing with shapes, but of the precarious nature of discourses. While William Bankes accepts Lily's explanation, he fails to realise what a destabilising image the triangle actually is. A moment's contemplation of Lily's response to him also makes us aware of the information that we do not have – whether the triangle is of equal proportions, whether it is upside down or upright, whether it is the only triangle in the painting.

The discussion between Bankes and Lily over the triangle in her painting follows Lily's reflection on her night-time visit to Mrs Ramsay when she found herself with her head against Mrs Ramsay's knee – in other words, taking the place of James. Here she thinks of her relation with Mrs Ramsay as a dyad but, of course, the 'absent presence' here is always the triangle:

> Sitting on the floor with her arms round Mrs Ramsay's knees, close as she could get, smiling to think that Mrs Ramsay would never know the reason of that pressure, she imagined how in the chambers of the mind and heart of the woman who was physically touching her, were stood, like the treasures in the tombs of kings, tablets bearing sacred inscriptions, which if one could spell them out would teach one everything, but they would never be offered openly, never made public. (p. 70)

Here the dyad clearly interrupts the Oedipal triangle and the idealised mother and son dyad perceived through the (male) gaze of William Bankes. But the love of the surrogate daughter is clearly associated with the *crypta* – tombs and secret chambers – and with the cryptographic, sacred inscriptions. 'Spell them out' is ambiguous, suggesting both 'decipher' and 'proclaim'. The 'absent presence' of the triangle means that the scene which Lily describes is one of exclusion as well as inclusion. Lily displays a half-articulated passion for Mrs Ramsay that blurs the boundaries between their two bodies. In a way that reminds us of Melanie Klein's research into mother–child relationships, Lily appears to want to enter the body of the mother. But the language that is employed of 'chambers', 'tombs', 'Kings', 'treasures' and 'sacred inscriptions' displaces the scene from the house in which it occurs to an exotic Middle East. In other words, the boundaries between the desire and the fantasy in which it is conceived are blurred.

Lily's passionate desire for Mrs Ramsay interrupts the novel's focus on the marriage of Mr and Mrs Ramsay and its privileging of heterosexual relationships in Mrs Ramsay's persistent desire to want to find marriage partners for her children and Lily. The centre of gravity of the novel shifts from the marriage of Mr and Mrs Ramsay to Mrs Ramsay and Lily's expression of her creativity as a woman in art. An important difference between *To the Lighthouse* and *Mrs Dalloway*, however, is that Mrs Ramsay does not act as a focal point for the relationships in the novel. Her presence, actual and remembered, influences relationships and in that sense she is a more active force in *To the Lighthouse* than Clarissa in *Mrs Dalloway*. Whereas James and Lily initially see Mrs Ramsay in ways that are centripetal, the novel locates Mrs Ramsay as a centrifugal presence. In this way Woolf resists essentialising Mrs Ramsay according to any one particular set of interpretations. In this respect Mrs Ramsay may be identified with the lighthouse itself. However, I do not wish to suggest, as some critics have, that Mrs Ramsay is merely the lighthouse to which others are attracted. As I noted earlier, neither Mrs Ramsay nor the lighthouse is open to a single interpretation. Their significance actually lies not in what they represent but in what is revealed of others in their attitude towards them.

One of the least satisfactory features of the novel from a feminist point of view is that, while Mrs Ramsay is a central part of other people's lives, she is marginalised within her own. Admittedly, through her self-suppression she may be viewed as manipulating and controlling others, but she risks sacrificing her own, full self-signification. These difficulties, however, are part of a larger problem in the novel with identifying women's art and mother–daughter and same-sex relationships as the *crypta*, which Woolf clearly does in the passage quoted above: the *crypta* might be taken as privileging that to which it is the *crypta*. Woolf, though, locates the *crypta* not only beyond but outside. If Lily and her secret passion for another woman, complicated as the secret desire of a woman for a mother, is associated with the *crypta* in this novel, it is also outside of time. Lily is outside of time in that we know nothing of her mother or of her past. Her status as an outsider figure is further underlined by her enigmatic Chinese features and by her position not only as a woman artist but as a painter working outside the dominant realist traditions of English art.

V

The relative nature of outsider status is an important dimension, too, in the novel's exploration of masculinity and mother–son relationships, areas in which *To the Lighthouse* can most obviously be seen as an interruption of *Jacob's Room*, unveiling, and developing what is implied in the earlier novel. If Mrs Ramsay is an interruption of the mental portrait that Woolf and her sisters had of their mother, Julia Duckworth, then Mr Ramsay is an interruption of their imaginary portrait of their father who, like Mr Ramsay, was a philosopher. But Mr Ramsay is more than a revised portrait, albeit a rather harsh one, of Sir Leslie Stephen. Given to quotation of poetry (which like Virginia's father he recites aloud), Mr Ramsay identifies himself with heroic victims, exemplifying a type of masculinity that Woolf associated with the empire. While this masculinity is satirised throughout her fiction for its chauvinism and aggression, it also gives rise in her novels to confusion in the wake of a disappearing social and symbolic order. In this novel the disappearing order is epitomised in the way in which the domestic life of the Ramsays appears to have been decimated by the war – they have no servants and do not seem to give dinner parties as they once did.

Jacob's Room exposes that type of masculinity Woolf believed was determined by the phantasm or ideals of heroic behaviour in which boys of Jacob's class were educated. It is suggested in *Jacob's Room* that Jacob's emotional and imaginative development is distorted by his socialisation within a phallocentric culture, the dominant discourses of which legitimise treating the feminine as inferior and the maternal as abject. The same can also be said for her son, James, who echoes the young Jacob – cutting pictures from an Army and Navy Stores catalogue, he conveys an 'image of stark and uncompromising severity' (p. 7), to which I will return in a moment. Indeed, *Jacob's Room* seems to have been so much to the forefront of her mind in writing *To the Lighthouse* that she recycles some of its imagery such as the seascape, the waves and the skull. The boar's skull, for example, serves the same metaphorical function as the ram's skull in

Jacob's Room; an image not just of male sexuality but of male sexuality laid cerebral and bare.

In writing *To the Lighthouse*, Woolf appears to have interrupted her line of thought about masculinity in *Jacob's Room* to pursue her suggestion in that novel that the traditional discourses of masculinity are based on a repression of the mother. Thus, the stories constructed by the Ramsay children, James and Cam, are posited on the renunciation of their mother's memory. Significantly, their retrospective narratives are composed in a boat under the aegis of their father, reminding us of Woolf's entry in her diary in which she conceived that 'the centre [of the novel] is father's character, sitting in a boat, reciting We perished, each alone, while he crushes a dying mackerel'.[18] Indeed, the episode which virtually opens the novel in which James enjoys a close relationship with his mother is interrupted by Mr Ramsay, and might be compared with the scene in *Mrs Dalloway* in which Clarissa and Sally are disturbed by Peter Walsh:

> But his son hated him. He hated him for coming up to them, for stopping and looking down on them; he hated him for interrupting them.... By looking fixedly at the page, he hoped to make him move on; by pointing his finger at a word, he hoped to recall his mother's attention, which, he knew angrily, wavered instantly his father stopped. (p. 51)

James's reaction to the interruption by his father – 'Had there been an axe handy, a poker, or any weapon that would have gashed a hole in his father's breast and killed him, there and then, James would have seized it' (p. 8) – is much more violent, however, than Clarissa's to Peter Walsh, as Elizabeth Abel has pointed out.[19] It is also redolent of the intense affection that D. H. Lawrence's Paul Morel has for his mother and his vehement hatred of his father in *Sons and Lovers* (1913). By contrast, Cam's dislike of her father does not find expression in analogous objects as does James's. In this respect the novel as a whole can be read as an interruption of the Freudian narrative, focusing not on the identification of the father as a sign of maturity, which is the point of Freud's narrative, but as a site of violence, unhappiness and repression within the male. It is no coincidence that the weapons that James thinks of are phallic objects and that the method of killing is a displacement of sexual penetration.

Despite his apparent severity, the image of the young James cutting pictures from a catalogue, like many images in the novel, is enigmatic. We feel that it is intended to be symbolic, and it seems to merge with other silent behaviours in the text, but it is difficult to define. What are these pictures? Is he interested in the shapes? What are these shapes a displacement of? As I pointed out in the previous chapter, the Army and Navy Stores, intended to provide for troops in the empire, became one of the glittering department stores, associated with upper-middle-class women as the principal consumers. Although he is only a young child, this connection undermines James's severity and gives him a feminine dimension in anticipation of his affection for his mother and apparent need even later to confirm his emotional bond with her. He is the child within his father who has similarly suppressed emotional needs, although he does not realise this until the journey to the lighthouse when he and his sister begin the trip disliking, even hating, their father but come to understand him.

Unveiling what is implied in *Jacob's Room*, *To the Lighthouse* foregrounds James's desire to reclaim his bond with his mother:

> It was sympathy he wanted, to be assured of his genius, first of all, and then to be taken within the circle of life, warmed and soothed, to have his senses restored to him, his barrenness made fertile, and all the rooms of the house made full of life.   (p. 52)

But *To the Lighthouse* also interrupts that narrative in the earlier novel. Instead of focusing on the rejection of the feminine in the principal discourses of masculinity in pre-war England, *To the Lighthouse* highlights the discourses of women as Woman that have been carried over into, or have been allowed to emerge in, the aftermath of the war. Critics have tended to think of *To the Lighthouse*, as Woolf did at times herself, as a psychoanalytic text, in which she sought to resolve her difficult relationships with her mother and with her mother's loss so early in her life. But the concern in the novel with the cultural construction of women as Woman circulating in post-war England has received far less attention. The novel highlights how James's view of his mother as Mother is not simply the product of his needs but of desires that have been shaped by the public discourse of the Mother. Even the description of Mrs Ramsay moving in her chair, 'animated and alive as if all her energies were being fused into force, burning and illuminating', is informed by poetic discourses of the Mother figure as the origin and source of life. Woolf is not primarily interested, as was the psychoanalyst Melanie Klein, in whether a child's love for its mother was biological or imaginary. Her concern is with discourses that were/are brought to bear when that close attachment is articulated in language that must inevitably have a public as well as a private dimension.

VI

Whatever desires we may harbour to return to the support and protection of the mother, Woolf recognises that they are invariably articulated through discourses about the status of the mother in relation to the male, about nurturing and the relative importance of different roles within the family and society as a whole. Moreover, the seamless nature of the phantasm of nurturing and of the ideal of mothering, Woolf suggests, is the product not only of discourses of the maternal but of what those discourses have occluded, 'obscured and concealed' (p. 24), presented in the novel as the *crypta* within family and mother–child relationships. This can be seen in the way in which *To the Lighthouse* unfurls the darkness and ominous brooding over the seascape in *Jacob's Room*:

> [t]he monotonous fall of the waves on the beach, which for the most part beat a measured and soothing tattoo to her thoughts and seemed consolingly to repeat over and over again as she sat with the children the words of some old cradle song, murmured by nature, 'I am guarding you – I am your support', but at other times suddenly and unexpectedly, especially when her mind raised itself slightly from the task actually in hand, had no such kindly meaning, but like a ghostly roll of drums remorselessly beat the measure of life, made one think of the destruction of the island and its engulfment in the sea, and warned her whose day had slipped past in one quick doing after another that it was all ephemeral as a rainbow – this sound which had been obscured and concealed under other sounds suddenly thundered hollow in her ears and made her look up with an impulse of terror. (pp. 23–4)

The cradle song might be seen as an example of the female voice and of women's creativity, in turn linked with nature and a wider sense of creativity, challenging the dominant creative traditions of men. However, the focus here is not on the soothing words and rhythms of the nurturing tongue but on what disrupts them. As soon as the words of the cradle song – 'I am guarding you – I am your support' – are put to the waves, they are interrupted by the entry of what is normally suppressed, thoughts of destruction, entrapment and death.

As in all of Woolf's fiction, one of the principal tropes of *To the Lighthouse* is the revelation of what is concealed or occluded. Thus, Lily turns Charles Tansley into an X-ray photograph and tries to probe Mrs Ramsay's inner, secret self, and Paul and Minta's secret passion occurs out of sight, literally behind a rock. But, as in *Jacob's Room*, the *crypta* within the text is associated with danger, death and even the annihilation of England – the reference to the 'island' in the above passage is double-edged. Mrs Ramsay's death is linked in the second part of the novel, 'Time Passes', to the war in which the universe seems to be 'battling and tumbling, in brute confusion and wanton lust aimlessly by itself' (p.183). And it is in this section that we learn that, in addition to Mrs Ramsay, Andrew and Prue are dead. Prue's death undermines not only Mrs Ramsay's commitment to ensuring the continuity of the maternal line but her idealisation of motherhood itself. Minta's loss of her grandmother's brooch – a weeping willow set in a pearl – might signify the loss of her virginity but the weeping willow in the brooch can be seen as representing the pain and despair that is passed inevitably, it would seem, from one generation of women to another, and which cannot be lost.

At several points, *To the Lighthouse*, like *Jacob's Room*, appears to suggest an essentialist view of gender identity, as in the account of Mr Ramsay's interruption of his son's sense of closeness with his mother: 'into this delicious fecundity, this fountain and spray of life, the fatal sterility of the male plunged itself, like a beak of brass, barren and bare' (p. 52). However, Woolf's perspective is more subtle than this, positing how hegemonic gender identities might well be a social consequence of the dominant ideologies that shape the male and female subjects, particularly those from a similar class and educational background. In *To the Lighthouse*, Woolf appears to be developing her interest, pursued in more detail in *The Years*, in the way in which the family as a social structure is a product not simply of kinship but of wider ideologies and socio-economic forces. In the last section of the novel the adult James admits that he has never lost the secret desire to stab his father in the heart. However, he has come to realise that it is not his father he wishes to kill but 'the thing that descended on him' (p. 248). This 'thing' is the discourse that has determined and limited his father's world-view and emotional development. Like Jacob in *Jacob's Room*, James is uncomfortable with the future laid out before him and men of his generation:

> Whatever he did – (and he might do anything, he felt, looking at the Lighthouse and the distant shore) whether he was in a business, in a bank, a barrister, a man at the head of some enterprise, that he would fight, that he would track down and stamp out – tyranny, despotism, he called it – making people do what they did not want to do, cutting off their right to speak. (pp. 248–9)

Once again, what is treated briefly in *Jacob's Room* is developed in this novel. But James's reference here to the way in which one discourse can silence another serves as a retrospective gloss on Mrs Ramsay's argument with her husband and the lower middle-class atheist philosopher Charles Tansley over whether the weather will permit a journey to the lighthouse. To interpret their attempt to silence her as a metaphor for the way in which the male takes the child from the mother is to overlook the point that Woolf is making about the gendered nature of discourse. Charles Tansley may be representative of the pacifists and socialists who tried to achieve power in the war years, but he is complicit in the same patriarchal system as Mr Ramsay whose class affiliations he detests. Woolf, then, is making the point that today needs no elaboration that in post-war English society, and certainly in the Victorian period, women's voices were not heard as often as men's, and what they had to say was not received with the same authority.

The way in which Mrs Ramsay sees the lighthouse – as part of the fantasy in which mother and son participate – is different from the way in which James sees it when he finally arrives there as an adult. At one level it reflects the kind of world created in the discourse of his father who literally and symbolically interrupted the journey he was to take there with his mother. However, some psychoanalytic readings of the novel interpret the difference between their perspectives here rather naively. Elizabeth Abel associates Mrs Ramsay's viewpoint with Freud's 'pleasure principle' which is destroyed by the intrusion of Mr Ramsay's 'reality'.[20] There are several problems here. Firstly, Mrs Ramsay cannot be divorced from a realistic view of the lighthouse. She is knitting a stocking for the lighthouse-keeper's child because she is only too aware that the keepers 'must be bored to death sitting all day with nothing to do but polish the lamp and trim the wick and rake about their scrap of garden' (p. 9). Secondly, it is as reductive to associate Mr Ramsay only with the symbolic male in Freudian discourse or with 'reality' as to see him only as a portrait of Virginia Woolf's father. Indeed, his insistence that the weather may not be fine is not simply the voice of realism opposed to his wife's optimism. In fact, later in the novel, Mr Ramsay accuses his wife of being a pessimist when she muses that it is a pity that children have to grow out of their innocence and lose their spontaneity, suggesting that in some respects Mr Ramsay is more optimistic than herself.

In the published version of *To the Lighthouse*, Woolf resists polarising Mr and Mrs Ramsay as binary opposites. Each of them is a contradictory character – Mr Ramsay fluctuates between optimism and melancholy, not entirely satisfied with what he has done in his life and feeling that if he had not got married he would have written better books. But without resorting to a crude essentialising of masculinity and femininity, Mrs Ramsay recognises that men, because of the way in which they are usually brought up, were likely not to notice or take an interest in the ordinary things. Mr Ramsay is interested in the extraordinary but his admiration of flowers is only surface deep, an attempt to please his wife. Her observation that he 'would sit at table with them like a person in a dream' (p. 96) indicates how he, like other men of his class, occupy a phantasmatic actuality. His frequent quotation of heroic verse suggests the nature of this actuality and that, because of the different ways in which men and women are brought up, men are more likely to be estranged from the immediate and the sensuous than are women.

An aspect of this phantasmatic reality that both he and Mrs Ramsay share is evident in the way she thinks of the lighthouse-keeper's son. In the manuscript version of the novel, the working class – the poor and the sick visited by Mrs Ramsay, the one-armed bill poster, the circus troupe, the Swiss maid and the cook – have a less muted presence than in the published work. But, unlike in *Mrs Dalloway* where the working-class characters make strategic interventions in the text, in *To the Lighthouse*, Woolf is interested, as Hermione Lee notes, in using such figures to illustrate how Victorian philanthropy has survived into the twentieth century.[21] The Ramsays have an attitude towards the sick, the poor and the working class that is comparable to Mr Dalloway's view of them in her first novel. One of Mr Ramsay's quotations in the manuscript is from Matthew Arnold's elegy for Arthur Clough, the archetypal Victorian poet, scholar and intellectual, in which the poet looks back on his Arcadia from 'the great town's harsh, heart-wearying roar' – in other words from the realities of the modern industrial state. But the conflict in the novel between the Ramsays, who see the poor as individuals, and Charles Tansley, who thinks in terms of the political organisation of the working class, reflects a dispute that dominated Parliament in the first two decades of the twentieth century. The closing years of the nineteenth century and the opening years of the new century witnessed the demise of the aristocratic politicians who never lacked for anything themselves. But ignorance of the realities of the modern industrial state among this class of politician did not die out with Salisbury's retirement in 1902, for Lloyd George made much political capital of the evidence he found of it in Balfour during the war.

To the Lighthouse, like Mrs Dalloway, thus reflects the different ideas and debates of its day, especially those circulating among the literary classes. It requires us to be as alert to the dangers of homogenising the past as in reading the earlier text. It would be too simple to see Mr Ramsay, on account of his recitation of heroic verse, his overbearing manner and the fact that his wife's relatives governed India, as emblematic of a Victorian nexus of patriarchy and empire. Not only is he personally more complex than this, as I have sought to point out, but he is only one voice in the novel, in turn reflecting only one strain of late nineteenth-century and early twentieth-century political thought. Tansley loathing the upper-middle class and reading about the French Revolution is another.

VII

In the course of the book I have suggested that Woolf works through some of the difficulties in writing about history by establishing, via the viewpoints of her various characters, a plurality of pasts. At one level Lily's relationship – real or fantasised – is analogous to the problems of imposing a false consciousness on the past and of interpreting historical events according to a contemporary rather than a contemporaneous agenda. Initially, she thinks of Mrs Ramsay as a mother figure to be seen and desired. In doing so she translates the real Mrs Ramsay, whom we see negotiating a number of roles associated with being a wife and mother, into an idealised Great Mother. While some critics, such as Makiko Minow-Pinkney, have argued that 'Mrs Ramsay's death is the bleak loss of total meaning',[22] I have maintained that the complex, and at times contradictory, delineation of Mrs Ramsay resists an association with the idea of closed meaning. In the course of the novel – for example, through her memory of Mrs Ramsay, Charles and Mr Ramsay on the beach together where Mrs Ramsay sat on a rock writing letters – Lily importantly comes to appreciate Mrs Ramsay as someone who has her own perceptions:

> And suddenly the meaning which, for no reason at all, as perhaps they are stepping out of the Tube together or ringing a doorbell, descends on people, making them symbolical, making them representative, came upon them, and made them in the dusk standing, looking, the symbols of marriage, husband and wife. Then, after an instant, the symbolical outline which transcended the real figures sank down again and they became, as they met them, Mr and Mrs Ramsay watching the children throwing catches.   (p. 99)

As throughout Woolf's fiction, imagining the past means confronting the discourses in which it is normally written – to which the 'symbolical outline' here can be seen as analogous – and is thereby constructed. Lily achieves a fuller understanding of this than Woolf's other daughter figures (Rachel Vinrace, Katharine Hilbery, Clara Durrant, Elizabeth Dalloway). Importantly, she is the first of these characters, as Heather Ingman notes, 'to succeed in inscribing herself into the symbolic without betraying the mother [figure]'.[23] Her work looks behind the 'symbolical outline' of historiography to the 'real'. However, since the 'symbolical' can be seen as 'descending' on the 'real', making it 'representative' – despite the fact that the characters in the above passage are conceived as having 'transcended the real' – in her fiction as a whole Woolf is concerned with the dialectical relationship between them.

Whereas the complex structure of *Mrs Dalloway*, as I suggested in the previous chapter, reflects the tension between competing perspectives of militarism, Englishness, empire and gender relationships, *To the Lighthouse* exemplifies modernist ideas about different levels of time co-existing and the way in which the past and the present relate to each other. Not only ideas about memory but the presence of *Jacob's Room* as one of the intertexts in *To the*

Lighthouse can be explained in terms of Freud's concept of 'deferred action', on the basis of which the novel, in turn, may be considered as the product, at different levels, of 'interruption'. The concept of the past being interrupted by the present, contradicting conventional notions of the progress of time, reflects Woolf's shifting interest in the problems of writing about the past. The idea of the present endowing the past with meaning might be viewed as legitimating a historiography which distorts the past by imposing upon it its own preoccupations. As I argued in the previous chapter, Woolf's use of a variety of focalisations in order to do justice to the plurality of the past, and of a narrator who allows herself to be accessed by the past, were strategies designed, in part, to avoid such a historiography in her own work. But the concept of *nachträglichkeit* actually makes the writing of a history over determined by the interests of the present less, rather than more, likely. Undermining our conventional ideas of the past acting independently on the present, as it were, the concept of the present as interrupting the past stresses how the significance of the past is relational, how past and present exist in a dialectical relationship to each other, and how history is invariably bound up with interpretation. These are ideas that Woolf pursued with more specific reference to British history and historiography in her subsequent novel, the subject of the next chapter.

7

History and Historiography: *Orlando* (1928) and *The Waves* (1931)

Memory is not an instrument for exploring the past, but its theatre.
Walter Benjamin, *One-Way Street*[1]

I

Written towards the end of the 1920s, *Orlando: A Biography* and *The Waves* are no less experimental than Woolf's previous three novels of this time. At first it may seem strange to discuss these two novels in tandem, not least because while *Orlando* has come to be seen as a 'political' novel, *The Waves* is approached more often as an aesthetic experiment. However, in each novel Woolf returns to the familiar triptych of Englishness, empire and gender identity. In *Orlando* Woolf pursues her interest, evident even in her first novel, in those aspects of gender identity that might be seen as the *crypta* within the dominant discursive formations, this time broached through a broader consideration of androgyny, disguise and masquerade. By contrast, *The Waves* prioritises the anxiety over identity, and specifically within masculinity, that developed in the wake of the projected demise of the empire, particularly of the British empire in India. Despite the differences between them, the novels share an exploration of the interconnection of space, political history and the imaginary through a range of cryptic references to Britain's cultural climate in the 1920s and to specific political events. They are each concerned with the emergent sense of national and cultural identity among the English upper classes during that decade and with questioning the nature of change itself.

There is also a strong satirical vein in each of the novels. But the main reason for linking *Orlando* and *The Waves* in this chapter is that they are more appropriately approached as apologues than satires. According to Sheldon Sacks, a satire is a work in which each part is employed for the single purpose of ridicule. But the apologue is a work 'organised as a fictional example of the truth of a formulable statement or closely related set of such statements'.[2] *Orlando* and *The Waves* exemplify, in fictional form, a closely related set of statements, in the Foucauldian sense, pertaining to gender identity, patriarchy, Englishness, empire and history, which together weave an intricate web of sexual repression, cultural superiority, domination and inferiorisation. Sacks' use of the word 'example' does not do justice, however, to the way in which apologues interrogate and challenge the statements on which they are based.

Woolf began *Orlando* in the autumn of 1927 when she was struggling to write a critical book on fiction that she never finished. As is well known, *Orlando* was initially intended as a mock biography of Vita Sackville-West, whom Woolf met in 1928 and with whom she fell in love. Many of the characters and events are in fact allusions to Vita's life. But, unlike a conventional biography, the novel ranges over three hundred years and involves the subject in a sex change. What, though, has been insufficiently discussed is that as a mock biography of Vita Sackville-West, *Orlando* establishes a dialectic relationship between biography and identity and in its time span and geography challenges the hegemony of formal biography.

Like *Jacob's Room* but in different ways, *Orlando* reflects the influence of critiques of Victorian biography such as Lytton Strachey's *Eminent Victorians* (1918). We are first introduced to Lord Orlando as a young man in the sixteenth century but then follow him to the Court of King James, where he has a relationship with the Russian Shasha (based on Vita's affair with Violet 'Lushka' Trefusis), and the Court of Charles II, where, redolent of Vita's bisexual husband Harold Nicolson who also appears later in the novel as Marmaduke Bonthrop Shelmerdine, he is appointed an ambassador. In Constantinople, Orlando has a disreputable marriage with Rosina Pepita (a character based on Vita's Spanish grandmother) and undergoes a change in gender. As an ex-ambassador, Lady Orlando lives for a while among a band of gipsies whom she upsets through her very English admiration of nature, her poetry and her enthusiasm for English ancestral homes. Although in the eighteenth and nineteenth centuries Lady Orlando lives the life of a literary aristocrat, she continues to be estranged from the societies in which she finds herself. In the eighteenth century she dresses as a man to meet London prostitutes and in the nineteenth century she marries an eccentric explorer and sea captain. In the 1920s she is a prize-winning author. The echoes of Vita Sackville-West's life are continued throughout the novel in Lord/Lady Orlando's travels in Eastern Europe, in her pursuit by the Duke/Duchess Scand-op-Boom and in her transvestism.

Woolf intended *Orlando* as 'an escapade' and described it 'all a joke'; a 'writer's holiday' with the 'spirit to be satiric' and the 'structure wild'.[3] Woolf also wrote another mock biography, *Flush*, the story of Elizabeth Barrett Browning's dog. Although, as Susan Squier points out, *Orlando* has been regarded at times rather like *Flush* as no more than 'a playful interlude in Woolf's *oeuvre*',[4] it is, in fact, part of Woolf's ongoing engagement with history and historiography. Within the context of the close interrelationship between intellectual debate, innovation and politics in her fiction, *Orlando* is an important novel. Indeed, although *Orlando* began as a joke, it ended as a more serious work in which Woolf had difficulty resolving the tension between satire and comic fantasy. But if the novel is approached as an apologue, then satire and fantasy become only two of a number of strategies employed in the book, including mockery, ridicule, farce and the carnivalesque.

II

Carnival is evidently a key image in the book. As Mikhail Bakhtin has pointed out, carnival developed in the folk culture of the Middle Ages, protecting the people's creativity and verbal expression in non-official forms.[5] Turning the world upside down, carnival provided a temporary opportunity for the ordinary people to subvert traditional hierarchies and to challenge authority. It offered a space in which they could demonstrate, for a while, the absurd truth of formulable concepts under which, and within which, they lived. Even though carnival can be seen as a safety-valve which releases social tensions in a safe environment, in fact permitting the status quo to persist,

Bakhtin's terms were those in which Woolf first conceived of *Orlando*. She recorded in her diary that 'everything [is to be] mocked....For the truth is I feel the need of an escapade after these serious poetic experimental books whose form is always so closely considered'.[6] However, despite Woolf's declared intention that *Orlando* should mock everything, the novel is not an unmitigated celebration of carnival and non-meaning. Rather, there are elements of deconstructive mockery – as in Lady Orlando's meetings with Alexander Pope or her encounters, while dressed as a man, with prostitutes. There is a difference, as Terry Eagleton has pointed out in a discussion of Bakhtin, Schopenhauer and Milan Kundera, between hostility to particular values, which is what we find in *Orlando*, and apologues generally, and the negativity of a larger cynicism displayed by writers such as Schopenhauer.[7]

Bakhtin argues that on feast days people were freed from 'the oppression of such gloomy categories as "eternal", "immovable", "absolute", "unchangeable" and instead were exposed to the gay and free laughing aspect of the world, with its unfinished and open character, with the joy of change and renewal'.[8] During the carnival in *Orlando*, the people are 'exposed to the gay and free laughing aspect' of both the world and of language. Laughter, as a mode of deconstructive mockery, emerges in the novel as the *crypta* occluded by the authority which the dominant discursive formations claim for themselves:

> The feast was a temporary suspension of the entire official system with all its prohibitions and hierarchic barriers. For a short time life came out of its usual, legalized and consecrated furrows and entered the sphere of Utopian freedom. The very brevity of this freedom increased its fantastic nature and utopian radicalism, born in the festive atmosphere of images.[9]

Woolf's account of the carnival in the novel may well have been inspired by Yeats' discussion of the end of the Anglo-French nation in his essay on Spenser. Yeats associated Merrie England with the Anglo-French nation that was swept away in the Elizabethan period by the new Anglo-Saxon values from which arose Puritan sermons and Marprelate tracts:

> This nation had driven out the language of its conquerors, and now it was to overthrow their beautiful haughty imagination and their

manners, full of abandon and wilfulness, and to set in their stead earnestness and logic and the timidity and reserve of a counting-house.[10]

Although Shasha, whose haughtiness, manners, abandon and wilfulness embody the spirit of the carnival, is a Muscovite, she sets up a binary opposition between the Norman and the English in the contrast between her fluent French and the monoglot English of the Court. And, of course, one of the literary antecedents for the name Orlando is the French medieval *Chanson de Roland*, thus associating this carnivalesque spirit of Merrie England with the novel as a whole. Throughout the novel, mockery and ridicule are the 'Other' to the earnestness that belies the imperialistic, patriarchal and monolithic assumptions of the English.

In writing of the spirit of Merrie England in *Orlando* and transposing the official and the formal into 'the key of gay laughter',[11] Woolf, consciously or unconsciously, follows the technique of medieval parodies. For, like *Orlando* and apologues generally, the medieval parodies were not formal, literary satires on what was regarded as sacred but transpositions of these into what Bakhtin calls the 'material bodily sphere':

> Who were those bumpkins [Shasha asked Orlando], who sat beside her with the manners of stablemen? What was the nauseating mixture they poured on her plate? Did the dogs eat at the same table with the men in England? Was that figure of fun at the end of the table with her hair rigged up like a Maypole (comme une grande perche mal fagotée) really the Queen? And did the King always slobber like that?[12]

Indeed, *Orlando* is one of the most lewdly physical of Woolf's novels. Throughout the book, the body, which sometimes as in Shasha's description of the Court verges on the grotesque, is situated as a site of conflict between the natural and the socially constructed. But in *Orlando*, in line with Bakhtin's thesis, the official and authoritarian are 'combined with violence, prohibitions, limitations and always contain an element of fear and intimidation'.[13] Despite the carnival atmosphere on the Thames,

> Great statesmen, in their beards and ruffs, despatched affairs of state under the crimson awning of the Royal Pagoda. Soldiers planned the conquest of the Moor and the downfall of the Turk in striped arbours surmounted by plumes of ostrich feathers. (p. 34)

In *Orlando*, laughter, an idiom which is never employed in violence or authority, provides a means of combating fear, oppression and guilt over what is repressed.

III

While it is important to recognise, as Hermione Lee points out, that much of Woolf's thinking about sexuality, biography, history and class in *Orlando* was bound up with Vita Sackville-West, the principal relationship of her forties,[14] the novel was also the product of a wide range of reading, including Jules Michelet's history of France, Yeats' *The Tower*, Defoe's *Moll Flanders*, Sterne's *Tristram Shandy*, Dickens' novels and Shakespeare's *As You Like It*. Woolf even returns to parody aspects of her earlier novel, *To the Lighthouse*. From this wide reading, and especially from the work of Michelet, Woolf derived an approach to history that anticipates Foucault's *The Archaeology of Knowledge* (1969), and in particular his essay 'Nietzsche, Genealogy and History'. This is not surprising, for Foucault too was indebted to Michelet who, as J. G. Merquior reminds us, worked 'for a "resurrection" of past life, away from the placid, detached reconstructions sought by run-of-the-mill historiography'.[15] Both Woolf and Foucault render the past unfamiliar in contrast to the conventional historian who is usually intent upon familiarising readers with the past.

The response that Jules Michelet's history of France prompted in Woolf – 'that history is one of the most fantastic concoctions of the human brain'[16] – provides an insight into the nature of *Orlando*. For both Foucault and Woolf, Michelet's work clearly generates an intrinsically foreign and, at times in *Orlando*, a bizarre past. In defamiliarising the three hundred years over which *Orlando* ranges – for example, the Elizabethan Age, the Courts of King James and Charles II, seventeenth-century Constantinople, the eighteenth-century coffee-house society, London at the time of the Great Exhibition – *Orlando* encourages its readers to reconsider their own cultural identities. Characters such as Elizabeth, Shakespeare, Nell Gwyn and the prostitute Nell introduce alternative narratives to the 'official' histories, including literary histories, that call into question the nature of historiography.

Woolf, of course, is not a historian. Her interest is not in public events *per se* but in how events are incorporated into public discourses, in distinguishing between history and historiography, and in contemplating what might be released when we permit ourselves freedom from 'history'. Thus Lord Orlando's release from historical time permits him freedom from the imprint of his forefathers, escape from the self-contained notion of English cultural identity with which he has grown up, and an alternative to a (largely) masculine categorisation of both gender identity and sexual experience. The thaw that follows the Great Frost literally and metaphorically unfreezes historical time but also connotes through the suggestion of orgasm the release of female sexuality and through the unfreezing of the 'ego' the release of the unconscious (the 'id').

Yeats' *The Tower* no doubt had an important influence on *Orlando*. Like *Orlando* it can be seen, as Denis Donoghue has said, 'as symbolism, glancing ruefully at history'.[17] Both texts share a similar dialectic between history, in Yeats' terms what the imagination recognises as distinct from itself, and symbolism, which mediates between the individual's consciousness and the given world. The rueful nature of *Orlando* as a mock biography cannot be over-estimated. Indeed, like Yeats' *The Tower*, it can be seen as an act of imagination in excess of its historical stimuli. But the realisation of our alienation from history is not the only basis of *Orlando*'s rueful glance at the past. It also alienates us from our shared cultural understanding in the present. In many respects, *Orlando* is not so much about three hundred years of history as the decade that followed the Great War.

The Great Frost of the seventeenth century may be seen as analogous to the Great War of the twentieth century. The emphasis in the account of the Frost upon the enormous mortality, the suddenness of death and the frozen corpses clearly bring the front lines of the Great War to mind. The language itself is occasionally redolent of war. A young country woman is '*blown* in a puff of dust over the roofs as the icy *blast* struck her' (pp. 32–3; my emphasis). The Frost is the product of the 'severity that then marked the English climate' (p. 32), analogous to the cultural climate that Woolf suggested in *Jacob's Room* created a particular concept of masculinity that led to war. The way in which ordinary people engaged in traditional tasks in the countryside are suddenly 'struck stark in the act of the moment' (p. 33) suggests both the impact of the war on the country and the way in which poets such as Thomas Hardy and Edward Thomas emphasised the disruption of war by placing it alongside the

so-called unchanging life of the English countryside. The church is
of little help in the Great Frost, echoing the disillusionment with
religion that characterised much poetry and fiction about the
Great War.

But if the Great Frost can be read as a metaphor for the Great War,
the carnival on the Thames brought about by the Great Frost would
seem to be a metaphor for the Roaring Twenties. At the end of the
decade, Woolf seems to have concluded that whether the Roaring
Twenties was to be celebrated as a decade of change and liberation
depended upon how the participant was positioned in relation to
it through geography, class, age and gender: 'But while the
country people suffered the extremity of want, and the trade of
the country was at a standstill, London enjoyed a carnival of the
utmost brilliancy' (p. 33).

IV

Anticipating postmodern theories of the nation state, Woolf eschews
the historicism that dominated discussion of nationhood in the nineteenth century, and focuses upon nationhood as a form of social and
textual affiliation. Within this framework the English people are seen
as the objects of a range of literary and social narratives. *Orlando*,
then, reconfigures the role of history in the formation of national
identity and particularly the way in which a nation's past is seen in
terms of continuous lines of development to a necessary future.
Orlando highlights what the linear, progressive model of time in
relation to the nation state occludes: the ghostly (*Gespenstermas-
siges*), the terrifying (*Unerfreuliches*) and the unaccountable (*Unzu-
berechnendes*).[18]

The young, male Orlando's pastime of slicing at the head of a
Moor swinging from the rafters of his room suggests that within
English culture there is an anxiety about difference – his fathers
had 'struck many heads of many colours off many shoulders' (p.
13) – which has found expression in various imperialist projects.
Woolf suggests that the inferiorising of non-English races by the
English is not a product but an integral part of the construction of
one strain of Englishness. Here Woolf confronts a crucial contradiction in the modern nation state. While it purports to be an autonomous or sovereign form of political rationality rooted in Enlightenment
thinking, it is based on the existence of the 'Other'.

To some extent the arguments about Orlando's forefathers within the text anticipate Edward Said's views, on which his book *Orient-alism* (1978) is based, that all systems of Western cultural description are contaminated by its politics, interests and strategies of power. But although Said maintains that different historical periods perceived the Orient differently, as Bart Moore-Gilbert has pointed out, 'it often seems that the continuities within colonial discourse are much stronger than [the] discontinuities'.[19] But clearly *Orlando* reflects the critical stance towards colonialism and imperialism that emerged in the metropolitan centres, and may itself be seen as an example of a metropolitan intervention in the debate about imperialism. For a novel written in 1928, it is significant that Orlando is made King Charles's ambassador in Constantinople at a difficult time, that he is able to complete delicate negotiations satisfactorily but that a revolution breaks out in the course of his period of office. Six years earlier, Britain had confronted the Turks – the last occasion on which the country came close to war before 1939. In 1920 the treaty of Sèvres had made peace with Turkey, installing a shadow sultan at Constantinople and neutralising the Straits under the control of allied garrisons. However, the Turks, freed from their empire, under Kemal Pasha, a hero of Gallipoli, created a new national state within the interior of Turkey on the back of a new national spirit. In the following twelve months Italy, France and Soviet Russia made their peace with Kemal, leaving only the Greeks holding on at Smyrna. While British politicians were divided, Lloyd George struck a pro-Greek stance, but the Greeks, forbidden by the allies to take Constantinople, were increasingly impatient. Kemal seized the advantage and took Smyrna amidst scenes of massacre. Without the support of France and Italy, who were anxious to keep on good terms with Kemal, Britain managed by the skin of its teeth to secure the pact of Madunia whereby Turkey agreed to respect the neutral zone. It would be difficult to imagine a reader in the 1920s encountering Orlando's experiences in Constantinople without thinking of Britain's near-war with Turkey. The whole episode was one which Lloyd George misunderstood and might have had more serious consequences if the British ultimatum had not failed to be delivered to the Turks. A majority of the public apparently felt that Britain was being rushed recklessly into another war.

A further significant presence, however, in Woolf's description of seventeenth-century Constantinople, is that of the modern Turkish state which emerged in the first part of the twentieth century. Although the novel describes seventeenth-century Constantinople, there is a clear allusion to the twentieth century in the description of it as a 'strident multicoloured and barbaric population' (p. 116). 'Strident multicoloured' is an appropriate description of Turkey after 1915, which became an ethnically homogeneous nation, forcibly assimilating Greeks, Armenians, Kurds and others who, as Hobsbawm says, 'were not either expelled *en bloc* or massacred'.[20] But the words 'multicoloured' and 'barbaric' in Woolf's description refer us to the opening of the novel and to the deeds of Orlando's fathers, an implicit reminder that since the seventeenth century the Ottoman empire had been pushed out of Europe. The label 'barbaric' reminds the reader that Turkey was regarded as such because the violence of Orientals to each other – strange and exotic punishments, hideous tortures and 'barbaric' executions – was a salient theme in Western representations of the Orient. But Orlando's actions at the opening of the novel remind the reader that a recurring absence in Western representations of the Orient is the violence wrought by Europeans in the East.

'Strident' introduces a temporal element into the description of Constantinople which was often missing from Western representations of the Orient in which the East was generally depicted immutable. The adjective brings to mind not only the ethnic policies of modern Turkey but its presence in post-war Asia as one of the first nation states 'committed to progress and enlightenment against tradition, "development" and a new sort of populism untroubled by liberal debating'.[21] The modernisation of Turkey, of course, was a process begun in earnest in the middle of the nineteenth century. Certainly that was when Britain, France, Russia and Austria took a keen interest in what was happening in Constantinople. In 1863 the Ottoman Bank was founded and in 1867 the Sultan visited Paris to receive recommendations about setting up a system of public education, public works and communications. But in alluding to the modern nation state of Turkey in her description of seventeenth-century Constantinople, Woolf implies that Western views of it may still be mediated by the observer's involvement in a particular kind of Englishness and in British imperialist history. The particular details in the description of Constantinople may seem gratuitous, but they authenticate the myth of the Orient as backward, which in turn implicitly associates the barbaric with Islam.

The absurdity of the notion of England as a self-contained nation and culture is exposed in the novel through its acknowledgement of the permeable nature of boundaries. Orlando falls in love with a Russian and, sent to Constantinople, he ponders whether one of his ancestors in the Crusades had taken up with a Circassian peasant woman and begins to detect evidence of mixed blood in his pallor. The account of Constantinople is from Orlando's point of view and an equal amount of time is devoted to what it is not – England – as to what it is. But the England that is the absence against which Constantinople is defined is that of the Home Counties – 'the counties of Surrey and Kent or the towns of London and Tunbridge Wells' (p. 116). If England has a geographical centre, it is in the triangle of Oxford, Cambridge and London.

At several points in *Orlando*, Woolf draws attention to the extent to which English national identity is bound up with the English countryside. In other words, how the English landscape is the inscape of English national identity. Orlando is rendered an outsider among the gipsies because she writes poems, in Romantic vein, admiring sunsets. Without realising it, Orlando is confirming how the rhetoric of national affiliation is naturalised through the imagery of landscape. Her experiences among the gipsies are important to the novel not because she is rendered an outsider – she is such in all the societies in which she lives – but because their reaction to two of the staples of English national identity – nature and ancestral houses – defamiliarises them. 'Englishness' is thus highlighted as a cultural construction based upon particular narratives of heritage. This thesis may have been suggested to Woolf by the growing interest in the ancestral house in English tourist guides throughout the 1920s to which I referred in the discussion of *Mrs Dalloway*. The importance of the ancestral home to the upper-class sense of identity is mocked in *Orlando* by the inclusion of family portraits from Vita Sackville-West's ancestral home, Knole, as pictures of the young, male Orlando and of Sherlmerdine whom the female Orlando eventually marries. The exchange between Orlando and the gipsies debunks English pride in an ancestry that can be traced back only several hundred years through contrasting it with the much older lineage of the gipsies. A linchpin of monolithic national pride, ancestry is also challenged on the grounds that most families have skeletons in the cupboard. Pride in ancestral lines, like notions of a pure Englishness, is undermined by miscegenation.

Some of these arguments are developed in Woolf's subsequent novels and may have been inspired by Defoe's long poem *The True Born Englishman*, originally published as a pamphlet in 1701. The poem is a defence of the introvert and unpopular King William of Orange, who came to the throne in 1688. Defoe's argument is that it is unfair to abuse William for being a foreigner because all English people – labelled 'offal outcasts' – are foreigners, being descendants of Vikings, Normans, Picts and Scots. This calls into question not only the notion of England as a self-contained nation and culture but the sense of distance from peoples deemed the 'Other' upon which the worst excesses of imperialism were based. Within this context the initial location in Elizabethan England is significant as the site of the origin of the Heart of Oaks formulation clearly alluded to in Orlando's manuscript poem 'The Oak Tree'.

Throughout the novel, Woolf returns to the theme, raised in its first few pages, that what Englishness defines as unEnglish is an inextricable part of its definition of itself. Orlando sees Shasha according to ideas about Russians with which he has been brought up:

> He suspected at first that her rank was not as high as she would like; or that she was ashamed of the savage ways of her people, for he had heard that the women in Muscovy wear beards and the men are covered with fur from the waist down; that both sexes are smeared with tallow to keep the cold out, tear meat with their fingers and live in huts where an English noble would scruple to keep his cattle.
>
> (pp. 46–7)

The Russians are placed in a narrative, indicating how the English define themselves in relation to others, which elides their ethnocentricism with civilised values, confuses the 'Other' with the sub-human, and projects on to the 'Other' what they deny in themselves. Sublimated fears of invasion associate outsiders with the carnal and the savage. But while the discourse of empire highlights external sources of corruption, the real threat to the empire comes from within the discourses themselves – from the attitudes that may rebound upon them. The key words 'English noble' not only oppose the 'civilised' English and the 'uncivilised' Russians, but equate the 'essence' of Englishness with a particular class – the nobility – and with a bloodline. In Sasha herself, and in her behaviour, established narratives and hierarchies are turned upside down. Like the carnival,

Sasha is situated outside conventional discourse. Although she is Russian she does not live up to the English stereotype of her people – even criticising the English Court for its lack of etiquette. In other words, she serves to defamiliarise some of the assumptions around which the affective life of the national culture is constructed.

How the concept of Englishness is tied to a definition of the unEnglish as 'Other' is pursued in the novel on a general level, but is also developed with reference to specific political issues of the 1920s. The reference to the King already having 'had trouble enough with the Irish' (p. 63) is clearly an allusion to the Irish question. Defence in Ireland was a major preoccupation during James I's reign as in the post-war years – Orlando blames the flood from the Great Thaw on the Irish rebels, an allusion to O'Donaghy's rebellion that occurred in the same winter as the Great Frost (p. 61). But they are also allusions to the way in which the Irish had become framed as the 'Other' in discourses of English national identity. In a novel which goes on to debunk the upper-class English preoccupation with lineage, it is significant that Orlando becomes betrothed to a young Irish woman with a family tree so old it challenges his own. Aspects of the description of the Turks – shawled women, innumerable donkeys, men working with horses – might be taken as a description of Ireland. For Ireland had become fixed in anti-Irish English discourse as backward and barbaric compared with the civilised English. In other words, in the account of the Turks, Ireland is the 'absent presence'.

V

As an apologue, *Orlando* renders two principal areas of cultural life absurd – the myth of a self-contained 'pure' Englishness and the way in which gender is perceived in absolute and essentialist terms. Like *Jacob's Room*, *Orlando* suggests that there is collusion between monolithic masculinity and biographies of male subjects written by males. At times the novel parodies the style of the traditional biography and suggests that biography, like the kind of memoir Edward Marsh provided of Rupert Brooke, is based not upon real memory but a kind of unreal loyalty to the subject. As in *Jacob's Room*, however, with its challenge to Marsh's *Memoir* of Brooke, the principal cause of concern is not so much the writing of memoirs or biographies based upon 'unreal' memory as the insufficiently rigorous mode of thinking out of which it has developed.

As a metropolitan intervention in debates about empire, the exposure of the gendered nature of imperialist discourse in *Orlando* is clearly important. Like Jacob, Orlando appears to be an imprint of his father. But unlike *Jacob's Room*, *Orlando* is firmly located at the intersection of cultural politics, collective memory and biological determinism. On a wider philosophical level, it questions the extent to which Orlando is the product of 'nature' or discourse. The narrator's observation of gendered behaviour – 'He was young; he was boyish; he did but as nature bade him do' (p. 27) – turns into questions about the validity of the term 'natural'. Even before his transformation into a woman, Orlando experiences androgyny – calling into question the 'either...or' binarism – and is excited by it. After Orlando's sudden transformation into a woman, the centre of gravity of the novel shifts. It overtly assumes the focalisation of a woman who is outside the male rite of passage and the shared cultural understanding of what constitutes masculine norms. The effect of this sexual transformation is to render the history of Orlando as a young male strange. But while in the initial part of the novel we observe Orlando, in the second part of the novel – where we see through Orlando's eyes – the effect is to defamiliarise the female subject.

The central concerns which critics have identified in *Orlando* – for example, its exploration of monolithic definitions of gender and sexuality, whether social conventions such as clothes reflect or create sexual difference, the extent to which sexual difference is biologically determined or socially constructed – reflect the decade in which it was written. As L. C. B. Seaman has observed, the 1920s created an image of women that was self-consciously 'modern' and 'androgynous':

> The female shape became flat-chested, and the female head was shorn of its long hair which, with monotonous iteration, had been called 'women's crowning glory'. This created a so-called 'boyish' look. It was boyish only in the sense that it was not feminine in the way that Edwardian fashions had been. These had emphasised the curves of the female body to the extent of amplitude if not of caricature.... The compensation to the male for the loss of femininity involved in the short hair and the tubular torso was the rapid shortening of the skirts. To the Edwardian young man the sight of so much as a female ankle was an almost pulsating experience; but in the twenties the female knee was revealed to all.[22]

Androgyny in female fashion in the 1920s was related to (young) women's increased mobility and freedom to occupy public spaces. Orlando's experience of wearing a crinoline dress may well be a projection of what would be lost if people went back to the traditional modes of dress: 'No longer could she stride through the garden with her dogs, or run lightly to the high mound and fling herself beneath the oak tree' (pp. 233–4). But *Orlando* pursues some of the deeper psychosexual implications of the androgyny which became a more obvious trope in upper-class life in the 1920s. I say trope because androgyny was often associated with social spectacle and display. This suggested that human sexuality was not defined by the categories of 'heterosexual' and 'homosexual' but existed in each individual as a continuum between the two. Not only Orlando herself but other characters, too, are multiple-sexed beings. The Archduchess Harriet of Scand-op-Boom becomes Archduke Harry and s/he and Orlando act the parts of male and female alternately. After she has wed Captain Marmaduke Bonthrop Shelmerdine, they accuse each other of being of the opposite sex. The novel, then, reflects Woolf's convictions that gender identity is not determined by anatomy as Freud believed and that sexual identity is more fluid than is conventionally supposed. It also conveys the excitement which Woolf herself, according to Quentin Bell, found in the concept of sexual transformation:

> Sheppard enacted the part of an Italian *prima donna*, words and music being supplied by a gramophone. Someone had brought a newspaper cutting of a pretty young woman who had become a man, and this for the rest of the evening became Virginia's main topic of conversation.[23]

And, of course, it hardly needs pointing out that such excitement had been the linchpin of her relationship with Vita Sackville-West who, as Sandra Gilbert has reminded us, was 'a notorious "Sapphist", who made no effort to conceal her attraction to, and affairs with, women'.[24]

Androgyny is one of the most obvious themes in the novel and not surprisingly most critics have approached *Orlando* from this perspective.[25] Orlando's name itself reminds us of Orlando in Shakespeare's *As You Like It*, as well as the French medieval *Chanson de Roland*, as I observed earlier, so associating her with masculine roles. Clare Hanson has identified a paradox in the novel, in that

Woolf appears to stress a constructed 'femininity', which is open to change, while valuing certain aspects of femininity as if they were given.[26] However, what seems to most interest the narrator of *Orlando* is not the balancing of gender differences within the androgynous subject but the narratives within which the gendered subject is placed.

As an apologue, *Orlando*, can be seen as demonstrating the absurdity of conceiving of male and female gender and sexual identities in fixed and absolute terms. Exploring how males and females are complicit in the way in which both genders are imagined, the novel suggests that meanings normally attached to sexuality lie outside the body itself. Orlando's transformation into a woman does not seem to change the appearance of his legs, which, we are told at the beginning of the novel, are 'shapely', though they produce different reactions from the different sexes, depending upon what his/her sex is perceived to be. Thus, his legs drive Nell Gwyn wild, while a sailor is almost killed because he catches sight of the ankles of Orlando as a woman:

> 'To fall from a masthead', she thought, 'because you see a woman's ankles; to dress up like a Guy Fawkes and parade the streets, so that women may praise you; to deny a woman teaching lest she may laugh at you; to be the slave of the frailest chit in petticoats, and yet to go about as if you were the Lords of Creation. – Heavens!' she thought, 'what fools they make of us – what fools we are!'
>
> (p. 152)

The thinking here is very close to that which pervades Defoe's *Moll Flanders* – clearly, as Susan Squier has explained, an important influence.[27] When Woolf first conceived the idea for the book she was thinking in terms of a 'Defoe narrative for fun'.[28] There are a number of parallels between the two novels. As Squier says, both novels have protagonists who disguise themselves as men; who consort with prostitutes and gipsies; who are experienced international travellers; who are mothers; and who explore the different strata of London society. Yet there are important differences between them. Moll develops from a position as social outcast to an accommodation with social values; Orlando moves from 'a position of privileged centrality' to a position of marginality as a woman and poet.[29] But the most important question that needs to be asked is why Woolf turned to *Moll Flanders*.

Part of the explanation of the influence of *Moll Flanders* on *Orlando* is that it provided Woolf with an example of an apologue concerned with the 'truth' or 'freedom' of the outcast,[30] and, like *Orlando*, *Moll Flanders*, although written by a man, is concerned with the female protagonist's emotional life, her encounters in the social world and relations between the sexes. But, equally importantantly, the episodic structure of the eighteenth-century novel provided a way of loosening up the novel as a form as it had become increasingly realised in the Victorian period. The picaresque mode of writing allows for a fusion (even confusion) of realism and fantasy. The sense of complicity to which I drew attention above – 'what fools they make of us – what fools we are!' – is developed in *Orlando* into an exploration of how social relations between the sexes involve strategies of disguise and recognition. The various disguises which Orlando assumes in the course of her narrative can be seen as a feminist inflection on the masks and poses assumed by modernist authors,[31] but the novel also explores the performative nature of women's identity, distinguishing between women as Woman and women masquerading as Woman. Women are seen as acting out fantasies which are themselves representations. As Isobel Armstrong has observed, Orlando finds that her social identity is defined increasingly in carnival, fiesta, masques, parties and social gatherings.[32] The apologue can be seen as using masks to unmask masks, and it is in this respect, rather than in defence of the position of the outcast, that the influence of *Moll Flanders* is most clearly discernible in Woolf's novel.

One of the reasons why Woolf may have looked back to the eighteenth century, both in terms of the form of *Orlando* and in terms of Orlando's preference of living in that century, is that it was a period in which, as in the years that followed the Great War, England was anxious to define itself. Much eighteenth-century writing, as Madeleine Kahn has suggested, is preoccupied with the nature and permeability of boundaries and with the consequences to the individual of transgressing them.[33] While Woolf is more interested than Defoe in the implications of cross-dressing for debates about the origins and nature of gender identity, both writers share a concern with the way in which men and women engage in a kind of 'sexual commerce', mixing business with pleasure. Moll's accounts of herself in disguise include occasions when she cross-dresses, for example as a pickpocket, and has to assume various personae to protect herself in a predatory environment. This in itself becomes metonymic of the way in which the whole of society in Defoe's fiction is based on masquerade. But in *Orlando* the focus on the 'truth' of masks, rather than the revelation of a true self through masks, leads to a general doubt about the validity of all social categories. In other words, Woolf's interest is not so much in the reality behind the mask as the relationships between masks.

At one extreme, strategies of disguise and recognition are illustrated in Orlando's encounter with a prostitute, Nell. Finding it impossible to walk on the street without attracting the unwanted attentions of men who seem to think of all unattached women in a public space as 'working-women', Orlando is forced to return to her former (male) identity. But even in this encounter, masks are taken up and dropped in an intriguingly subtle game of dare and response. Nell, believing Orlando to be a man, employs approaches and responses which she thinks he would expect of her. Orlando having recently been a man recognises that this is what Nell is doing. But the way she holds on to Orlando's arm arouses feelings in her which, in turn, makes her feel masculine. As a woman herself, Orlando recognises that the prostitute's behaviour is a charade. She is playing, in Orlando's view, to what she thinks are men's expectations. As soon as Orlando reveals herself to be a woman, Nell changes her mode of behaviour. In other words, both Orlando and Nell rid themselves of their disguises. The conversation between them, despite the differences in their backgrounds, appears to assert the primacy of the union of two female friends who can share in the delight of similar perspectives, again despite the differences between them. Set within the androgynous frame of the novel, it betrays, perhaps, a hidden desire for female love.

Orlando's encounter with a prostitute, a blatant example of sex as commerce, is immediately juxtaposed with a summary account of how business and pleasure are intermingled in social activities at the opposite end of the social spectrum. The way in which Orlando is said to exchange the 'seductiveness of petticoats' for 'the probity of breeches' (p. 211) emphasises the fluid and the relative nature of gender identities. But Woolf also anticipates Angela Carter in deploying masquerade to expose the fictional nature of femininity while challenging the male fetishising of women as Woman that sustains the Masquerade. *Orlando* emerged from the same milieu as Joan Riviere's 'Womanliness as Masquerade' (1929), the groundbreaking study of how ambitious women often employed an exaggerated femininity to mask their supposedly masculine aspirations and intellectual capacities. This milieu was marked by increased opportunities for women's social and intellectual mobility, particularly middle-class women for whom masquerade was often a way of countering male hostility to their new-found presence in the professional sphere.

VI

The Waves shares *Orlando's* concerns with normative assumptions about sexuality, gender and a particular codified Englishness. However, writing *The Waves* proved a very different experience from working on *Orlando*. It is commonly known that it was 'the most hard-won'[34] of all Woolf's novels. The original idea for the book – a solitary woman's flow of thought – came to mind in 1926, but was very different from the one which she eventually realised. The novel actually came slowly and hesitantly – Woolf returned to it frequently over a period of three years – leaving us to wonder what provided the impetus for that last push. The novel which we now have was not written until quite late in the revision process. In fact, the first draft was not finished until after Woolf had completed *Orlando* and *A Room of One's Own* (1929). At that time she thought of the narrator telling the stories of six characters, first as children and then as adults. Only when she was working on the second draft did she conceive of the characters taking responsibility for their own narratives.

A Room of One's Own – much of it written in about six weeks while she was confined to bed – can be linked to the exploration and historicising of the cultural context of women's lives in *Orlando*.[35] It continues the interest in women's lives in different historical periods, in imagining the occluded histories of women such as Judith Shakespeare, and researching the lives of women writers such as Lady Winchilsea and Margaret of Newcastle. The book confirms what more recent criticism of Woolf's fiction has gleaned from her novels. Woolf is interested in the kind of cultural materialism that post-structuralism initially tended to shun. *A Room of One's Own*, like *Orlando* whose conversational style it shares, stresses the important differences in the opportunities for women of different centuries and of different classes, although Woolf does not embrace the traditionally Marxist thesis that social being determines consciousness. For Woolf there is an important dialectic between the individual consciousness and society.

On a cursory reading there appear to be two aspects to the book – the external world which prevents women from writing, particularly in the way it deprives them of education and independence, and the private world into which the woman can withdraw. However, these two dimensions are fused in Woolf's understanding of what Foucault called discourse. It is not just historical and material circumstances, but dominant discursive formations that mitigate against women pursuing professional careers or becoming writers, encapsulated in the world they inhabit. Thus when Woolf offers evidence of the material conditions that deny women access to education and publishes the fact that they are not allowed to enter an Oxbridge library unless accompanied by a Fellow, she is also exposing the discourses about gender identity that legitimates such absurdity. Throughout *A Room of One's Own*, Woolf demonstrates the encrypted presence of the *a priori*, from her observation that 'biography [is] too much about great men', to her reflection that a book is made of sentences built 'into arcades or domes. And this shape, too, has been made by men out of their own needs for their own uses' (pp. 142, 100). Indeed, these discursive formations also create psychological obstacles for women when they are alone, which Woolf wittily envisaged as the Angel at her shoulder. The lack of a tradition of women's writing that provides a further obstacle to women's creativity is not only an absence which women must correct by thinking back through their mothers but a vacuum which oppressive masculinist discourses have filled. At times, *A Room of One's Own* appears to be open to the same criticism as *Jacob's Room*, that Woolf comes close to essentialism in suggesting that the norm of British culture is a masculinity that automatically guarantees authority. But, as in *Jacob's Room*, Woolf's focus is not on 'masculinity' or 'femininity' *per se* but on discourses that essentialise gender and render gender differences in absolute terms:

> A scene in a battle-field is more important than a scene in a shop – everywhere and much more subtly the difference of value persists. The whole structure, therefore, of the early nineteenth-century novel was raised, if one was a woman, by a mind which was slightly pulled from the straight, and made to alter its clear vision in deference to external authority. . . . What genius, what integrity it must have required in face

of all that criticism, in the midst of that purely patriarchal society, to hold fast to the thing as they saw it without shrinking. (pp. 96–7)

While *A Room of One's Own* is normally regarded as a lecture, it is more than that. Exemplifying the experiences of women and recording some of the social conditions that obstruct them in ways which, through a variety of strategies such as mockery, satire, fantasy and irony, challenge the dominant discursive formations, *A Room of One's Own* is located between the lecture and the apologue:

> And what was London doing? Nobody, it seemed, was reading *Antony and Cleopatra*. London was wholly indifferent, it appeared, to Shakespeare's plays. Nobody cared a straw – and I do not blame them – for the future of fiction, the death of poetry or the development by the average woman of a prose style completely expressive of her mind.
>
> (p. 124)

Thus, as in *Orlando*, Woolf is interested in demonstrating the 'truth' of related cultural assumptions that constitute what Foucault called the 'archive'. She mocks the way in which Tolstoy was able to tour Europe for the sexual experiences he incorporated in his fiction while George Eliot was ostracised for living with a man whose wife, albeit seriously mentally ill, was still alive.

Much of the criticism of *A Room of One's Own* implies that Woolf has split herself into two personae – one interested in the social world that women inhabit and the other concerned with the random and mysterious workings of the mind. But Woolf is interested in the relationship between the collective and the intensely personal in individual consciousness:

> [The mind] can separate itself from the people in the street, for example, and think of itself as apart from them, at an upper window looking down on them. Or it can think with other people spontaneously, as, for instance, in a crowd waiting to hear some piece of news read out. It can think back through its fathers or through its mothers, as I have said a woman writing thinks back through her mothers. Again if one is a woman one is often surprised by a sudden splitting off of consciousness, say in walking down Whitehall, when from being the natural inheritor of that civilisation, she becomes, on the contrary, outside of it, alien and critical. (pp. 126–7)

The issue raised by *A Room of One's Own* is not that Woolf split herself into two personae – one located in the social world and the other in the deeper recesses of consciousness – but the capacity and potential of the mind, particularly in the case of women, to situate itself positively outside the dominant, male-oriented discursive formations. This is something that Jacob in *Jacob's Room* glimpses but does not pursue. Unlike *Jacob's Room*, *The Waves* has a more sustained focus on young men, as well as women, who feel contrary to and critical of the inheritance of civilisation as realised in the world around them.

Woolf was both pleasantly surprised and disappointed by *The Waves*' critical reception. Many reviewers tended to think of it as a poem rather than a novel. For example, Frank Swinnerton considered it 'a series of rhapsodies', Louis Kronenberger believed 'its true interests are those of poetry' and described *The Waves* as 'not a poetic novel but a poem, a kind of symphonic poem...in prose'.[36] But as John Mepham has said, what she wanted to be told, we know from her diary, was 'that this is solid & means something'.[37] This, however, begs further questions as to how Woolf thought *The Waves* 'solid' and as meaning 'something'.

Many reviewers expressed an interest in, and some admiration for, the way in which 'consciousness' was realised in the novel. However, most of them saw this aspect of the book as articulating the fragmentary, chaotic and random nature of the mind. Few reviewers addressed Woolf's interest in how consciousness is constructed by and within the historical *a priori*. Indeed, some reviewers felt that the novel did not engage with the external world at all. Gerald Bullett argued that although each of the characters had an independent name, and a private independent existence, each was 'lifted out of the circumstances of daily life'.[38]

The narration of the inner workings of the mind in Woolf's fiction is not simply a Modernist experiment. Woolf sought techniques that would enable her to represent the random nature of thought and perception, but also to explore the extent to which individual consciousness is determined by the *a priori*. An exploration of the relationship between individual consciousness and dominant discursive formations that did justice to the complexity of the mind was not possible in a traditional mode of writing based on a unitary, less random and more rational model of consciousness. Woolf evidently chose to reject her initial idea of a novel based on a woman's solitary thoughts for a narrative composed of different voices in which individual senses of self are threatened by being incorporated within the vision of others. But even more importantly, the multifocal format enabled her to explore how the social and gender divisions of power restrict the individual's capacity to be both subject and object within another's field of vision.

VII

It is surprising that *The Waves* has been excluded from most critical discussions of Woolf as a political writer. Like *Jacob's Room*, it challenges the way in which masculinity within the pre-war officer class is constructed. While *Jacob's Room* is an implied critique of Edward Marsh's *Memoir* of Rupert Brooke, the act of writing a memoir – Bernard's elegy for Percival – is actually incorporated into the narrative of *The Waves*. Up to a point Bernard is in control of his own discourse as Edward Marsh was of his *Memoir* of Rupert Brooke. However, in his use of other people's views and voices, which as in the case of the Romantic poets he frequently misquotes, he is, like Edward Marsh, the object of a discourse about Englishness, patriarchy and empire. And, like Edward Marsh, he is unwittingly engaged in helping write a post-war hegemonic English identity.

It is hard not to see Percival – the Arthurian Knight Parsifal transferred to the early twentieth century – as one of the young men passing into service in King's College chapel in *Jacob's Room*:

> Look now, how everybody follows Percival. He is heavy. He walks clumsily down the field, through the long grass, to where the great elm trees stand. His magnificence is that of some medieval commander. A wake of light seems to lie on the grass behind him. Look at us trooping after him, his faithful servants, to be shot like sheep, for he will certainly attempt some forlorn enterprise and die in battle.[39]

The military metaphors used to construct Percival here and throughout the novel, and the fusion of military and religious connotations, clearly bring *Jacob's Room* to mind. And Percival himself is redolent of the young Jacob for he, too, lives, as Judith Lee argues, 'in completely unconscious conformity with his culture'.[40] Percival's future, like that of Jacob Flanders, is contingent upon the past – signified in the passage by the great elms and the word 'medieval' – into which he grows up. Significantly, all the light is behind him.

The name Percival and the description of him as a 'military' commander marks Woolf's return to the concern in *Jacob's Room* with the 'meanings of abstractions' and the significance of abstractions to the cultural stability of pre-war England. Not only were Greek myths and heroes important to how the young officer class saw itself, but, as I suggested in the discussion of *Jacob's Room*, also the medieval romance quest. Paul Fussell points out that:

> The experiences of a man going up the line to his destiny cannot help seeming to him like those of a hero of medieval romance if his imagination has been steeped in actual literary romances or their equivalent. For most who fought in the Great War, one highly popular equivalent was Victorian pseudo-medieval romance, like the versified redactions of Malory by Tennnyson and the prose romances of William Morris.[41]

On entering the chapel, Louis has a sense, comparable to that described in King's College chapel in *Jacob's Room*, of the objects as signs and symbols of an affective national identity. But in this novel, where the focalisation is that of an insider, there is a greater emphasis than in *Jacob's Room* upon *how* one is located through the ambience and the objects in a narrative of national identity to which the past and its place in a line of continuous development is important:

> 'Now we march, two by two,' said Louis, 'orderly, processional, into chapel. I like the dimness that falls as we enter the sacred building. I like the orderly progress. We file in; we seat ourselves. . . . I like it now, when, lurching slightly, but only from his momentum, Dr Crane mounts the pulpit and reads the lesson from a Bible spread on the back of the brass eagle. I rejoice; my heart expands in his bulk, in his authority. . . . Now all is laid by his authority, his crucifix. . . . I recover my continuity, as he reads. I become a figure in the procession.
>
> (pp. 25–6)

The image of the chapel may well have been suggested to Woolf by the epitaph from Eliot's 'Little Gidding':

> A people without history
> Is not redeemed from time, for history is a pattern
> Of timeless moments. So while this light fails
> On a winter's afternoon, in a secluded chapel
> History is now and England.

Woolf asks whose history is now and whose England is being talked about. The myths of a coherent, empowering sense of historical purpose and of the modernity of England may not be shared by all the people. Certainly not as much by women as the majority of men, for the foundation myth of England is a narrative that denies women their past and their present 'realities'. And the same may be said of some men, such as Neville, who do not have the same relationship to imperialist England as Percival's class, or to the patriarchy represented by Dr Crane:

> Unwarmed by imagination, his words fall cold on my head like paving-stones, while the gilt cross heaves on his waistcoat. The words of authority are corrupted by those who speak them. I gibe and mock at this sad religion, at these tremulous, grief-stricken figures advancing, cadaverous and wounded, down a white road shadowed by fig trees where boys sprawl in the dust – naked boys. (p. 26)

There are allusions here to discursive formations that would have been familiar to the post-war literary upper classes. As Paul Fussell observes, the presence of European roadside calvaries changed the relationship of many soldiers during the war to the crucifix. It became an image which reflected back to them their own status as sacrifice.[42] The juxtaposition of the cadaverous and wounded with naked boys challenges the homoerotic war writing which equated love for a boy soldier with a melancholy – presumably the melancholy of unrequited love – located in his early heroic death. These allusions suggest that those such as Neville are not to be redeemed, like Louis, by the traditional symbols and codified narratives. Their lives may remain a meaningless and patternless series of timeless moments unless they reclaim histories and patterns which the dominant myths and narratives of English history have occluded.

VIII

The imagery of the italicised interludes in *The Waves* concerns the 'shadow' side of Englishness and empire. The sun that rises in the second interlude in *The Waves* may be the old sun of empire but it exposes the savagery of the oppressors and, in the images of the 'poisoned assegais' and the 'turbaned warriors', the violence with which the empire threatens to strike back:

> The wind rose. The waves drummed on the shore, like turbaned
> warriors, like turbaned men with poisoned assegais who, whirling
> their arms on high, advance upon the feeding flocks, the white
> sheep. (p. 60)

Jane Marcus points out that *The Waves* draws attention to the part
played by the Stephen family in constructing cultural hegemony in
nineteenth-century India. Kathy Phillips sees the turbaned warriors
of the second interlude as an allusion to the Sepoy Mutiny of 1857.[43]
But neither Marcus, who actually challenges ahistorical interpretations of the novel, nor Phillips sees the novel as engaging with the
events of the years 1919–30 even though they were among the most
turbulent as far as British relationships with India were concerned.
This may be because neither really develops a cryptanalytical reading
of the novel which links it to Woolf's reading of contemporary and
historical events as cultural texts.

It would be difficult to imagine any author writing a novel in the
period 1928–30 concerning the fusion of religious, military and
imperialist elements in the English national identity and including
the subject of English involvement with India not being influenced by
the events of the 1920s. The Government of India Act of 1919, when
India was denied Dominion status, had provided that a Commission
be set up after ten years to examine the possibility of further advance
for India. However, in response to the Congress Movement's
demand for complete independence, the Simon Commission was
appointed two years earlier in 1927. When the Congress Movement
realised that 'Dominion status' would not in fact be granted, the
Commission's report in June 1930 was received amidst widespread
disorder in India itself that led to the arrests of Mahatma Gandhi and
Jawaharlal Nehru. At the end of October, Lord Irwin, the Viceroy,
announced the decision to grant India Dominion Status. While
retaining a Viceroy appointed from London, India would be ruled
by Indians at both national and local levels.

The agreement between the Government and Shadow Cabinet
over India had important consequences for the public mood and for
domestic politics in Britain. It led eventually to the much-
publicised split between Stanley Baldwin and Winston Churchill,
whose evocation of the 'warrior races' when he took up the cause
of the Indian princes in 1930, attacking the conciliation of Indian
nationalism, mirrors Woolf's image of the 'turbaned warriors' and

their assegais. In an article in the *Daily Mail*, Churchill stressed the Hindu contempt for the millions of Untouchables and that Dominion Status could not be obtained by those who treated their 'fellow human beings, toiling at their side' so badly.[44] He resigned from the Shadow Cabinet because of what he saw as the frightful prospect of losing India. *The Waves* articulates the anxieties of the 1920s about India and demonstrates the 'truth' of the formulable statements circulating among the upper classes about the empire. But it does so in a way which challenges and interrogates the *a priori* about the British in India and its consequences for cultural and gender identity.

While there is a strong elegiac element in *The Waves* as Marcus and Phillips argue – there are frequent references to elegies that are meant to be taken as the elegy for empire – there is also the 'frightfulness' of the prospect of the end of empire. It is this perceived 'frightfulness' that is the basis of Woolf's approach to the events of 1919–30. The critique of empire in *Jacob's Room* and *Orlando* exposes the homosocial and patriarchal bonds within the upper class that Woolf believed supported imperialism. *The Waves*, like *Jacob's Room*, however, concerns the effect of the prospect of the end of the British empire on members of that class.

The death in India of Percival, who is a stereotypical product of the English public school system, combined with the Arthurian knight Parsifal transferred to the early twentieth century, can be read as analogous to the demise of the British in India. But his death focuses not so much on the demise itself as the anxiety over Britain's involvement in India. This anxiety is heightened rather than alleviated by the various intellectual and cultural frameworks that confronted anyone in the 1930s engaging with Anglo-India. The predominant anti-imperialist literary modes of the 1930s were irony and parody. As an apologue, *The Waves*, like *Orlando*, employs a range of strategies including satire, irony, ridicule, mockery and parody. The end of the Anglo-Indian empire may easily have been incorporated in a less speculative text than *The Waves* in a way that had become commonplace. In encrypting the dominant discourses of Englishness and masculinity in *The Waves*, Woolf provides fresh critical depth to the critique of the British in India.

Bernard's elegies to Percival invoke the use of India in popular romance where loved ones or brothers meet their death, while the intertext in the details of Percival's death – he is thrown from a flea-bitten mare – is the absurd figure of Don Quixote which under-mines both the romance and the heroism in Britain's imperialist project. Bernard's assessment that, in righting a bullock cart, Percival solved the Oriental problem is not only absurd but, read within the context of the parliamentary debates at the time Woolf was working on the novel, caustically ironic. Bernard's references to half-naked Indians only able to 'swarm' and 'chatter' and to an old man only able 'to contemplate his navel' (p. 111) express both the arrogance of his class towards the peoples of the empire, in this case India, and its view of the Indians as unable to assume responsibility for their own government. As soon as he envisages India, Bernard sees 'crenellated buildings which have an air of fragility and decay' (p. 111). At one level this may foreshadow the collapse of the British empire in India, but it also reflects Bernard's view of India as a social and political economy. The bullock cart travelling along the sun-baked road may be read cryptanalytically as India under Dominion Status. The cart 'sways incompetently from side to side' – the use of the word 'incompetently' is particularly provocative and clearly invokes more than just how a cart is driven – and eventually, almost pre-dictably, it becomes stuck in a rut (p. 111). Percival is envisaged as solving the problem by 'applying the standards of the West' and by 'using the violent language that is natural to him'; a fusion that demonstrates Woolf's Foucauldian interest in how traditional con-cepts and thematic continuities are transferred from one domain to another; in this case, from the language of the public school to the application of British standards of progress and behaviour in the administration of empire.

The Waves puts at least as much emphasis upon the reactions to Percival's friends to his death as upon the education system and the social forces which shaped him as a particular type of English hero. Percival's death inaugurates the second half of their day, the declining sun analogous to the declining empire. But once again the focus is upon the intellectual anxiety created by the prospect of the loss of empire. The waves in the penultimate interlude, having lost their light – a cryptic allusion perhaps to Enlightenment notions of history and progress – now fall 'in one long concussion' (p. 173). The image of former cornfields evokes a traditional, rural Englishness with which notions of empire were bound: 'Now the corn was cut. Now only a brisk stubble was left of all its flowing and waving' (p. 173). The cut corn clearly signifies the physical end of empire but 'waving'

– evoking the celebration of nation through the waving of flags – also suggests that, equally importantly, the psychological empire has come to an end. Although the effect of patriotic flag-waving in countries where the radical left had acquired an anti-colonial tradition is complicated, colonial exhibitions, military parades, jubilees and state occasions encouraged the people to identify with the nation and the imperial state.

The interlude is as much prophetic as descriptive: 'The tree, that had burnt foxy red in spring and in midsummer bent pliant leaves to the south wind, was now black as iron' (p. 174). The seasonal changes in the tree suggest the stages of empire, the colonisers bending to the needs and demands of the colonised Indians, but also betrays anxiety over what kind of India will emerge under Dominion Status: not only 'black' but defiant. The next line – 'The land was so distant' – encapsulates anxieties about Britain's removal from the region's affairs; distanced physically, historically, economically and culturally.

The sense of youth and endless possibility focused on Percival in the first part of the novel, analogous to that enshrined in the empire, are replaced by anxiety, sober reflection, and even pessimism: 'The door will not open; [Percival] will not come. And we are laden' (p. 176). Percival, like the empire to which he is analogous, served as a binding power for his friends who belong to or have affiliations with the social class in whom cultural and economic power resides. Despite the last-ditch defiance in the final section of the novel by Bernard who is writing about Percival, we are left with the dominant impression of the six friends fragmenting and with a dwindling sense of possibility.

After his death, what Percival's friends imagine he might have accomplished in India becomes, as Phillips points out, increasingly grandiose.[45] But this argument can be taken further. Bernard believes that Percival would have protected people dying of famine and disease and would have done justice to the empire. These views of him seem analogous to the defence of empire by those fearful of how the period of British rule might come to be seen after Indian independence.

The anxiety that all Percival's friends suffer following his death is exacerbated because they are unable to imagine an alternative to the interconnection of English national identity and empire with which they have all grown up. Louis, the son of an Australian banker, was so desperate to be accepted by his English upper-class friends that he fabricated a past with roots in Ancient Egypt. As a reflection of Woolf's cryptic reading of the events of 1919–30, this is doubly ironic because Egypt was taken under British control to facilitate trade with India. Even Rhoda's exotic fantasies, through which she seeks to escape from the discomforts of school, are shaped by the ideologies of empire. The white petals that at one point she floats in a brown basin are inflated to become ships and then an Armada. While the sinking of her Armada anticipates her suicide – as a female she is never able to realise her dreams like Louis – it also anticipates Percival's death and the loss of India. But Rhoda also prefigures, like Louis, the failure of England to envisage an alternative identity for itself, to free itself from the concepts and ideologies of empire. The expulsion of England from India, although it could never – can never – be complete, is a worrying prospect for those of Bernard's generation and class. It signifies the demise of what has impelled the development of England as an imperialist power. Empire is fraught not only with the weight of its burden but with the anxiety of its loss.

While, at one level, Woolf might be accused in *The Waves*, as in *The Years* which is the subject of the next chapter, of not making sufficient distinction between the different ethnic populations of the empire, she pursues the concerns of her experimental fiction written in the 1920s with the 'othering' of empire, and of its importance to a mythical, homogeneous Englishness. Her discovery of the apologue, in working on *Orlando* and *The Waves*, enabled her to explore connections between various forms of exploitation based on 'othering' by gender and race, and the discrepancies between the complexity of private, lived experience and dominant, public ideologies. Importantly, the apologue enabled her to produce novels that slipped easily between a variety of modes of writing – satire, ridicule, mockery, carnivalesque, cultural commentary – without sacrificing their overall coherence, their seriousness of purpose, or her cryptic analyses of what she perceived as the cryptographic *modus operandi* of social discourse. But much of the 1920s was a period of intense intellectual and political anxiety over empire, fuelled by debates in parliament and the press over Dominion Status for India. Although both *Orlando* and *The Waves* may be regarded as apologues, the impact of the India crisis on the latter helped make them different kinds of novels. However, acknowledging that *The Waves* is an apologue, highlights aspects of the novel that until recently have been overlooked, particularly the employment of a variety of modes of writing for specific 'political' purposes. The structure of *The Waves* is, again, not merely an aesthetic experiment but an attempt to explore the emergent post-empire perspectives in their variety of manifestations. As in *Orlando*, Woolf seeks to extrapolate the multivalent cultural processes at work in the way events are interpreted and constructed. In her subsequent work she sought to further these aims in a mode of writing more appropriate than the apologue to the 1930s, a politically more troubled decade than the 1920s. As historical narrative itself acquired a new-found public importance, burdened by the crises of the time, Woolf found herself having to work through the issues of her earlier fiction from different and more disturbing perspectives.

8

Private and Public Spaces: *The Years* (1937)

> *In order to fix a date it is necessary to remember what one saw.*
> Virginia Woolf, 'The Mark on the Wall'[1]

I

The Years proved to be Woolf's best-selling and most popular novel. Although it displays at times the verisimilitude associated with traditional, social realist fiction, it undermines that mode of writing through the many interruptions, discontinuities and ellipses in the text. While it appears to be a novel of historical change, it is based on a debate between different discourses in circulation during the period 1880–1937 concerned particularly with the family and the nature of public and private space. However, I want to suggest that Woolf employs an enigmatic and disconcerting version of the social realist novel to narrate the inner experience of the social and public discourses of this period, itself dominated by discourses of change, discontinuity and the unknowable.

Woolf originally conceived of *The Years* as a 'Novel Essay' – *The Pargiters*. Once again she was experimenting with form in ways determined by her interest in historiography. Between the episodes dramatising the fictional lives of her characters she had intended to place essays on their sociohistorical contexts. But as she worked on the initial draft, the chapters themselves became grounded in what seemed closer to social realism than anything she had written since *Night and Day*. Whereas in her earlier work she had developed ways of writing about her characters' inner worlds, here she appeared to be writing about the social world which affected them in a way that she had abandoned at the beginning of the 1920s – even starting the book with a description of the Pargiter family home. *The Pargiters* appeared to represent, in John Mepham's words, an 'astonishing turnabout' in her views of the novel.[2] However, perhaps feeling that she was preaching too much, by the time she had completed revising *The Years* (as the novel came to be called in 1935), Woolf had pruned much of it, including the dialogue of Sara, Rose and Maggie, who in the earlier manuscript express more clearly defined points of view.[3]

Critics who see the book in terms of a conventional kind of social realism and stress its verisimilitude, however, ignore many of its disconcerting, cryptic qualities. Much is present in the novel by allusion, while conversations and patterns of thought are interrupted and situated as part of wider, confusing cross-currents. Although *The Years* is a historical novel covering the period from 1880 to 1937, the major events of those years are barely touched upon, as reviewers at the time pointed out.[4] Thus the novel marginalises the Boer War, the death of Queen Victoria, the First World War (to which only one page is devoted), the Suffragettes, the rise of the Labour Party, the demise of the Liberals, the General Strike, the Wall Street Crash and the British Union of Fascists. Moreover, as Janet Montefiore, has pointed out, it avoids 'the subject of politics in the traditional, recognizable guise of power struggles between representative individuals'.[5]

In *The Years*, despite its apparent concessions to social realism, Woolf was still working within the parameters of the approach that she first employed in *Jacob's Room* and *Orlando*. Indeed, the novel can be seen in terms of her quarrel with realism in her essay 'Modern Fiction' (1919) and her argument that novels should be less concerned with 'realism' and 'materialism' and more with the inner experience of 'reality'. In her later essay 'Character in Fiction' (1924), in which she defended *Jacob's Room* against Arnold Bennett's criticism that the characters 'did not vitally survive in the mind', she shifted the argument to the nature of 'verisimilitude' as it enters the inner consciousness of individuals. In *The Years* her subject continues to be that of *Jacob's Room*, the codified nature of social 'reality' and of the historical *a priori*. As Pamela Hansford Johnson pointed out in her review of the novel, 'each member of the Pargiter family is strengthened or devitalised, as the case may be, by the influence of externals hardly realised subjectively'.[6] The 'queer simultaneousness of life, with all those incongruous threads which now run parallel, now intersect, and then part as unaccountably'[7] on which the novels of the 1920s are based, have their roots in *The Years* in a firmer sense of social experience. Although Woolf admitted that she might have 'muted the characters down too much' in order 'to keep their faces toward society',[8] she was not necessarily implying that she thought of *The Years* as social realism. What critics have taken for traditional social realism in *The Years* is Woolf's interest in how the incongruous threads within which individual subjectivity is constructed not only reflect a wider and entrenched *a priori*, but place the *a priori* in a bolder sense of history. After all, the 1930s, which saw the Depression and the rise of Fascism, did not permit the same kind of intellectual detachment from history and historiography.

What is oppression, Woolf appears to be asking, if not certain collective experiences of generations repeated generation after generation? When we think of the novel as being concerned, like *Jacob's Room* and *Orlando*, with the construction of history and of experience, particularly female experience, it appears to be a less radical shift in her *oeuvre* than critics who have seized on its apparent social verisimilitude have suggested. But it does reflect the influence on her work throughout much of the 1930s of *Three Guineas*. Although *The Years* was not completed until 1938, Woolf began thinking about the project in the early 1930s as a book about 'the sexual life of women'. The various titles considered, 'Professions for Women' and 'On Being Despised', suggest the particular approach to women in *The Years*. Ostensibly addressing a male reader, *Three Guineas* addresses women of the class with which *The Years* is concerned and whose own education, financial and emotional independence had been eschewed in favour of their brothers' opportunities. Although eventually Eleanor becomes a charity worker, Rose becomes involved in political work, and Peggy becomes a doctor, the men fare better than the women, becoming university teachers, lawyers or colonial administrators. History here, as in *Jacob's Room* and *Orlando*, is seen as premised on significant absences in women's lives – the absence of power, agency, self-determination and of language.

Until recently, even critics who have pursued the multivalent nature of Woolf's narratives have tended to discuss them as if they were monological rather than dialogical works. In other words, they have approached the novels as containing different speaking characters or monologues but have failed to see any genuine dialogue between the different voices. The narrative method in many of Woolf's novels, however, is to compare and contrast. As Lynne Pearce, in a rare Bakhtinian reading of Woolf's fiction, argues, in *The Waves* Woolf is interested in 'the differences between subjectivities and in the differences within a single identity'. A careful Bakhtinian reading of Woolf's fiction must focus on the dialogic nature of the subjectivities represented, how identities 'have been formed through their relationships with multiple others'.[9] However, in order to take the argument further than this we have to draw upon recent scholarship on Bakhtin. Critics who have employed Bakhtin's dialogical theory in literary criticism, in assuming that he posits an ahistorical or universal subject, have failed to acknowledge, as Lynne Pearce says, that not only does he allow for the dominance of one subject over another, but, additionally, that authority need not be conceived as absolute or permanent[10] – as is the tyranny ascribed to the Symbolic Order in psychoanalytic criticism.

II

Like *Jacob's Room* and *Orlando*, *The Years* revises a traditional genre in order to reclaim social experiences marginalised or occluded by the dominant discursive formations comprising the Symbolic Order in order to suggest that the Symbolic Order is neither absolute nor permanent. The novel is a sustained focus on women within an upper-middle-class family who are relatively impoverished and further marginalised by their father's failure to provide for them after his death. And, as has been recognised, it is a novel which presents the family, from a feminist perspective, as an anti-social institution.

The Years lends itself to being read within the framework for understanding the organisation of public space suggested by Michel de Certeau to which I drew attention in Chapter 1. In *The Years* Woolf explores the nature of the traditional Victorian family along the axes recommended by de Certeau: the rational organisation that seeks to, and must, repress all mental, physical and political pollutants that would challenge and compromise it and the ruses and combination of power that lie outside and have no obvious identity.

Indeed, de Certeau's argument that what lies outside and challenges the rational organisation of public space is not readily recognisable is especially pertinent to *The Years*. The novel exposes what might be seen as the *crypta* within the solid, public structure of the Victorian family, especially since the large house is analogous to the family as a social institution. As such, it returns to an idea that Woolf suggested but did not develop in *The Voyage Out*. As I said in the discussion of that novel, Rachel's home has a public, patriarchal front that hides an alternative, feminine space. In *The Years*, the *crypta* includes a number of incestuous relationships – Abel and Eugénie, Martin and Maggie, and Peggy and Morris – reflecting the fact that Woolf was abused by both her half-brothers. The *crypta* within the dominant discourse of heterosexuality, the range of relationships between women that is identified if not fully explored in all Woolf's fiction, is evident in this novel in, for example, Rose's lesbianism and Sara's devotion to her sister Maggie.

In advocating the family as an anti-social institution, contemporary social theory insists, as Michèle Barrett and Mary McIntosh point out, that 'the "family" is not merely an economic unit, nor merely a kinship structure; it is an ideological configuration with resonance far beyond these narrow definitions'.[11] Because of the emphasis in post-war England on ensuring the stability of social codes or 'texts', contemporary social theorising of the anti-social family, with its emphasis upon the hegemonic status of the familial perspective and familial ideology, is particularly pertinent to a discussion of *The Years* as a politically radical novel. Critics such as Alex Zwerdling have stressed the novel's critique of the Victorian family. However, the novel goes further than this and is engaged by a dialogical representation of the family, comparing and contrasting the various discourses of the family in circulation in the period 1880–1937. In other words, while certain views of the family acquire legitimacy, the family in *The Years*, in anticipation of Foucault, is seen as a precarious ensemble of statements that are not necessarily unifiable and coherent. This is reflected in the opening of the novel in the play of light in the Pargiters' rooms – 'here was a pattern; here was a bald patch' – and in the street – 'changing from gold to black, from black to gold' (pp. 11 and 18). But it is also reflected in the rhythm of the novel as a whole and in its patterns of interruption, discontinuities and ellipses.

Not imposed from outside, the discourses of family in *The Years*, again anticipating Foucault's conception of discourse, are 'caught up in the very things that they connect': Woolf's initial description of the Pargiters focuses on the archive of late-Victorian bourgeois values responsible for the construction of a particular ideology of the family – financial prosperity, property, empire, individual achievement, social advancement through personal effort and 'cultivated' taste. These are all values salient to Victorian patriarchy. But the oppressive nature of the family as a patriarchal institution that critics have tended to emphasise is only one aspect of the critique. Despite the commitment to rituals and routines that maintain its oppressive structures – such as the status accorded the father, the privileges enjoyed by the male child, the infantilism of the daughters – there is a *crypta* within family life that is not simply destabilising but shifts its centre of gravity.

The cryptic details of the Pargiter family life, taken together, contradict and undermine the initial impressions its routines and public face are meant to convey. The ritual of afternoon tea, for example, is a public acknowledgement of the family as a social unit which it also links with the empire, especially India and Ceylon. The Colonel's special cup, inherited from his father, is symbolic of the law of the father passed down through generations. But he takes no more than a few sips from it and actually dislikes tea. In other words, he only pays lip service, literally and metaphorically, to this convention, as to the others that are undermined by his visits to Westminster. Moreover, while there is a benign element to the family as to the empire – Martin is rewarded by his father for coming top at school – it is undermined by cryptic references to a darker side of both – the Colonel's mutilated hand is like a claw and the children are frightened of his gloomy moods.

The formal relationships around the Pargiter family table are displaced by a cryptic 'reality' in which the children are bonded to a truer sense of each other through their fear of their father, an anxiety to get things right (for example, to make sure that the kettle is boiled), solace in the presence of their elder brothers and sisters (for example, the calming presence of Eleanor), and (wittingly or unwittingly) subverting the law of the father (for example, Martin sitting in his father's chair, Eleanor being late and Rose going alone to Lamley's).

In the course of the novel, Martin Pargiter declares that family life 'was an abominable system...Abercorn Terrace. No wonder the house would not let. It had one bathroom, and a basement; and there all those different people had lived, boxed up together, telling lies' (p. 212). His denunciation of the family is clearly a far cry from what is generally referred to as the 'social paternalist' view of the family as a benign hierarchy that could be found in some nineteenth-century realist, and particularly Victorian magazine, fiction. However, Woolf cannot be seen here simply to be revisioning the nineteenth-century social paternalist ideal of the family even though social paternalist ideologies were explicitly and implicitly invoked in advertising, posters and popular magazines in the aftermath of the First World War. Post-war images of the bourgeois family extolled the co-operative associations of family life as a model for class relationships in society even though in doing so they reinstated the disjunction of the private and the public that they sought to overcome. Even in the mid nineteenth-century, hegemonic narratives, for all their exploitation of the family-society metaphor, tended to hoist themselves on their own petards, ultimately privileging the private family as a transcendent signifier. John Ruskin, for example, in *Sesame and Lilies* (1865) apotheosised 'the true nature of home – it is the place of Peace; the shelter, not only from all injury, but from all terror, doubt, and division'.[12] In *The Years*, the family, unequivocally integrated with the public sphere, is anything but a transcendent signifier.

The model of the family extolled in post-war Britain was not one with which advocates of nineteenth-century social paternalist ideologies of the family would have been familiar. The nuclear family of post-war Britain signified an implicit criticism of the oppressive nature of the conventional upper-and upper-middle class Victorian family with its frequent childbearing that often brought about the mother's premature death, its time-consuming rituals, its filial obligations, its ceaseless rounds of visits and its management of a large household including servants.

Representation of the family as an anti-social institution can be found in a wide range of works including Samuel Butler's *The Way of All Flesh* (1903), H. G. Wells' *Ann Veronica* (1909) and the plays of Bernard Shaw. The preface of Shaw's *Misalliance* (1910), which talks of a 'family system' – a phrase which Alex Zwerdling reminds us Victorian rebels and reformers were fond of using[13]

– summarises the view of the family that Woolf may have derived
from Shaw:

> Our family system does unquestionably take the natural bond between
> members of the same family, which, like all natural bonds, is not too
> tight to be borne, and superimposes on it a painful burden of forced,
> inculcated, suggested, and altogether unnecessary affection and
> responsibility which we should do well to get rid of by making rela-
> tives as independent of one another as possible.[14]

This familial structure, in which individual beings are functional
units in a system over which they have no control, was criticised as
coercive and oppressive by Shaw, but viewed positively in Victorian
social-paternalist family narratives. However, *The Years* does not just
emphasise the oppressive nature of the traditional Victorian family
occluded in the social-paternalist family narratives. Rather, it
explores the implications of the ways in which attitudes to the family
were codified.

Martin's denunciation of the family has often been taken at face
value as summarising the theme of *The Years*.[15] It is close not only to
the views of Shaw, Butler and Wells, but Lytton Strachey's denunciation of the Victorians as a 'set of mouthing bungling hypocrites'.[16]
But it is important here to remember Foucault's concept of the
historical *a priori*. Martin's denunciation of the family is the product
of the influence of a number of anti-family discourses which cannot
be reduced to the work of specific writers. Woolf is working, to
appropriate Foucault's words, in 'a more extensive space than the
play of influences that have operated from one author to another'.[17]
The anti-social view of the family to which Martin gives voice is an
example of 'the positivity' that Foucault argued discourses achieve
through time. By this he meant that discourses, that are essentially
precarious ensembles, do achieve 'unity' and can be seen as inter-
secting an author's unique discourse in 'a web of which [the authors]
are not the masters, of which they cannot see the whole'.[18]

The view of the family as an anti-social institution was a 'radical'
position; a counterpoint to Victorian 'social paternalist' ideologies.
Leonard Woolf in his autobiography remembered that they 'were
living in an era of incipient revolt', but he also acknowledged that
'we did not initiate this revolt', and there is the complication. The
radical position had become codified – even Alex Zwerdling who
sees *The Years* as primarily an attack on the traditional Victorian

upper- or upper-middle-class family, acknowledges that Martin's comments reflect 'the rhetoric of the disaffected'.[19] Martin in the novel is not merely the mouthpiece of the anti-social family perspective, but an example of the way in which radical views of the family had become locked into a particular mode of thinking and writing.

III

The Years, rather than being a continuity of or a challenge to any one particular narrative of family, occupies a space opened up by the dialectic between the three principal, and often interrelated, narratives of family available to writers in the 1920s and 1930s. First, the synchronic narratives of which there were principally two: those that relied on social-paternalist ideologies of the family and were based on family–social metaphors and those that might be described as 'domestic integrationist' narratives in which family relationships are metonymic of those in the wider society.[20] Second, diachronic, time-based, 'social context' narratives that were directly or indirectly indebted to late Victorian sociological and anthropological inquiry. They perceived the organisation of domestic life almost as sceptically as Martin Pargiter and recognised its subjection to larger social forces and changing social assumptions.[21] Third, the anti-social family narratives that moved, or in their own terms progressed, from a consideration of family or marriage to recommending personal independence and liberalism in social structures.

That Woolf is writing within a space opened up by the dialogism between different narratives of the family is evident in the way in which the critique of the social-paternalist ideology of the family is pursued in relation to diachronic and anti-social narratives of the family. The notion of protection that is so essential to this ideology of the family is seen as protection of the female by the male, and is developed by Woolf to the point where the boundaries between protection and imprisonment are blurred, as in the Pargiter drawing room and in the episode in which Lady Eugénie Pargiter is reprimanded by her husband over forgetting to replace the lock on the kitchen door. Prior to his return home, Eugénie has been persuaded to dance as she did as a young woman, revealing a more spontaneous and physical sense of herself that has been hidden beneath the weight of her marriage to Sir Digby. The notion of the cryptic informs the entire episode. That Eugénie should dance is itself an illicit activity – reminding us that female relationships are associated with the *crypta* in Woolf's work – and she dances in a space cleared by another female. When Eugénie is reprimanded by Digby they have just finished checking the security of the basement, the 'crypt' of the house.

The repression of women's bodily awareness and of divergent sexualities in the social-paternalistic ideology of the family is contrasted in *The Years* with the liberalism permitted within the ideology of the family as an anti-social institution. Nicholas and Rose are both associated with such a view of the family and with homosexuality. The ideology of the family as an anti-social institution, placing characters outside the tyranny of the social-paternalist family, is seen as permitting a redefinition of gender identity. Rose's view of the Pargiter family 'going on and on and on' (p. 161) is a critique of the way in which female sexuality in the traditional large family was defined largely in terms of the reproduction function. For Rose, outside of these repressive structures, sexuality can be defined in different ways and in terms of her own sense of fulfilment.

In setting the repressive social-paternalist model against the anti-social family ideologies, Woolf overturns ideologies that see the family as metonymic of social integration and structuring. North directly attacks the domestic-integrationist model of the family as metonymic of social integration by depicting the family as a basis for social disintegration. Women within families, he argues, are 'not interested in other people's children.... Only in their own; their own property; their own flesh and blood, which they would protect with the unsheathed claws of the primeval swamp' (p. 359). While the 'absent presence' here is the domestic-integrationist model of the family, the other principal Victorian model of the family – the social-paternalist – is represented negatively. The importance that the Victorian bourgeoisie attached to property is here extended to children, and the increasing insularity of the family through the increasing Victorian separation of 'private' and 'public' and of 'work' and 'home' gives rise to pre-'human' behaviours. The references to the child as 'property' and to the importance of protection brings to mind the Digby and Eugénie episode while the reference to the claw recalls Colonel Pargiter's mutilated hand that 'resembled the claw of some aged bird' (p. 13).

The dominant discourse of the family in the novel is the diachronic model. Its plot is literally based on the loosening of family structures and the break-up of upper-class families during the period between 1880 and 1937, and how the changing nature of 'family' life in post-Victorian Britain resulted in a diversity that even embraces non-family structures: Eleanor achieves physical and emotional independence; Edward lives as a College student; Rose lives with a female lover and then alone; Delia lives in a flat above offices. The text, however, is not simply exploring the nature of these new forms of living but their relationship or lack of relationship to the historical *a priori* of the family.

The diversity of structures within which people live in *The Years* is not easily incorporated even within the diachronic model of the family. As is evident in Rose's situation, the new structures are often not an evolution but a radical break from the dominant discourses of the past. Although the synchronic, diachronic and anti-social family ideologies adopted very different perspectives on the family, there was a fundamental coherence around an identifiable entity known as the 'family'. The dispersion of the Pargiter family is a movement into forms of living in which there is not as readily an identifiable notion of the family. Once again, the influence of *Three Guineas* is apparent in this novel. In *Three Guineas*, perceiving a connection between patriarchy and the causes of war, Woolf urges the adoption of the values of 'Outsiders' – those who withdraw from participation in many of society's functions – re-establishing professions and higher education on new values and promoting women's economic and social rights.

When Peggy and Eleanor travel across London together, Peggy tries to persuade her to talk about the 1880s: 'It was so interesting; so safe; so unreal – that past of the 'eighties; and to her, so beautiful in its unreality' (p. 316). The traditional Victorian upper-class family presented vividly at the outset of the novel is now invoked as a nostalgic presence that reflects the wider confusion of the 1930s. The nostalgia stands in contrast to the *crypta* within the family revealed in the conversation between Martin, Eleanor and Rose when Rose returns from a byelection in the north of England. Together they remember family rows that constitute a cryptic life within the family that they all seem to have suppressed. Eleanor's observation, 'what awful lives children live' (p. 152), sounds more like a revelation than an observation. Rose particularly surprises Eleanor with her account of how she had locked herself in the bathroom with a knife and cut her wrists, about which Eleanor knew nothing. This negative view of the family comes to the fore again in 1937 when Delia, alluding cryptically to what went on at Abercorn Terrace, interrupts Nicholas's speech, exclaiming that life at Abercorn Terrace, which she could still no longer be driven past, was 'hell' (p. 396).

In the closing section of the novel, a number of characters recall and/or discuss the past. Whereas throughout the novel characters occupy their own private spaces, in the last section of the book this space is more overtly one of memory. The extent of change and the difficulty of coping with the new pervades most of the conversation and private thoughts. If Peggy and the Pargiters, who were the new generation in the 1880s, now find it difficult to discover a pattern in their own lives, then it is equally difficult to place the 1930s and what was happening in Europe in a narrative that makes sense according to the principal discourses of progress, order and history. The private and the public fused at the beginning of the novel are confused in the last (1937) section. Sara observes: 'how can we make laws, religions, that fit, that fit, when we don't know ourselves?' (p. 299). In the last section of the novel, this sense of confusion and the difficulty of deciphering the historical *a priori* is heightened by the return of North:

> 'How strange it must be', she resumed, 'coming back after all these years – as if you'd dropped from the clouds in an aeroplane', she pointed to the table as if that were the field in which he had landed.   (p. 301)

Whereas the novels of the 1920s were engaged by a decipherable symbolic order, *The Waves* and *The Years* confront a society in a state of flux. One of the most radical aspects of *The Years* is that the war is not seen as the watershed but the social change for women, however limited, that predated the war because of the changes in the family. In the chapter '1914', Kitty's confusion is the product of pre-1914 events, not of 1914:

> She stood in her travelling-dress, wondering if she had forgotten anything. Her mind was a perfect blank for a moment. Where am I? she wondered. What am I doing? Where am I going? Her eyes fixed themselves on the dressing-table; vaguely she remembered some other room, and some other time when she was a girl. At Oxford was it?   (p. 255)

At one level, both novels stress a discontinuity that in *The Waves* is explored as a site of anxiety for those of a particular class and generation but in *The Years* enables release from falsifying discourses of family, sexuality and empire. But, at another level, *The Years* is a more complicated novel driven not so much by historical change *per se* as by a heightened awareness of the precarious, partial and changing nature of the social and cultural archive. Hence Eleanor's housing schemes for the poor, Peggy's medical work and Rose's work as a Suffragette are sites of engagement with private aspirations, socio-historically determined possibilities, socio-economic restraints and culturally determined discourses that are in a state of flux and between which the boundaries are confused. One of the ironies of the last section of the novel is that the realisation that most of the characters come to, that nothing now is fixed and knowable, has itself become a dominant socio-cultural discourse.

IV

The chronotopic structuring of *The Years* is part of the overall tension in the novel between different discourses. The geography of the novel is dialectic, permitting Woolf to explore tensions, contradictions and complexities – within as well as between, say, Abercorn Terrace, the dingier parts of Westminster, Pestwick Terrace and Browne Street – denied by conventional social topographies. After Abercorn Terrace and Browne Street are sold, the Pargiter family disperse to live in flats and rented homes, reflecting how this period saw the emergence of new ways of living. Traditional rigid distinctions between the various streets and regions are overturned as characters move in and out of different locations.

One of the aspects of the novel that appears to reinforce its status as a social-realist text is the attention given throughout to the chronotope of the street. The street, however, is both 'text' and chronotope, and as a 'text' reflects the changing nature of the 'social'. The street, of course, was developed as an important chronotope in the fiction of the French realist writers Flaubert and Balzac. In a discussion of their work Mikhail Bakhtin implies, but does not develop the point, that the street had already become a social text prior to its incorporation in the nineteenth-century novel.

The street as a chronotope in a work of fiction differs from the older literary chronotope of the road. As Bakhtin argues, the road is associated in literature with chance, since it provides opportunities for freak accidents and chance encounters, and as the basis of linear journeys it mirrors the onward progress associated with the post-enlightenment model of history. The street, as is evident from the way in which it is deployed in *The Years*, is more contained. It can be observed within a single panoramic view. Unlike the road, that may be deserted or only sparsely populated for much of its route, the street provides a fuller and more immediate snapshot of the society or community in which it is situated. It provides a view of what Bakhtin calls 'materialized history'.[22] In this respect the street reveals the 'sociohistorical heterogeneity' within the familiar so that, of course, there are what Bakhtin calls exotic elements to the street that include the 'social exotic' such as 'slums', 'dregs' and 'the world of thieves'.[23]

The point I made earlier that Woolf was interested in the figurative nature of space is well illustrated by the focus in *The Years* on the extent to which space represents and is structured by the discourses that determine social relations. The chronotope of the street in *The Years* is employed to reveal the changing 'materialised history' of England during the period 1880–1937 and the 'sociohistorical hete-rogeneity' within the familiar. When Mrs Pargiter's funeral cortège reaches the main road, Delia observes from her carriage:

> the pace quickened, for the drive to the cemetery was a long one. Through the slit of the blind, Delia noticed dogs playing; a beggar singing; men raising their hats as the hearse passed them. But by the time their own carriage passed, the hats were on again. Men walked briskly and unconcernedly along the pavement. The shops were already gay with spring clothing; women paused and looked in at the windows. (p. 81)

While critics have noted Woolf's interest in shopping, as we saw in the chapter on *Mrs Dalloway*, it is less important in her work than the spectacle of the commercial street itself. As Judith Walkowitz has pointed out, 'in the West End, the presence of perambulating prosti-tutes, window-shopping ladies, "girls in business," and idle male civil servants in one public area provoked territorial tensions'.[24] The fact that the novel begins in the year 1880 is significant because it was in the 1880s that the West End of Mayfair and St James became secure as the centre of the empire, finance, commerce, entertainment and communication. But the chronotope of the street is also employed in the description of what Bakhtin calls the 'socially exotic' – for example, the dingy district of Westminster where Colonel Pargiter visits his mistress, or the streets through which North Pargiter drives, searching for Sara Pargiter's flat:

> Every time [the Colonel] approached the little street that lay under the huge bulk of the Abbey, the street of dingy little houses, with yellow curtains and cards in the window, the street where the muffin man seemed always to be ringing his bell, where children screamed and hopped in and out of white chalkmarks on the pavement, he paused, looked to the right, looked to the left. (p. 6)

The chalkmark links this street with Milton Street through which North drives fifty-seven years later and observes the symbol of the British Union of Fascists, to which there are a number of cryptic allusions in the text:[25]

> 'Where the dickens am I now?' [North] asked, peering at the name on the street corner. Somebody had chalked a circle on the wall with a jagged line in it. He looked down the long vista. Door after door, window after window, repeated the same pattern. There was a red-yellow glow over it all, for the sun was sinking through the London dust. Everything was tinged with a warm yellow haze. Barrows full of fruit and flowers were drawn up at the kerb. The sun gilded the fruit; the flowers had a blurred brilliance; there were roses, carnations and lilies too. (p. 294)

Woolf does not simply present the reader with the verisimilitude of the 'sociohistorical heterogeneity' or the 'social exotic' of London's streets. The heterogeneity that Delia observes raises a fundamental issue for Woolf about the nature of modernity, while the social exotic of Westminster's streets and Milton Street raises questions about the different discourses within which urban space is textualised.

V

In the account of what Delia sees from her carriage window, Woolf anticipates the French social theorist Jean Baudrillard's observation that 'modernity is not the transmutation but the commutation of all values, their combination and their ambiguity'.[26] Delia's window in the funeral coach, acting as a frame for the commutation of the Victorian street, and of all its heterogeneity, draws attention to modernity in the Victorian period as both spectacle and a site of contradiction.

The window displays of the latest clothes incorporate fashion as spectacle, festival and even squandering. But, as Baudrillard has pointed out, 'fashion exists only within the framework of modernity, that is to say, in a schema of rupture, progress and innovation'.[27] Viewed from this perspective, *The Years* can be seen as questioning the extent to which modernity itself is really about change, or whether it involves merely the spectacle of change. The reference to the spring fashions reminds us that modernity sets up both a linear time of technical progress and a cyclical time of fashion. Hence, the whole notion of change in the novel is thrown into question. If fashion is at the core of modernity – which it is Delia's role at this point in the novel to suggest – then subversive and emancipatory developments may not be developments because fashion is able to recuperate everything. 'Spring' may be a key word here, suggesting, as Baudrillard says, that 'the dialectic of rupture very quickly becomes the dynamics of the amalgam and recycling'.[28] Moreover, if fashion is at the heart of modernity, then notions of 'tradition' and 'change' lose their meaning. What fashion announces is the myth of change, maintaining it as 'the supreme value in the most everyday aspects'.[29] Debates about the pre-eminence of tradition, of the old over the new, become irrelevant, for modernity has invented both.

There is a further anxiety, though, reflected in the descriptions of London streets in *The Years*. The apparent freedoms signified by the dogs, the lower orders represented by the beggar, and the shop window displays offer Delia a site of visual abandonment akin to what Woolf felt the department store 'fairies' palaces' offered her in the 1920s – a world both enchanting and vertiginous. But Delia does not appear to distinguish between dogs, beggars and fashion; they are all elements within a wonderful visual feast. As a commutation of the values of modernity, the commercial street is disturbing because it is so distracting, occluding cultural assumptions and contradictions that ought to be the real focus of the street as a social text.

The word 'gay' that Delia employs to describe the window displays in the shops is one that Woolf used to describe the carnival city built on the frozen Thames during the Great Frost in *Orlando*. It suggests an intensity of pleasure that one strain of Victorian culture, with its emphasis upon sobriety and respectability, would have found disturbing. What Woolf reveals in her fiction are suspicions surrounding the sensuous world of consumption that anticipate those highlighted in contemporary cultural theory. Although he does not distinguish between the different types of shops in different historical periods, Mike Featherstone has pointed out that the forerunners of the department stores were the fairs. In the way in which they brought together, albeit in a much more controlled way, the exotic and the familiar, the stores contained a trace of carnival.[30] This fantasy element of modern consumerism is exposed in *Mrs Dalloway*, particularly through Clarissa. But Woolf's focus in *The Years* is a different one, highlighting not the stores, or even shopping, as such, but the mooted carnivalesque elements of the modern street which, in turn, challenge the authority and sobriety of Victorian public ritual.

What Delia glimpses from her carriage in 1880 is echoed in Kitty's view of the street in '1914':

> It was a clear still night and every tree in the square was visible; some were black, others were sprinkled with strange patches of green artificial light. Above the arc lamps rose shafts of darkness. Although it was close on midnight, it scarcely seemed to be night; but rather some ethereal disembodied day, for there were so many lamps in the streets; cars passing; men in white mufflers with their light overcoats open walking along the clean dry pavements, and many houses were still lit up, for everyone was giving parties. The town changed as they drew smoothly through Mayfair. The public houses were closing; here was a group clustered round a lamp-post at the corner. A drunken man was bawling out some loud song; a tipsy girl with a feather bobbing in her eyes was swaying as she clung to the lamp-post... but Kitty's eyes alone registered what she saw. (pp. 255–6)

This description catches the primary qualities of spectacle. Kitty is impressed by the 'ethereal' and the 'disembodied', and although she would not express it in these terms herself, with images that have become divorced from their referents. The unreal quality of it all is reinforced by the fact that it 'scarcely seemed to be night' and by the reference to the 'strange patches of green artificial light'. The different elements that Kitty sees are removed from the diachronicity in which they are located to the synchronicity of spectacle. Here, we have not modernity but, in Baudrillard's terms, modernity as the commutation of social values, including the ambiguities and contradictions. In other words, the spectacle that is evident here, like that which Delia observed, acquires further meaning in the context of the times. Delia's observations acted as a focal point for late-century anxieties about modernity, not all of them held, of course, by the same Victorians in the same way. Even in the 1880s, London high streets were becoming a visual manifestation of a different, more consumer-oriented type of society; of the increasing, and in some quarters strongly resisted, 'democratisation' of public spaces; and of doubts about the true nature of modernity. The unreality that Kitty witnesses is analogous to the unreality that accompanied the start of the First World War and the way in which the war itself tended to be regarded in the early days as a spectacle. The failure of the upper class to take on board the 'hour' in Kitty's description is analogous to their failure to take on board the hour in another sense – to realise fully what the war would entail. In the account of the street lamps, the white mufflers and the clean pavements there is an innocence that anticipates the naive confidence of 1914.

Although the First World War might seem barely to enter into *The Years*, the novel presents a critique of it as part of the spectacle, the delusion and the excitement of modernity. Throughout '1914' there are references to time, to whether there is enough time, and to time passing unnoticed. For modernity has invented its own solipsistic sense of time that positions the individual, as Kitty is positioned on the train, within its own spectacle:

> 'Just in time,' Kitty said to herself as she stood there. Then the train gave a gentle tug. She could hardly believe that so great a monster could start so gently on so long a journey. Then she saw the tea-urn sliding past.
> 'We're off,' she said to herself, sinking back on to the seat. 'We're off!'   (p. 257)

Kitty's reaction to the train mirrors the public's attitude to the war by 1916 – disbelief that such a monster could have started so innocuously.

'Just in time' is open to several interpretations – the most obvious one that Kitty has just caught her train; and a privileging of the diachronic over the synchronic (ironically, since modernity had come to privilege the synchronic). While Kitty is excited at the prospect of beginning a journey, her excitement is also the thrill of modernity – of movement as spectacle. Kitty is transported back into her past and into a fantasy that bears no relation to reality: '"What fun!" she said to herself, as if she were a little girl who had run away from her nurse and escaped' (p. 257). And this is a point reinforced by the disappearance of the platform and the people on it. Her fantasy, like the reference to the tea-urn, trivialises modernity and suggests a failure to experience it other than in terms of a naïve excitement. But Woolf also stresses the sense of disorientation Kitty experiences:

> She turned away from the light. *Now* where are we? she said to herself. Where is the train at this moment?. . . A blank intervened; her thoughts became spaced; they became muddled. Past and present became jumbled together. (p. 259)

The experience here – of spatial disorientation, of discontinuity and jumbled thoughts – reminiscent of sensory deprivation is analogous to the wider experience of modernity and anticipates the greater degree of confusion expressed by nearly all the members of the younger generation of Partigers in the last section of the novel.

Nothing in Woolf's fiction operates at one level, however. As in the depiction of the aeroplane in *Mrs Dalloway*, Woolf realises the capacity of the train journey for articulating erotic desires, the *crypta* within discourses of the feminine. In the account of Kitty's train journey, the engine becomes a focus for a displaced erotic imaginary of the body: 'It seemed all body, all muscle; even the neck had been consumed into the smooth barrel of the body' (p. 256). Kitty's indulgence in this fantasy is interrupted, as is Clarissa's relationship with Sally in *Mrs Dalloway*, by a man – in this case the guard with his whistle. The journey itself is analogous to lovemaking, female orgasm or even female masturbation. Undressed, Kitty feels the vibration of the train which 'seemed to fall into a regular rhythm' and experiences the train getting into its stride. And there is even the postcoital experience of fragmented thoughts and memories.

VI

The dialectic between the chronotopes in *The Years* uncovers the preoccupation in Victorian discourse of public space with control and the loss of control. The carnivalesque, however, always disrupts the chain of signifiers through which unity and stability in cultural meaning are achieved, as in Kitty's train journey or the novel's street spectacles.

While the embourgeoisment of British society, linked to the expansion of consumerism and the establishment of a secure middle class, brought about, in Mike Featherstone's phrase, a 'controlled decontrol' of British emotional life,[31] Woolf's fiction reveals Victorian society's concomitant preoccupation with boundarylessness. The description of the Westminster street Pargiter visits is characterised by a display of the uncontrolled – the screaming of the children at play is stressed, as is the apparent relentlessness of the muffin seller's bell – and the house is characterised by the smell and the presence of dirty washing. There are echoes here of the way in which the Victorian novelist, in seeking to depict the poor as an aspect of middle-class experience, illustrated a dominant fear of the time that respectable homes might be invaded by disease and disgrace. The dangers of loosening controls over British emotional life and behaviour are displaced to the description of Mira's dog's eczema, a red patch redolent of sexual disease. The satirical, anti-authoritarian elements of the carnivalesque are evident in the way in which Mira treats Pargiter – thinking of him as the 'old boy', snatching his spectacles and placing them on the dog's nose and flaunting herself before him – in contrast with the respect accorded his severe presence in the drawing room at Abercorn Terrace. In that room the portrait of the red-haired woman in a white muslin dress signifies the way in which passion and sexuality are supposedly kept under control while also suggesting the *crypta* that undermines it.

Living in Abercorn Terrace and having a mistress in a dingy street in Westminster, Colonel Pargiter transgresses the rigid geographical distinctions established in Victorian London in the 1880s. But while he is in one or the other, the liminal space which he occupies is between the two as it is also located between the private and the public. The doorway is a key image in this novel. In the first section, Rose waits outside the schoolroom, Delia waits at the door of her mother's sickroom, the ladies at the Lodge watch the rain from the doorway, Kitty hesitates at Mrs Robson's front door and, of course, what the Colonel most loathes about his visits to Mira is the wait at the lodging-house door. Later in the novel, at Milton Street, North Pargiter is baffled by the names at the entrance to the building in which Sara lives:

> Names mounted one above another; here on a visiting-card; here engraved on brass – Foster; Abrahamson; Roberts; S. Pargiter was

near the top, punched on a strip of aluminium. He rang one of the
many bells. No one came.   (p. 295)

Bakhtin identified the chronotope of the threshold with a moment of
'crisis' or of a 'break' in life.[32] As Bakhtin suggests of Dostoevsky's
work, in Woolf's later fiction thresholds, together with related chronotopes of stairs and corridors, are extended into the street as the site
of anxiety, significant meetings, decisions and even crises. Milton
Street presents North with a specific confusion that mirrors a larger
sense of confusion. The colours over the houses, red and gold, are the
ones used in *The Waves* to suggest the empire – the red of the
Merchant Navy flag and gold for the spoils of empire. The setting
sun was also employed in that novel to suggest the demise of the
British empire in India. Here North has returned from a sheep farm
in Eastern Africa at a time when anti-imperialist sentiments are
beginning among the farmers who were cheated out of the best
grazing land by the British. The demise of the empire has left a
vacuum that on the streets of the East End of London is already
beginning to be filled by the rise of the British Union of Fascists.

   The 'controlled decontrolling' which occurs in *The Years* suggests
Bakhtin's argument that 'the personal and detached human
being . . . [has] lost the unity and wholeness that had been a product
of his public origin'.[33] But 'detached human beings' are often sites of
subversion in *The Years*. Although Kitty is the daughter of a famous
historian, she is excluded from his version of history and from the
education establishment so that he is no more to her than 'the damp
feel of a heavy hand on her knee' (p. 64). The lodge by which St
Katharine's is epitomised stands in contrast to the ugly little houses of
Miss Craddock, who makes a living teaching history, and also to
Professor Robson's family, excluded by their gender and their working-class background respectively from the discursive formations
that define the 'real' Oxford so that they are also outside of the
university and the wholeness of that background. When the reader
is first introduced to Miss Craddock she is caught with her pen
suspended in mid-thought. In a sense she is suspended between the
Oxford world she envies but from which she is excluded, and her
female background with which the flowers sent to her by her sister
keep her in touch. But there are cryptic suggestions that she is no
longer in touch with the wholeness of the feminine. In verbally
chastising Kitty she has to make a conscious effort to suppress the

sentimentality that she associates with her sister and flowers. Her red-tipped nose associates her physically with the red ink with which she corrects her students' work. When Kitty makes to tell her of her mother, she is cut short because Dr Malone does not pay her to talk with Kitty about such things.

The working-class culture from which Professor Robson is estranged is now a site of anxiety for him. He is obviously uncomfortable with mending the hen coops – his long-fingered white hands mark his separation from his background – but he feels obliged to do so because he remembers his father mending boots on a Sunday. The nails that split the wood or are driven in sideways signify how the 'public unity' enjoyed by his father's generation is now split and how Robson is now situated outside two discourses. But the apparently seamless culture of Oxford epitomised by St Katharine's is also splitting. The ancient tree in the garden of the lodge under which kings and poets sat is now half fallen and propped up by a stake. Indeed, to the 'modern' eye of Kitty, in 1880, Oxford seems 'obsolete, frivolous, inane'; the undergraduates look 'silly' and 'portentous old men with their exaggerated features, looked like gargoyles, carved, medieval, unreal' (p. 72). The absurdity which Kitty sees instead of the unified chronotope of Oxford is mirrored in Robson's view of his hens as 'imbecile fowls' (p. 65). It is significant that the grand old men of Oxford are compared to gargoyles, for their function was to channel off roof-rotting rain. But the rain, like the presence of Miss Craddock and Professor Robson, persists. The rain may seem innocuous, making a faint mist in the fields, 'chuckling and burbling' – baby sounds that associate the amniotic rain with the feminine – but it smears windows (disrupting taken-for-granted views) and slices the ancient tree.

The public street in *The Years* is a chronotope that is glimpsed in the novel often from a private home or on the way from or to it. Those who spend any time there are hawkers, flower sellers, barrel organists or working-class children. But once again they are detached from the unity and wholeness of their public origins:

> The shabby street on the south side of the river was very noisy. Now and again a voice detached itself from the general clamour. A woman shouted to her neighbour; a child cried. A man trundling a barrow opened his mouth and bawled up at the windows as he passed. There were bedsteads, grates, pokers and odd pieces of twisted iron on his

> barrow. But whether he was selling old iron or buying old iron it was impossible to say; the rhythm persisted; but the words were almost rubbed out.   (p. 155)

Very few people in the novel seem to belong entirely to their locations. *The Years* presents the situation described by Bakhtin that 'once having lost the popular chronotope of the public square, [the personal and detached human being's] self-consciousness could not find an equally real, unified and whole chronotope'.[34] Much in the novel – Colonel Pargiter's secret affair, Rose's secret journey to Lamley's store, Delia's ambivalent feelings towards her mother, the anxieties and private ambitions that are not expressed – confirms Bakhtin's point that, in the absence of a 'unified and whole chronotope',

> a vast number of new spheres of consciousness and objects appeared in the private life of the private individual that were not, in general, subject to being made public (the sexual sphere and others), or were subject only to an intimate, conditional, closeted expression. The human image became multi-layered, multi-faceted. A core and a shell, an inner and an outer, separated within it.[35]

In Woolf's later fiction, what Bakhtin would call the multi-layered and multi-faceted private life is mirrored in the diverse nature of the *a priori* discourse of urban space. As the fantasy which Rose invokes as a child to support her on her journey to Lamley's shop indicates, Woolf is interested in the difficulty of separating the imaginary 'texts' of the streets from their 'reality'. The irony is that Rose's imperialist fantasy that she is on her way to rescue a besieged garrison is one from which women are excluded. The horrid pock-marked face leering at her from under the gas lamp is also incorporated into the fantasy. While, at one level, he is part of the mythology – in part embedded in reality – that inhibits women from using the streets, he is also an index of the way in which the lower classes have become a social text. The issue in Woolf's work is not so much the boundary between the imaginary and 'reality', but the power that social texts or social mythologies can assume, exemplified here in the way in which the man under the gas lamp reappears in Rose's nightmares as a robber. The dream has more to do with what the middle class project onto the lower orders than with the latter in reality. This bourgeois fear of the lower classes goes back a long way, certainly to the impact which the French Revolution had on the bourgeoisie in many parts of Europe. But it is all the more potent here in that the man, as a villain in Rose's dreams, enters her bedroom, the most private part of the bourgeois house where the middle and upper classes – especially women and children – were perceived to be at their most vulnerable. The escaped convict Magwitch's threat that he will tear out the child Pip's heart in Dickens' *Great Expectations* is all the more terrifying for his promise that should Pip betray him he will reach him even when he is asleep in his locked bedroom.

In post-war Britain there were a number of principal narratives of public space available to the writer as there were of the family: narratives which had their origins in the mid-nineteenth-century 'gaslight' era when, as Judith Walkowitz says, 'the Great Unwashed lived in chaotic alleys, courts, and hovels just off the grand thorough-fares' in 'a Dickensian cityscape of dirty, crowded, disorganized clusters of urban villages'.[36] The city was exhilaratingly a place of disconnection and anonymity, but also a site of contamination. The configuration of London in the late Victorian era into a 'civilised' West End and an East End 'Other' mirrored the imperial West/East global topography, evidenced in the way in which social writers of the time employed imperialist discourse to describe the latter. But narratives of the city were also gendered, as the narrative of the urban (male) voyeur, epitomised as Walkowitz points out by Henry James, who, enjoying the anonymity, is able to find social and intellectual elbow room in the city, denied the majority of women.[37] These are narratives which, like those of the family, cannot be attributed to any one writer or group of writers, but are discourses which, as Foucault argued, have achieved unity through time.[38] Woolf's later fiction is written in a space opened up by a dialectic between them, but, nevertheless, in *The Years* particularly the *a priori* of urban space is included in an obverse form or in a form which is challenged.

The imperialist mode of comprehending space is obverted at several points in *The Years*. Rose's fantasy journey to Lamley's, in which she thinks of herself crossing deserts and fording rivers, is almost a parody of the way in which, as Judith Walkowitz says, 'urban explorers never seemed to walk or ride into the slums, but to "penetrate" inaccessible places where the poor lived, in dark and noisy courts, thieves' "dens", foulsmelling "swamps", and the black "abyss"'.[39] Rose's imaginary journey is an attempt to appropriate the power of the presence of the adult imperialist adventurer. The way in which North, who has recently returned from Africa, perceives the streets of London in the 1930s overturns how the two were usually seen as social texts. London is exciting after Africa, reversing how the guests at Eleanor's party see that continent. The former is described in figurative language normally used by travellers of the latter. The emphasis is upon the kind of outdoor life one would associate with Africa; people 'swarm' on the pavements; the barrows of fruit and vegetables are impressive; there is the kind of iconography travellers might be led to find in Africa, a chalked circle on the wall with a jagged line in it; and street hawkers.

Woolf also regularly alludes to narratives of the 'gaslight era' which presented a threatening, chaotic labyrinthine London. When North becomes lost among the London streets, he thinks 'Where the dickens am I?' Where the 'dickens', indeed, for the Victorian novelist contributed to, and was the product of, the *a priori* gaslight discourse of urban topography, invoked, for example, in the description of the working-class man Rose as a child configures as much as sees under the gas lamp, and in the account of Hyams Place, lit by the yellow glare from the public-house lamp, which reveals the bourgeois fascination with, and fear of, what Bakhtin called the 'social exotic' of the street. The 'battered and red-nosed' man selling violets on the street bears the trace of the 'gaslight narrative'. The brief physical details we are offered are enough to suggest the grotesque body marginalised in nineteenth-century discourse of the body. As Mike Featherstone has pointed out,

> The grotesque body of the carnival is the lower body of impurity, disproportion, immediacy, orifices, the material body, which is the opposite of the *classical body*, which is beautiful, symmetrical, elevated, perceived from a distance and which is the ideal body. The grotesque body and the carnival represent the otherness which is excluded from the process of formation of middle-class identity and culture. With the extension of the civilizing process into the middle classes the need for greater controls over the emotions and bodily functions produced changes in manners and conduct which heightened the sense of disgust at direct emotional and bodily expressivity.[40]

How far the lower-class body became associated with the grotesque body as a site of revulsion is suggested by the man's mispronunciation of the flowers he sells as 'vilets', emphasising how he might be seen by the people who pass him by as 'vile'. He describes his flowers as 'nice' and 'sweet', words that suggest the bourgeois ideal of the feminine, and which stand in contradistinction to the withered violets he offers for sale. But, importantly, his association with Hyams Place links him with the London Jewish population, and with another excluded – and feared – group in Victorian discourse.

The process of 'controlled decontrolling' which the commercial street came to represent extends throughout society. Whereas the decline of the large Victorian family is a social fact reflected in the dispersion of the younger members of the Pargiter family to smaller houses or to rooms, sometimes in less than salubrious areas, it also brings the middle class into more proximity, albeit in a controlled way, with the grotesque and carnivalesque. North sees the district in which Sara's rooms are situated as a 'slum', an historical *a priori* itself associated with corruption, decay, pollution and infection. As a threat to respectable, middle-class society, North's invocation of the slum initiates a chain of signifiers which suggest middle-class anxiety about the loosening of controls and the greater proximity of the carnivalesque. He is anxious that dinner is late and not satisfactory. Meals are paid considerable attention in the course of the novel; they are an index of the well-regulated ideal of upper-class/upper-middle-class Victorian family life. At Abercorn Terrace, Eleanor finds security in what her father's carving of the chicken at lunch represents. But the meal in Sara's rooms is closer to what Baudrillard calls a 'negative ideal'; it brings North into proximity with what the well-regulated routine of the English middle class was designed to distance. There are a number of allusions to the grotesque, carnivalesque body; the girl servant with red hands and jaunty white cap is a lodging-house 'skivvy' – she moves noisily around the table, holding knives and forks in a bunch, and breathes heavily. There is a yellowed stain on the table cloth, the undercooked mutton runs with blood, the yellow potatoes look hard and the 'slabbed-down mass of cabbage' is 'oozing green water' (p. 302). The references to an excess of blood and water suggest the impurities, orifices and leakages of the lower body excluded from the classical ideal body while the chain of colours – red, yellow, green – are those which signify bodily infection and disease. The butchery and cannibalistic trace which prepared meat on the Victorian family table was often dressed so as to deny is clearly present in the description of the leg of mutton as a 'rather stringy disagreeable object' which left the willow-patterned plate 'daubed with gory streaks' (p. 304).

North comes to represent an 'I' positioned in a space vacated by discourses that have been discredited. Conrad's *Heart of Darkness* is invoked in both *The Voyage Out* and *The Years*. Whereas *The Voyage Out* takes us into the heart of darkness, in *The Years* Woolf thinks of the heart of darkness as the condition of being embroiled in the 'truths' of empire and Englishness:

> He felt that he had been in the middle of a jungle; in the heart of darkness; cutting his way towards the light; but provided only with broken sentences, single words, with which to break through the briar-bush of human bodies, human wills and voices, that bent over him, binding him, binding him.   (p. 391)

Again, whereas in *Night and Day* Woolf is concerned with the articulation of silence, in *The Years* she articulates the condition of being caught in mid-sentence, of not being able to complete a sentence because one does not know what is 'solid' any more. In this sense North thus comes to speak both for the text as a whole and for its exploration of the concept of 'real', as something in the end unknowable:

> But what do I mean, he wondered – I, to whom ceremonies are suspect, and religion's dead; who don't fit, as the man said, don't fit in anywhere? He paused. There was the glass in his hand; in his mind a sentence. And he wanted to make other sentences. But how can I, he thought . . . unless I know what's solid, what's true; in my life, in other people's lives?   (p. 390)

The uncertainty which pervades the text, and the generally more sombre treatment of the themes and preoccupations of her earlier work, reflects the mood of the late 1930s. The new significances with which the decade had burdened concepts of history, civilisation, progress and nationhood, evident in *The Years*, Woolf pursued, in a different vein, in her next novel, *Between the Acts*.

9

The Last Years:
'The Shooting Party' (1938)
and *Between the Acts* (1941)

> *We pour to the edge of a precipice ... & then? I cant conceive that there will be a 27th June 1941*
>
> Virginia Woolf, *Diary*[1]

I

The version of Virginia Woolf's 'The Shooting Party' published in 1938 marks the transition from *The Years* to *Between the Acts*, published posthumously in 1941, a few months after her suicide in March. Woolf began thinking about the story in 1932, drawing up a list of caricatures – 'Scenes from English life/The Pheasants/Scenes: Life on a Battleship', 'Country House Life', 'The Royal Navy', 'The Great Jeweller' – some of which reflected tropes she had used in her critique of Englishness in many of her novels. But 'The Shooting Party' shares with *Between the Acts* a fusion of the apocalyptic with a dark carnivalesque:

> Out in the King's Ride the pheasants were being driven across the noses of the guns. Up they spurted from the underwood like heavy rockets, reddish purple rockets, and as they rose the guns cracked in order, eagerly, sharply, as if a line of dogs had suddenly barked.
> In the deep-cut road beneath the hanger a cart stood, laid already with soft warm bodies with limp claws and still lustrous eyes. The birds seemed alive still, but swooning under their rich damp feathers.

> They looked relaxed and comfortable, stirring slightly, as if they slept
> upon a warm bank of soft feathers on the floor of the cart.[2]

This is the upper-class version of the carnivalesque, for the shoot is
like a fiesta – the birds are like rockets, the guns crack (like fire-
works?), and it is an occasion of thrill and excitement. But there is
also a displaced sexuality, as in the carnivalesque, in the allusions to
body parts and fluids – 'noses of the guns', 'up they spurted', 'rich
damp feathers' – and death and sexuality are conflated in the description of the pheasants where the boundaries between life and death
are deliberately confused.

As in *Between the Acts*, there is a sense of traditional upper-class
English life, based upon patriarchy and empire, as coming to an end.
Miss Antonia and her elder sister old Miss Rashleigh represent a
family line and an aristocratic Englishness that do not seem to fit
easily with the modern world, signified by the doors and windows of
the house that no longer fit, and which is dying out – they have
no children and their brother, the Squire, has left only illegitimate
children. Milly, the housekeeper, mutters pointedly to herself after
knitting the jersey for her illegitimate son, 'the end o' that', and
after she helps empty the cart of the dead pheasants, 'The last of
the lot!' (pp. 256 and 257). At one level there is order to their world
evident in the precise way Miss Antonia puts her sewing away and
arranges the vegetables on the plate at dinner. But while the metonymic in the story suggests the public face of order, the metaphorical foregrounds what threatens to destroy it. There is a great deal of
violence in the narrative, not only in the shoot itself but more mena-
cingly in the way in which Antonia 'drew the carving knife across the
pheasant's breast firmly' (p. 257) – perhaps cryptically displacing her
regrets about not having borne children but also signifying the
neuroses of her class generally – and the way in which the hunting
dogs attack the sister's spaniel. Indeed, anxiety is as an important
trope as the violence – the 'hens peck nervously' (p. 254), the sun
mocks the hole in the carpet (p. 255) and the Squire has a 'hang-dog,
purple-stained face' (p. 255) – and is linked again to the apocalyptic
in the increasing concern with the gathering storm.

The fusion of the apocalyptic with a carnivalesque that borders on
the grotesque is employed to suggest the *crypta* concealed by the
public face of the aristocracy. The shooting party – an uneasy juxtaposition of the joyous with killing – signifies a muted but nevertheless

real indifference to suffering evident also in the way in which Antonia and her sister chuckle over memories of the shooter who accidentally shot himself through the heart and John who, thrown from his horse, was ridden over by the hunt. The *crypta* within the aristocracy exposed by the story also extends to what the sisters can barely articulate themselves – that the housekeeper is their brother's mistress and her son their illegitimate nephew. The loose morality and sexual appetite of the men emphasise the apparent lack of sexuality in the sisters' lives. But in rendering the *crypta* almost in carnivalesque terms – in the way in which the sisters chuckle over tragic accidents – the story blurs the boundary between the external threat – the story was published a year before the outbreak of the Second World War – and the seeds of internal destruction. This is particularly evident in the fusion of the carnivalesque and the apocalyptic in the chaotic climax analogous to the impending chaos unleashed in Europe by Fascism. As the hunting dogs attack the spaniel, Woolf conflates the impending storm with the frenzy of the dogs and highlights the absurd slap-stick in the Squire swinging his tawse wildly, cursing his sisters and the dogs, old Miss Rashleigh flaying the air wildly with her stick as she falls, and the shield of the Rashleighs and the picture of King Edward falling.

The end of the story returns the reader to the train journey which frames it and to a sense of the ordinary that belies but does not entirely erase the chaos that the reader has just witnessed. The message at the end of the story anticipates a salient theme in *Between the Acts* – that the apparently ordinary is not to be trusted and is threatened by the *crypta* which it conceals and which points to a different version of 'reality'.

Woolf began *Between the Acts* (initially to be called *Pointz Hall*) in the year in which 'The Shooting Party' was published, the last year of peace, when she was also working on a biography of Roger Fry and the proofs of the political pamphlet, *Three Guineas*, locating the origins of war in male psychology as institutionalised in patriarchal, capitalist culture. Much of the criticism of the novel emphasises its apocalyptic tropes. In the novel as a whole, thoughts are frequently not of beginnings and possibilities but of endings. The narrative itself is structured around endings: the end of peace, the end of England and of European civilisation, the end of the fine weather and the end of the play. The book concludes with lights being turned out and the final image is of a field in darkness that anticipates the blackout but is also an ominous symbol of the end of civilisation. Although the novel is set in a single day, its time-scale extends to post-history through the prospect of a world war and pre-history in Mrs Swithin's reading of an *Outline of History*. In the final page of the novel, pre- and post-history are conflated:

> The window was all sky without colour. The house had lost its shelter. It was night before roads were made, or houses. It was the night that dwellers in caves had watched from some high place among rocks.
> Then the curtain rose. They spoke. (p. 197)

There are two death rattles, then, in *Between the Acts*: the end of European civilisation and the end of the European concept of history. Each is closely related to the other in a novel in which a revision of the concept of nation, particularly of England and Englishness between the wars – one possible interpretation of the title of the book – is inextricably linked to a revision of post-Enlightenment concepts of history and historiography.

Between the Acts was not well received in *Scrutiny*, where the review seemed a vehicle for the Leavises' dislike of the Bloomsbury group, nor in *Nation* (New York), where Louis Kronenberger believed it the weakest of Woolf's novels. There were other reviewers who found the book puzzling but interesting, and a few who thought very highly of it. Edwin Muir praised it as 'one of her most ambitious and most perfect novels', and a reviewer in *Nineteenth Century* argued against those who might think the novel 'a falling away from her individual outlook, a concession to the wider public'.[3] It was not universally understood and was sometimes misunderstood by reviewers. Frank Swinnerton missed the point in maintaining that in the 'pageant play which summarises old moral and social attitudes and their equivalents in successive periods of time [Woolf] shows the unchanging nature of men and women'.[4] But there were reviewers, pursuing the implications of the title, who realised that what should really engage the reader is the cryptic element within the text. As Hudson Strode in the *New York Times* observed, 'her peculiar interest was not in surfaces but in mysterious motivations and subterfuges that do not meet the eye'.[5]

The novel is set in an English village, symbolically the heart of England, preparing for its pageant in a mid-June afternoon 1939, six weeks before the start of the Second World War. I have argued throughout this book that Woolf's novels are subversions of pre-established genres and modes of writing and this novel is no exception. The pageant is literally and metaphorically the centre of the text which, despite the sombreness of its subject – the last few weeks of peace before the Second World War – has a strong theatrical element and overturns the distinction between prose narrative and drama.

Although the mood is overcast by the prospect of war, the afternoon of the pageant turns out better than expected, anticipating the period of calm that followed the declaration of war and which came to be known as the 'phoney war'. What critics have understated is the way in which the holiday atmosphere in the village that afternoon is reflected in the style of the novel itself, in its linguistic playfulness and mocking of Englishness, family and sexual relationships. Literary references, allusions to events in the community, songs, rhymes, noises and gossip are interwoven throughout the text in a non-hierarchical, at times carnivalesque, manner that does not distinguish between their relative cultural status. But, as in 'The Shooting Party', there is a teasing contradiction between the apocalyptic and the carnivalesque.

Throughout the novel there is a heightened sense of the way in which words in a different context can carry different meanings and of how with particular emphasis a word can glimpse something beyond its usual referent – something cryptic, half-articulated:

> 'The nursery,' said Mrs Swithin.
> Words raised themselves and became symbolical.
> 'The cradle of our race,' she seemed to say. (p. 66)

That words can 'raise themselves' and become 'symbolical' reflects the influence of being on the threshold of war on people's inner thoughts, their behaviour and the way in which they communicate with each other.

> 'Now up, now up again.' Again [Mrs Swithin and her guest] mounted. 'Up and up they went,' she panted, seeing, it seemed, an invisible procession, 'up and up to bed.'
> 'A bishop; a traveller; – I've forgotten even their names. I ignore. I forget.'
> She stopped at a window in the passage and held back the curtain. Beneath was the garden, bathed in sun. The grass was sleek and shining. Three white pigeons were flirting and tiptoeing as ornate as ladies in ball dresses. Their elegant bodies swayed as they minced with

> tiny steps on their little pink feet upon the grass. Suddenly, up they rose
> in a flutter, circled, and flew away. (pp. 63–4)

The act of leading someone upstairs becomes imbued with a symbolic significance it would not have at another time. The mind seems unable to concentrate on ordinary tasks at hand; a rhyme intrudes into a pedestrian piece of conversation and suddenly we glimpse the way in which even the ordinary in the last years of peace could become ominous. At another time, Mrs Swithin would not stop in the passage and consider the view from the window in the way she does here. The garden again reflects the unreality of this period before the start of the war, while it is not the pigeons themselves but what they signify that holds Mrs Swithin's attention. The ladies in their ball gowns in turn signify a way of life that is soon to disappear and which for Mrs Swithin is the essence of European civilisation. The curtain here is a key image, associating the garden scene with the images in the pageant, but also placing the ladies signified by the pigeons (and the civilisation that the ladies in turn represent) as one of the acts between which the villagers now seem to be living. Throughout the novel, the cryptic and the pedestrian are sharply interwoven and frequently characters communicate on different levels. In the early afternoon before the pageant begins, Mrs Swithin observes:

> 'It's very unsettled. It'll rain, I'm afraid. We can only pray,' she
> added, and fingered her crucifix.
> 'And provide umbrellas,' said her brother. (p. 21)

'It' might refer to the unsettled weather or to the political climate. Mrs Swithin (appropriately given her name) begins by worrying about the weather for the pageant, but thinking of prayer and fingering the crucifix, she ends by reflecting on the prospect of war. Her brother responds to her remark only as a comment on the day's weather, redolent perhaps of Chamberlain's failure to read the signs in Europe before the war, and returns the conversation to the mundane problem of what they should do to protect the audience should it rain. Even so, the notion of providing umbrellas, given that Mrs Swithin has wandered into darker thoughts, articulates the sense of hopelessness of the individual community in the face of world war as well as the unreality that pervaded the last days of peace and the opening of the war. The crucifix that Mrs Swithin fingers is a much darker image, of course. It suggests solace in the promise of the resurrection, but stripped of the compensatory symbolism of the resurrection it is as an image of agonising death, doubt and despair.

The focus for the revisionism of *Between the Acts* is Woolf's interest, which first emerged in a significant way in *Mrs Dalloway*, in the way in which the chronotopes, the spatiotemporal locations, of fictional and historical narratives are symbolically associated with the psychology of its occupants and with various ideological conventions. But, as one would expect of a novel set in a country on the verge of war, there is a more concentrated focus upon how the cultural psychology of the chronotope enters into people's conversations and their interests, determines their perceptions and preoccupations, and structures their relationships with others. The novel tries to re-create and explore the 'cultural psychology' of 1939 when Europe was poised on the threshold between peace and war, between the old past and an unknowable future – Barcelona had fallen to Franco, Austria and Czechoslovakia had fallen to Germany, and Poland was under threat. But, as in *Mrs Dalloway*, there is a strong dialectic, informing the structure, language and imagery of the novel, between its spatiotemporal framework, in this case England between the wars, and the narrative focalisation which is outside of this framework. The narrative focalisation looks back on Britain in the last days of peace from a future coloured by the experiences of 1940 – the Dunkirk evacuation of May 1940; the Battle of Britain in the autumn; and the London Blitz of the winter of that year – and dark thoughts as to what was to come next. In many respects the war seemed difficult to win, a fear brought home to Virginia Woolf herself by the damage caused to their own house in Bloomsbury, as well as the destruction of another for which they still paid rent, and to Vanessa's studio.

The mood of 1940 rather than 1939 enters the novel through its culturally and psychologically potent imagery. This is evident, for example, in the description of the lily pond, symbolically, through the colours red, white and blue, associated with England as an allegory of origin – 'There had always been lilies there, self-sown from wind-dropped seed . . . . Water, for hundreds of years, had silted down into the hollow, and lay there four or five feet deep over a black cushion of mud' (p. 39). But in the description of the lilies, the pond becomes an apocalyptic projection – 'At that the fleet of boat-shaped bodies paused; poised; equipped; mailed; then with a waver of undulation off they flashed' (p. 40).

Like *Mrs Dalloway*, *Between the Acts* is a fictional account of England in a particular historical period, coruscated with competing interests, perceptions, preconceptions and ambitions. In both cases Woolf has tried to find a mode of writing which will do justice to, and enable her to explore, that diversity. But *Between the Acts* seems to be more obviously narrated from an imaginary spatiotemporal location that is later than that in which the book is set and later than the year in which it was written. This imaginary location into which Woolf appears to have projected herself, and from which *Between the Acts* views the period between the wars, drives the much more searching critique of Englishness, the more radical revision of historiography and the much more savage social critique in this novel compared with *Mrs Dalloway*.

II

At one level the pageant is a reminder of the wealth of historical memory that is transmuted into, and sustains, the myths of empire and of English national identity. But while *Between the Acts* looks back to *Mrs Dalloway* in its chronotope of a single day, the pageant reinvokes the carnivalesque element of *Orlando*. The two aspects of the novel – the carnivalesque and the apocalyptic – are fused in the cryptography of the text. Both dimensions are brought together in the way in which the novel not only presents a critique of notions of nationhood and empire, but of historiography itself.

In the eyes of both the villagers and Miss La Trobe, the pageant is a cryptographic representation. The villagers are looking forward to a representation of the past with which they can identify, a reminder of shared values and, as in all local pageants, cryptic allusions to the community in which they live. But they are confronted with attitudes and values that have brought Europe to the point of war and also brought about the rise of Fascism. This aspect of the pageant is encapsulated in the imagery such as Queen Elizabeth's ruff becoming unpinned and in the figure of the village idiot. Mirroring the Fool in Elizabethan theatre, the idiot prides himself in his knowledge of the villagers' secrets:

> I know where the tit nests, he began
> In the hedgerow. I know, I know –
> What don't I know?
> All your secrets, ladies,
> And yours too, gentlemen. (p. 78)

When the different social groups represented in the pageant join hands and dance around Queen Elizabeth, the idiot weaves his way symbolically in and out of the circle threatening the symbolic unity.

In *Between the Acts*, Woolf anticipates Karl Löwith's argument, proposed seven years after her death, that 'neither a providential design nor a natural law of progressive development is discernible in the tragic comedy of all times'.[6] In doing so, Woolf rings the death knell for history in the Hegelian sense that had informed the Victorian, or at least the Whig, concept of history as progress. That is history as 'a record of progress – a record of accumulating knowledge and increasing wisdom, of continual advancement from a lower to a higher platform of intelligence and well-being'.[7]

The novel challenges what has come to be called in contemporary theory a mode of 'totalizing' representation. The concept has been summarised by Linda Hutcheon:

> The function of the term totalizing, as I understand it, is to point to the *process* (hence the awkward 'ing' form) by which writers of history, fiction, or even theory render their materials coherent, continuous, unified – but always with an eye to the control and mastery of those materials, even at the risk of doing violence to them.[8]

In *Between the Acts*, Woolf highlights both the desire for and the suspicion of totalising narratives. In this respect she anticipates the challenge to unitary, closed narratives that have dominated much contemporary criticism. Much of what Linda Hutcheon says about novels like Salman Rushdie's *Midnight's Children*, for example, is applicable to Miss La Trobe's pageant sequence:

> we now get the histories (in the plural) of the losers as well as the winners, of the regional (and colonisal) as well as the centrist, of the unsung many as well as the much sung few, and I might add, of women as well as men.[9]

The pageant draws attention to the process of constructing history, of imposing order on the past. Each act demonstrates how representation is the product of the discourses that inscribe social and ideological contexts, highlighting the narrative nature of history and suggesting that historical meaning is 'unstable, contextual, relational and provisional'.[10] The reader is alerted that all past 'events' are potentially facts, but only those that are narrated become facts. More than Miss La Trobe intended, the pageant reflects how history is composed of events that have been inscribed with meaning. Deprived of its narrative, as the pageant is deprived of much of its connecting commentary through the sound of the faulty gramophone and voices that are not strong enough to carry over distance, history appears discontinuous and fragmentary. However, despite the carnivalesque element of the pageant, Woolf does not collapse history into a world of free play without notions of 'truth'.

The confusion with which the pageant is received by the audience anticipates what critics such as Linda Hutcheon have seen as 'the postmodern contradictory response to emplotment'.[11] The pageant is contradictory. It presents us with what the audience at the pageant know of the past while simultaneously questioning the nature of historical knowledge. The audience's memories of the past which they witness in Act Two of the pageant raise issues about the radical discontinuity between experience and knowing. The 'pastness' of the past involves also an absence of the past. Appearing as the constable in the pageant, Budge (the publican) draws attention to the violence and racialism occluded in paternalist narratives of empire: 'black men; white men; sailors, soldiers; crossing the ocean; to proclaim her Empire; all of 'em Obey the Rule of my truncheon' (p. 145). Here the influence of *Three Guineas* upon the pageant is very apparent, for like *Three Guineas* the pageant is as much anti-fascist as anti-war. But in *Between the Acts* Woolf explores some of the philosophical difficulties which any attempt to critique 'history' must confront.

Miss La Trobe's satire, in challenging the official histories of empire as edited narratives, appears to hesitate between the two irreconcilable positions identified by Hawthorn: that the 'reality' of history is formulated by discourse but that there is a 'reality' of empire that lies outside discourse and can be seen to have been edited out of the histories of the British empire. The most obvious example of this occluded 'reality' is the way in which the colonisers exploited the colonised. But, as if Woolf was aware of the limitations and dangers in seeing empire in terms of an exploiter/exploited model, the way in which peoples and cultures were exploited under empire is presented cryptically within the text. For example, the description of the play of light on the site of the pageant referring to red, the colour of the Ensign of the Merchant Navy, and to silver clearly brings the interconnection of the empire with commercial exploitation to mind. Red Admiral butterflies, whose name suggests naval officers involved in trade or even naval officers who have blood on their hands, 'gluttonously absorbed richness from dish cloths' (p. 58). The words here are carefully chosen for their ambiguity. 'Richness', of course, suggests 'riches' or even the destruction of the cultural richness of the colonies exploited by the British and Merchant Navies. 'Gluttonously absorbed' suggests not only the greed that impelled many imperialist projects but the extent of the exploitation. The Red Admirals' movements, together with those of the cabbage white butterflies – 'flitting, tasting, returning' – mirror the pattern by which the colonies were visited by British vessels.

Throughout the pageant, Woolf draws attention to how knowing the past involves representing it, which in turn involves processes of construction and interpretation and this acts as a commentary on Miss La Trobe's critique of England and Englishness. The prologue begins with a small child who introduces the pageant as a selected narrative of events:

> Come hither for our festival (she continued)
> This is a pageant, all may see
> Drawn from our island history.
> England am I.... (p. 70)

The opening lines are riddled with irony. The pageant begins against the background of the faulty gramophone. Its menacing buzz from the bushes is a reminder of the technology that now threatens Europe. The first line promises to bring the community together – 'our festival' – but the pageant will highlight many of the internal conflicts in the nation and its empire. It is also ironic that she announces a pageant 'all may see', for the audience's reactions reveal that they do not all see the same pageant, and the cryptic nature of the satire is such that only those who read cryptanalytically will appreciate Miss La Trobe's critique. Moreover, 'drawn from our island history' not only emphasises the selective nature of the narrative but begs the question whose island history is meant, for it will not be the same for both genders, all classes or all ethnic groups. Significantly, when the girl reaches 'England am I', she forgets her lines, as does Mrs Clark playing Queen Elizabeth later. In the course of the pageant, as in what Budge says, there are a number of occasions that illustrate how much has been (conveniently) forgotten. 'Lines' is ambiguous, suggesting both her lines to be spoken and her ancestral lines that the villagers are hoping that the pageant will celebrate.

The influence of *Three Guineas* on *Between the Acts* is also evident in the way in which the critique of Fascism is rooted in Woolf's feminism. The feminist critique of Englishness in the pageant is exemplified in the verse sung by pilgrims who, assuming the role of village rustics, toss hay on their rakes:

> I kissed a girl and let her go,
> Another did I tumble,
> In the straw and in the hay.   (p. 74)

The occluded narrative here is what happens to the girls who are 'tumbled' when they are pregnant with illegitimate children. Mrs Manresa – whose name ironically associates her with arousing or teasing men – recognises this as a scene epitomising 'Merry England', but it is 'Merry' for the men rather than the women. The 'tumbling' of women here parallels the attitude of the guards, reported in the newspapers, who tricked a woman to come into the stables to see a horse with a green tail and then sexually assaulted her.

Woolf's pageant sequence anticipates the two impulses within representations of the past to which Hayden White has drawn attention and which may be seen as centripetal and centrifugal forces: the extent to which the representation corresponds to the 'truth of correspondence' (the concept of an independent historical past) and its relation to the 'truth of coherence' (the narrative of that historical past).[12] The 'truth of coherence' is set up as the principal presence in the pageant informing the monologues of its key figures, Elizabeth, Reason and Victoria. All three, although Victoria does not actually appear, are united around English nationhood and empire. But throughout the pageant, the 'truth of coherence' is undermined by the *crypta* within the pageant, the 'truth of correspondence'. Despite allusions to the grandiloquence of empire, imperialism is portrayed as an economic project; a point that is reinforced by the fact that she is played by the village shopkeeper, itself a reminder of

Napoleon's jibe that England was a nation of shopkeepers. Elizabeth's opening lines are a celebration of the expansionist policies of the Elizabethan Age and of its navy that brings Spenser's *The Faerie Queene* to mind:

> Mistress of ships and bearded men (she bawled)
> Hawkins, Frobisher, Drake,
> Tumbling their oranges, ingots of silver,
> Cargoes of diamonds, ducats of gold,
> Down on the jetty, there in the west land.   (pp. 76–7)

Reason is not immediately identifiable as such and is mistaken at first for Queen Anne. But she is received rapturously by Old Bartholomew when she identifies herself, presumably for the promise she brings in the last days of peace and order. But, once again, the emphasis is upon trade and empire. What distinguishes her speech from Elizabeth's, however, is the expansion of civilisation as a justification of imperialism:

> Time, leaning on his sickle, stands amazed. While commerce from her Cornucopia pours the mingled tribute of her different ores. In distant mines the savage sweats; and from the reluctant earth the painted pot is shaped. At my behest, the armed warrior lays his shield aside; the heathen leaves the Altar steaming with unholy sacrifice. The violet and the eglantine over the riven earth their flowers entwine. No longer fears the unwary wanderer the poisoned snake. And in the helmet, yellow bees their honey make.   (p. 111)

The rationality with which empire is presented here belies its uglier aspects, cryptically presented in the novel in ways that keep them at the margins of discourse. The subject with which Woolf is wrestling, though, is not merely the disparities between historical past and narrative versions of that past but whether a history independent of discourse can ever be recovered. Thus Woolf unveils, as far as possible, a past that, while it cannot be entirely free of discourse, has not been as politically manipulated as the official histories.

Before they are inscribed with new and alien meanings suggested by the idyllic, English pastoral image of the last line, the colonies are first reinscribed as the 'Other' of civilisation, encapsulated here in the references to armed warriors, heathens and poisoned snakes. Throughout the novel there are references to violence which appear to place the 'violence' of the British empire in a wider context. The description of the thrush with a 'coil of pinkish rubber twisted in its beak' suggests that the violence of prehistory that Mrs Swithin reads about in her *Outline of History* is present as an aspect of life in the second millennium A D. But in the novel, Woolf makes a distinction between the violence of animal and bird life and the violence committed by humans on each other. The novel does not attempt to rationalise animal and bird violence. But it would appear from the monologues of Queen Elizabeth, Reason and Budge that violence committed by human beings is morally problematic and has to be justified by cultural rhetoric. In the novels of the 1920s, Woolf's emphasis is upon how participation in violence is a matter of obedience inculcated through an individual's participation in a codified 'reality'. In *Between the Acts*, however, the emphasis is upon the rhetoric that justifies violence and in this respect the novel reflects Woolf's quarrel with the younger members of the Bloomsbury group in the mid-1930s, particularly Julian Bell who, in his essay 'War and Peace: A Letter to E. M. Forster', advocated opposing Fascism by force. Indeed, the quarrel with Julian's views would seem to inform one of the most disconcerting images of violence in the novel – the killing of the snake:

> There, couched in the grass, curled in an olive green ring, was a snake. Dead? No, choked with a toad in its mouth. The snake was unable to swallow; the toad was unable to die. A spasm made the ribs contract; blood oozed. It was birth the wrong way round – a monstrous inversion. So, raising his foot, [Giles] stamped on them. The mass crushed and slithered. The white canvas on his tennis shoes was bloodstained and sticky. But it was action. Action relieved him. He strode to the Barn, with blood on his shoes. (p. 89)

There is no single interpretation of this passage and Woolf probably never intended one. Giles acts out of the kind of instinctual violence in which the officer class of the First World War was inculcated. He sees the destructive snake and his response is to destroy it without realising that this action will also kill what the snake has swallowed. Here Woolf may well be contemplating the number of people in the future who, in being liberated by war with Germany, will be killed either directly by allied fire or indirectly by strategies introduced by Germany as a result of the declaration of war. In March 1939, of course, Hitler invaded Czechoslovakia, violating the Munich accord. Any notion that the allies will emerge unscathed from the war is jettisoned in the image of the bloodstained shoes. But the fact that the shoes are sticky as well as bloody suggests the moral compromises and transgressions involved in war. The passage emphasises circularity – the snake is choking on a toad that it is killing and the snake is within a circle of green – which might suggest the nature of the situation in which any nation finds itself that embarks on war and also the cul de sac into which Germany had got itself by swallowing up territories that would eventually choke it. That the end will come as a monstrous inversion of its origins is reinforced by the allusions to the Bible story of origins – not only in the reference to the snake but to the ribs that are contracting – suggesting possibly that the modern Europe that began with expansion of empire into countries beyond Europe will be destroyed by the expansion of Germany within Europe.

In the pageant, what White called the 'truth of coherence' becomes the force behind the sense of an English national identity. The library at Pointz Hall reflects the role of English canonical authors – such as Donne, Keats, Byron, and Shelley – and biographies of the 'major' nineteenth-century figures – such as Palmerston, Wellington and Garibaldi – in shaping a particular configuration of nationhood. However, the pageant also reveals the disjunction of 'truth of coherence' and the 'truth of correspondence'. Victorian England as suggested by the figure of the constable is a myth constructed from the way different imaginary elements stand in relation to each other rather than by any correspondence with the external world:

> It only wanted a shower of rain, a flight of pigeons round his head, and the pealing bells of St Paul's and the Abbey to transform him into the very spit and image of a Victorian constable; and to transport them to a foggy London afternoon, with the muffin bells ringing and the church bells pealing at the very height of Victorian prosperity.
>
> (p. 146)

But Budge is both an apocalyptic and carnivalesque figure. And, once again, the influence of *Three Guineas* is evident where instead of distinguishing British culture from German or Italian, Woolf highlights the Tyrant – a virile uniformed man, his hand on his sword. The values espoused by the constable are undermined by the fact that he is played by the village publican, traditionally a village character at odds with the local constable.

The contradictions between the past and the narrative of that past are represented in *Between the Acts* differently from in *Three Guineas* through the emphasis upon what is perceived as the upper-middle-class fear of losing power and control. Much of what Budge has to say, if read in the cryptanalytical way that Miss La Trobe intended, represents the Victorian period as a site of a number of anxieties. The over-insistence upon order in the different parts of the empire, for example, betrays an underlying fundamental insecurity about rebellion: 'Some bother it may be in Ireland; Famine. Fenians. What not. On Thursday it's the natives of Peru require protection and correction; we give 'em what's due'. (p. 145). The working-class districts of London – Cripplegate, St Giles and Whitechapel – are also invoked as sites of anxiety and linked in the constable's monologue with those who 'sweat at the mines' and 'cough at the looms' in the colonies.

But this very Victorian theme of the metropolis being destroyed from the inside is given an even more sobering twist in the description of the Noble Barn which suggests that not only has the rot set in but that it is irredeemable. The image of the Noble Barn reflects what is thought of as modern England; it is over seven hundred years old, which means that it was built in the thirteenth century, the century with which the pageant opens. It reflects the grandeur of English national identity and, because it reminds some people of a Greek temple, even the way in which Victorian England idealised Greece and Rome as the cradles of civilisation. But unnoticed within the barn, analogous with England and empire, there are forces of destruction destroying it as the damp in the library is destroying that symbol of English culture. But while the mice, beetles and insects go unnoticed, a butterfly sunning itself on a sunlit pane symbolises the complacency of middle England. The language which describes the innocence of the short-lived butterfly – that might also symbolise the naïveté of Neville Chamberlain and his short-lived peace – stands in contrast to the violence and mechanical imagery in the description of the bluebottle that, mirroring the German occupation of Czechoslovakia, 'settled on the cake and stabbed its yellow rock with its short drill' (p. 90).

The ambiguity and the confusion of discourses of social-paternalism and of control in Budge's monologue highlight the disjunction of the altruistic ideologies of empire and the violent, oppressive 'realities' in some of the colonies. The constable is a key figure in the pageant's exposure of those attitudes that have brought Europe to war and have given rise to Fascism. This particular image of the constable also ironically invokes one of the narrator's opening comments on the pageant, that 'the human figure was seen to great advantage against a background of sky' (p. 70). After his delineation of what he calls the 'white man's job', he is portrayed (like Dr Crane in *The Waves*) as 'eminent, dominant, glaring from his pedestal. A very fine figure of a man he was, everyone agreed, his truncheon extended' (p. 146). Here, English nationhood and empire are linked, alarmingly and comically, to patriarchy. The carnivalesque mockery of Budge, evident in the final image, as a conflation of eminence and hostility is particularly disconcerting because it highlights not only a specific oppressive masculine authority but the extent to which it may be found in the principal institutions throughout Victorian England including law courts, schools and churches.

The pageant's two playlets, parodies of a Shakespearean romance and a Restoration comedy, provide comic renditions of the patriarchy in which Woolf believed Fascism was rooted. In both, confirming the links of Englishness and patriarchy, the mother's death and absence are axiomatic. In the first playlet the male child wins his claim to be the 'rightful heir'. Redolent of the stories of Moses and Oedipus, the playlet re-enacts the folk tale of the baby threatened, as Moses was by the Pharaoh's decree that all Hebrew children should be put to death, but saved by the intervention of a female. In this case an old woman places the baby in a basket in the rushes as Moses was rescued by one of the Pharaoh's 'daughters' (probably the daughter of one of his concubines). The Prince returns years later to claim the hand of Carinthia. The second playlet is a feminist revisioning of this tale. While Woolf retains the implied threat posed by the father, Flavinda is not rescued by the ingenuity of a surrogate mother (the old woman in the playlet, the Pharaoh's daughter in the Moses story). She is saved by a cradle in which she floats free of the shipwreck in which her father drowns. But whereas the son in the playlet is able to escape the tyranny of his father, the daughter in the second playlet is still controlled by her father's will, in both senses of the word. Flavinda is brought up by her aunt, Lady Harpy Harraden – executor of her brother's will – who strives to become its beneficiary by plotting to marry Flavinda to Sir Spaniel Lilyliver. The will bequeaths Lady Harraden half of her brother's fortune if Flavinda marries according to Lady Harraden's wishes. Flavinda, however, displaying the fiery independence of the radical young women in Woolf's earlier fiction, frees herself from her father's will.

Flavinda's behaviour is in contradistinction to that of Eleanor, Mrs Hardcastle's daughter, who agrees to marry Edgar as her mother wishes. While Edgar and Arthur sing 'Rule Britannia', tying themselves to the empire, patriarchy and a masculine version of history, Eleanor and her mother confirm and even celebrate the inconsequential role of women under patriarchy, singing 'I'd be a Butterfly'.

The shared aesthetic experience that La Trobe seeks to provide is an interruption of the shared illusions of history as a sequence of unchallenged, gendered narratives of nation, community and even art. The pageant interrupts the illusion of continuity by ellipses and rapid shifts in tone. But in displacing the boundaries between theatre and narrative, the pageant recasts history (literally and metaphorically) as narrative and as theatre and the characters in the novel as participants in a performative space. In this way Woolf begins to confront the objection that what lies outside the illusion of historical discourse is only recoverable through discourse.

The conclusion of the novel mockingly presents the prehistoric origins of what might be said, if we ignore all the complex ramifications of history, to have brought us to 1939: Prehistoric man 'half-human, half-ape roused himself from his semi-crouching position and raised great stones' (p. 197). Here, at its crudest, is encapsulated the endeavour of humankind, challenging the unquestioned legitimacy of notions of progress, of raising great stones. History, then, becomes 'performative' instead of a coherent, purposeful narrative. In *Between the Acts*, Woolf literally reconfigures her anxieties about the chanciness of life which she obtained from reading Darwin.[13] If history is recast as theatre, if historical pageants do not simply re-enact the *a priori*, then discourses themselves are exposed as precarious and fluid ensembles.

As Gillian Beer has observed, Woolf was 'fascinated by the persistence of prehistory as well as its impenetrable distance'.[14] There is a greater emphasis in *Between the Acts* than Woolf's previous fiction upon what has been part of the world since the beginning of time. However, it is not often presented in the novel in an unmediated way. For example, the swallows, a recurring trope of continuity, when observed by Mrs Swithin, are associated with Africa, that is the empire, and prehistory, the swamp. Mrs Swithin's sense of history is 'poetic', to say the least. The point is that Woolf has no wish to escape from history intellectually even if she, like most of the population of Europe, would have fled from 1939 if they could have done.

The ending of the novel mischievously recasts the primal scene of origins in the figures of Giles and Isa at the window as theatre, 'Then the curtain rose. They spoke' (p. 197). Giles is a stockbroker, one of the three exclusively male professions in *Three Guineas*, and a descendant of the Norman French responsible according to *Orlando*, as we have seen, for conquering 'Merrie England'. Isa is an 'Angel in the House' and is descended from the O'Neils, Kings of Ireland. So in the closing stages of the novel we are presented with the Eden myth, the conquest of Ireland by England and of the English by the Normans, heterosexuality and the suppression of the female within patriarchy. But the novel does not confirm the Eden myth, and all its ideological and gendered assumptions, for it recasts Giles and Isa as enormous shadows against the window. In other words they are phantasms. And because the rising curtain places them in a performative space instead of the *a priori*, the novel ends in mid-breath (literally and metaphorically). We do not know what they will say. The performative nature of the novel, with a pageant that recasts history as narrative, has taken away the inevitability of the *a priori*. Thus despite the note of uncertainty, the novel's conclusion is in some respects quite positive, given the circumstances both within the text and within Europe. It is ultimately rescued from its own apocalyptic strain by the reclamation of the subversive irony so characteristic of Woolf's earlier fiction of the 1920s.

10

Conclusion

One of the earliest critical works to attempt to stem the tide of anti-Bloomsbury criticism initiated by F. R. Leavis and the *Scrutiny* group was published in France, where Woolf's fiction had always been more sympathetically received than in England. However, Jean Guiguet's philosophical approach, influenced by Sartrean existentialism, did little to challenge the view of Woolf as an intensely subjective writer.[1] Indeed, sexual/textual deconstructionist and psychoanalytic criticism of her fiction developed in Europe, and in America, ahead of wider political interpretations of her work. Criticism of Woolf as a political writer that did eventually emerge, mainly from American presses in the1980s, rested upon a narrow selection of her novels.

This study has sought to address the paradox at the centre of Woolf's work which has not received due consideration even in recent cultural materialist and anti-imperialist approaches to her fiction; that is, given Woolf's interest in domestic and international politics which recent scholarship has established, why do so many key events enter her novels only cryptically, if at all? While critics have found that the fragmentary elements of Woolf's work do constitute a coherent pattern after all, if we are prepared to search for it, the cryptic and enigmatic nature of her fiction has remained inadequately theorised beyond an acknowledgement that modernists jumbled naturalistic elements at random. But Woolf's fiction, repeatedly resisting history that links one political event or moment to another, foregrounds an interest in historiography. As we have seen, as early as 1919 Woolf was contemptuous of what she called 'historians' histories'. Instead, the focus of her work falls on the cultural practices embedded in organised, social life that impinge on the lives of individuals and determine their course, on the way historical events are turned into 'history' and on what is legitimated, privileged and occluded in the writing of history.

This realisation projects a trajectory for her writing whereby her oblique approach to events can be seen as shaping rather than contradicted by her interest in politics. Her fiction, as I have tried to illustrate, is engaged not simply by the cultural, philosophical and psychoanalytic issues of her day, but by how those issues are rendered in different discourses. In her novels, 'reality' is a coded reality that needs to be deciphered before it can be reinterpreted. Even though the interconnection in her work of narrative experiment, political analysis and intellectual debate has been brought to the fore in more politically oriented criticism, her true sophistication as a political thinker lies in the way in which the codified or 'textual' nature of her social milieu is incorporated, challenged and rewritten in her writings.

Drawn to what she described in 'Phyllis and Rosamond' as 'that dark and crowded place behind the scenes' and the 'many wires... upon whose jerk or twist the whole figure of the dance depends' (p. 17), not only did Woolf incorporate historical and political events in her work to be read cryptanalytically, but she read the external world herself cryptanalytically. This concern with the codified nature of public discourse gives a distinctive edge to her treatment of themes that are to be found in numerous post-1918 novels by women: the greater preponderance of women in the public sphere, the emergent sexualities, the changing nature of the Symbolic Order, the relationship between war and masculinity, the gendered nature of national identity, the politics of the urban environment and the changing role of the family as a social institution.

Studies that address the cryptic nature of Woolf's writing are overdue because it was an aspect of her work about which, as we have seen, she had reservations even while awaiting the publication of *The Years*, normally regarded, wrongly as I have tried to show, as the least cryptic of her novels. The linchpin of my argument is that Woolf's sophisticated grasp of the ideologically coded nature of 'social reality' is most illuminatingly approached through the ideas developed by Michel Foucault and his assertion that meaning can only be understood in relation to wider discursive systems. Anticipating Foucault, Woolf is engaged by the statements, attitudes and practices that have acquired currency and legitimation over time or have been excluded from dominant discourses. For Woolf as for

Foucault, discourses are 'precarious ensembles'. Reading historical and political events cryptanalytically, she is interested in her fiction in the formal identities, thematic continuities, translation of concepts and polemical interchanges in and across a range of principal discourses. Her fiction is written in the space opened up by what is not unifiable or coherent in the historical *a priori* and, while this returns us to the fragmentary nature of modernist art generally, Woolf anticipates Foucault's thesis that what he calls the cultural archive can only be uncovered in fragments and at different levels of the social structure. While the recurring concern in Woolf's fiction with travel and movement of all kinds opens up the fluid nature of empire, places, institutions, customs and behaviours, it also signifies Woolf's preoccupation with the migration of ideas from one domain to another.

Woolf's writings are also located in a space between two binarisms that have determined the direction and tone of twentieth-century debates about history: between the past as viewed as inert beneath the historian's microscope, and the past as a site for the free play of signifiers and difference. In her dialogical engagement with the past, Woolf sees events as 'texts', established, as for Foucault, not only as nodes within a network of meanings but also as brought into being by these networks. Events in her fiction, then, are precarious and mutable; the product of interpretative strategies, they are dependent upon a complex group of relations that are themselves always changing. The cultural geography of space, on the other hand, repeats and is structured by the real determinants of social relations. Her novels frequently break open the deep structures of metaphor in which space is gendered and challenges the Symbolic Order which imbues space with meaning.

A product of the Victorian as well as the Modernist period, indebted to the New Woman of the late century and the Suffragettes, widely read and interested in numerous contemporary debates, Woolf's breadth and depth have been confirmed by recent scholarship. In all the ways listed above, and for all the reasons given, Woolf deserves to be read as a sophisticated, political writer.

Notes

CHAPTER 1: INTRODUCTION

1. Jeffrey N. Cox and Larry J. Reynolds, 'Introduction', in *New Historical Literary Studies: Essays on Reproducing Texts, Representing History*, ed. Jeffrey N. Cox and Larry J. Reynolds (Princeton, NJ: Princeton University Press, 1993), p. 1.

2. Iain Wright, 'History, Hermeneutics, Deconstruction', in *Criticism and Critical Theory*, ed. Jeremy Hawthorn (London: Edward Arnold, 1984), p. 83.

3. Jacques Derrida, 'Structure, Sign, and Play in the Discourse of the Human Sciences', in *The Structuralist Controversy*, ed. Richard Macksey and Eugenio Donato (Baltimore, MD, and London: Johns Hopkins University Press, 1970), p. 264.

4. Jonathan Culler, *On Deconstruction: Theory and Criticism after Structuralism* (London: Routledge, 1983), p. 129.

5. Wright, 'History, Hermeneutics, Deconstruction', p. 87.

6. Lee Patterson, 'Making Identities in Fifteenth-Century England: Henry V and John Lydgate', in Cox and Larry (eds), *New Historical Literary Studies*, pp. 69–107.

7. Wright, 'History, Hermeneutics, Deconstruction', p. 84 and Jeremy Hawthorn, *Cunning Passages: New Historicism, Cultural Materialism and Marxism in the Contemporary Literary Debate* (London: Arnold, 1996), p. 71.

8. Hans-Georg Gadamer, *Truth and Method* (London: Sheed and Ward, 1979), pp. 107 and 104.

9. Wright, 'History, Hermeneutics, Deconstruction', p. 95.

10. Hawthorn, *Cunning Passages*, p. 192.

11. *Ibid.*, p. 191.

12. Elizabeth Abel, *Virginia Woolf and the Fictions of Psychoanalysis* (Chicago, IL, and London: University of Chicago Press, 1989), p. 1.

13. Roland Barthes, 'Criticism as Language', *The Times Literary Supplement*, 27 September 1963, p. 740.

14. Judith Hattaway, 'Virginia Woolf's *Jacob's Room*: History and Memory', in *Women and World War I: The Written Response*, ed. Dorothy Goldman (London and Basingstoke: Macmillan, 1993), pp. 14–15.

15. Hawthorn, *Cunning Passages*, p. 192.

16. Hayden White, *Metahistory: The Historical Imagination in Nineteenth-Century Europe* (Baltimore, MD, and London: Johns Hopkins University Press, 1973), p. x.

17. Eric J. Leed, *No Man's Land: Combat and Identity in World War I* (Cambridge: Cambridge University Press, 1979), p. 195.

18. Michel Foucault, *The Archaeology of Knowledge* (1969; trans. 1972; rpt London and New York: Routledge, 1994), p. 104.

19. *Ibid.*, p. 105.

20. *Ibid.*, p. 25.

21. *Ibid.*, p. 45.

22. Edward Soja, *Postmodern Geographies: The Reassertion of Space in Critical Social Theory* (London: Verso, 1989), p. 43.

23. Michel de Certeau, *The Practice of Everyday Life* (Berkeley, CA: University of California Press, 1988), pp. 94 ff.

24. I am indebted here to Donatella Mazzoleni, 'The City and the Imaginary' (trans. John Koumantarakis), in *Space and Place: Theories of Identity and Location*, ed. Erica Carter, James Donald and Judith Squires, pp. 285–301 (pp. 286–7).

25. M. M. Bakhtin, *The Dialogic Imagination: Four Essays*, ed. Michael Holquist (Austin, TX: University of Texas Press, 1981), p. 84.

CHAPTER 2: CONTEXTS

1. Virginia Woolf, 'Solid Objects', in *The Complete Shorter Fiction of Virginia Woolf*, ed. Susan Dick (London: Hogarth Press, 1985), p. 102.

2. Jane Marcus, 'Wrapped in the Stars and Stripes: Virginia Woolf in the U.S.A.', *The South Carolina Review*, 29:1 (Fall 1996), 17–23 (22).

3. Vera and Ansgar Nünning, 'From Thematics and Formalism to Aesthetics and History: Phases and Trends of Virginia Woolf Criticism in Germany', *The South Carolina Review*, 29:1 (Fall 1996), 101–8 (101).

4. Hermione Lee, *Virginia Woolf* (London: Chatto and Windus, 1966).

5. Mark Hussey, 'Living in a War Zone: Virginia Woolf as a War Novelist', in *Virginia Woolf and War: Fiction, Reality and Myth*, ed. Mark Hussey (Syracuse, NY: Syracuse University Press, 1991), p. 2.

6. Vera and Ansgar Nünning, 'From Thematics and Formalism to Aesthetics and History', 101.

7. Pierre-Eric Villeneuve, 'Virginia Woolf and the French Reader: An Overview', *The South Carolina Review*, 29:1 (Fall 1996), 109–21 (115).

8. Cited by Villeneuve, 'Virginia Woolf and the French Reader', 114. The original source is Hélène Cixous, 'Rethinking Differences', in *Homosexualities and French Literature: Cultural Contexts and Critical Texts*, ed. George Stambolian and Elaine Marks, trans. Isabelle de Courtivron (Ithaca, NY: Cornell University Press, 1979), p. 83. Cixous' influence can be seen in Anne Bragance, *Virginia Woolf: La dame sur le Piédestal* [*Virginia Woolf: The Lady on the Pedestal*] (Paris: Edition des Femmes, 1984); Françoise Defromont, *Virginia Woolf: Vers la maison de lumière* [*Virginia Woolf: Towards the Lighthouse*] (Paris: Edition des Femmes, 1985).

9. Marcus, 'Wrapped in the Stars and Stripes', 16 and 23.

10. *Ibid.*, 21 and 18.

11. Hussey, 'Living in a War Zone', p. 6.

12. Alex Zwerdling, *Virginia Woolf and the Real World* (London and Los Angeles, CA: University of California Press, 1986).

13. Villeneuve, 'Virginia Woolf and the French Reader', 263.

14. Noel Annan, 'Bloomsbury and the Leavises', *Virginia Woolf and Bloomsbury*, ed. Jane Marcus (London and Basingstoke: Macmillan, 1987), p. 31.

15. F. R. Leavis, *The Common Pursuit* (London: Chatto and Windus, 1952), p. 257.

16. Marion Shaw, 'From a Room of One's Own to a Literature of One's Own', *The South Carolina Review*, 29:1 (Fall 1996), 58–66 (62).

17. Marcus, 'Wrapped in the Stars and Stripes', 19.

18. Tom Paulin, 'Self-regard, Pomp and Circumstance', *Irish Times*, 30 September 1991.

19. Zwerdling, *Virginia Woolf and the Real World*, p. 26.

20. *Ibid.*, p. 27.

21. Annan, 'Bloomsbury and the Leavises', p. 23.

22. Villeneuve, 'Virginia Woolf and the French Reader', 110.

23. Zwerdling, *Virginia Woolf and the Real World*, p. 28.

24. Lee, *Virginia Woolf*, p. 223.

25. Virginia Woolf, *The Voyage Out*, ed. Lorna Sage (Oxford: Oxford University Press, 1992), p. 289. All further references are to this edition and are given in parentheses in the text.

26. *The Diary of Virginia Woolf*, ed. Anne Olivier Bell and Andrew McNeillie, 5 vols (London: Hogarth Press, 1977–84; Penguin Books, 1979–85), vol. II, p. 210 (29 October 1922).

27. Lee, *Virginia Woolf*, p. 460.

28. *Ibid.*

29. S. P. Rosenbaum, *Victorian Bloomsbury: The Early Literary History of the Bloomsbury Group* (1987; rpt with corrections, London and Basingstoke: Macmillan, 1994). Rosenbaum tends to under-emphasise the modernist context and the dialectical relationships that often existed between the members of the group and Victorian philosophy and religion.

30. Gary Day, 'Introduction: Past and Present – The Case of Samuel Smiles' *Self Help*', in *Varieties of Victorianism: The Uses of a Past*, ed. Gary Day (London and Basingstoke: Macmillan, 1998), p. 1. See also 'The Victorians in Virginia Woolf: 1832–1941', in *Virginia Woolf: The Common Ground. Essays by Gillian Beer* (Edinburgh: Edinburgh University Press, 1996), pp. 92–111.

31. John Peck, *War, the Army and Victorian Literature* (London and Basingstoke: Macmillan, 1998), pp. 162, 138 and 140.

32. Virginia Woolf, *Moments of Being*, ed. Jeanne Schulkind (1976; Brighton: Sussex University Press, 1985), p. 201. See also Lee, *Virginia Woolf*, p. 207.

33. Lee, *Virginia Woolf*, p. 207.

34. Hussey, 'Living in a War Zone', p. 3.

35. Hattaway, 'Virginia Woolf's *Jacob's Room*', p. 14.

36. Leed, *No Man's Land*, p. 193.

37. *Ibid.*, pp. 193–4.

38. Peck, *War, the Army and Victorian Literature*, pp. 141, 142.

39. Truti Tate, '*Mrs Dalloway* and the Armenian Question', *Textual Practice*, 8:3 (Winter 1994), 467.

40. *Ibid.*, 470.

41. James Longenbach, 'The Women and Men of 1914', in *Arms and the Woman: War, Gender and Literary Representation*, ed. Helen M. Cooper, Adrienne Auslander Munich and Susan Merrill Squier (Chapel Hill, NC: University of North Carolina Press, 1989), pp. 97–123 (pp. 98 and 115).

42. Elaine Showalter, *The Female Malady: Women, Madness and English Culture, 1830–1980* (London: Virago, 1987), p. 196.

43. *Ibid.*, pp. 196–7.

44. Lee, *Virginia Woolf*, p. 279.

45. *Ibid.*, p. 280.

46. *Ibid.*, p. 343.

47. Virginia Woolf, *Diary*, vol. I, p. 138 (13 April 1918).

48. Kathy Phillips, *Virginia Woolf Against Empire* (Knoxville, TN: University of Tennessee Press, 1994), p. xi.

49. Zwerdling, *Virginia Woolf and the Real World*, p. 15.

50. Isobel Armstrong, 'Woolf by the Lake, Woolf at the Circus: Carter and Tradition', *in Flesh and the Mirror: Essays on the Art of Angela Carter*, ed. Lorna Sage (London: Virago, 1994), p. 260.

51. Zwerdling, *Virginia Woolf and the Real World*, pp. 9–10.

52. *Ibid.*, p. 13.

53. I am indebted here to Stephen Slemon, 'The Scramble for Post-Colonialism', in *De-Scribing Empire: Post-Colonialism and Textuality*, ed. Chris Tiffin and Alan Lawson (London and New York: Routledge, 1994), pp. 15–32.

54. Zwerdling, *Virginia Woolf and the Real World*, p. 31.

55. Review of D. Bridgman Metchim, *Our Own History of the War: From a South London View*, in *The Times Literary Supplement*, 9 January 1919; rpt. in *The Essays of Virginia Woolf*, ed. Andrew McNeillie, 6 vols (London: Hogarth Press, 1988), vol. III, pp. 3–4 (p. 3).

56. See not only Isobel Armstrong, above, but Hermione Lee, 'A Room of One's Own, or a Bloody Chamber? Angela Carter and Political Correctness', in Sage (ed.), *Flesh and the Mirror*, pp. 317–20.

57. Armstrong, 'Woolf by the Lake', p. 258.

58. Angela Ingram, ' "The Sacred Edifices": Virginia Woolf and Some of the Sons of Culture', in Marcus (ed.), *Virginia Woolf and Bloomsbury*, p. 126.

59. A review published in the *Athenaeum*, 16 July 1920; rpt. in *The Essays of Virginia Woolf*, ed. McNeillie, vol. III, pp. 238–41 (p. 240).

60. Zwerdling, *Virginia Woolf and the Real World*, p. 12.

61. Virginia Woolf, 'Phyllis and Rosamond', in *The Complete Shorter Fiction of Virginia Woolf*, ed. Dick, p. 17.

62. Juliet Dusinberre, *Virginia Woolf's Renaissance: Woman Reader or Common Reader?* (London and Basingstoke: Macmillan, 1997), p. 232.

63. *Ibid.*, p. 46.

64. *Ibid.*, p. 53.

65. Armstrong, 'Woolf by the Lake', p. 258.

66. Lyn Pykett, *Engendering Fictions: The English Novel in the Early Twentieth Century* (London: Edward Arnold, 1995).

67. The *Oxford English Dictionary* defines cryptanalysis as 'the art of deciphering a cryptogram by analysis'. Susan Stanford Friedman, in recommending a geopolitical approach to Woolf's work, is the only critic to suggest, albeit in passing, that Woolf's fiction be read in this way. She uses the word 'cryptographic' which means 'to write' rather than 'to read or analyse' what is hidden. Cryptography and cryptanalysis are the two aspects of what is called cryptology. 'Uncommon Readings: Seeking the Geopolitical Woolf', *The South Carolina Review*, 29:1 (Fall 1996), 24–44 (35). The increasingly wider adoption of the term 'cryptanalysis' was signified perhaps by its inclusion as a category in the European Society for the Study of English Conference (Hungary, 1997).

68. Virginia Woolf, 'The Journal of Mistress Joan Martyn', in *The Complete Shorter Fiction of Virginia Woolf*, ed. Dick, p. 39. All further references are to this edition of the story and are given in parentheses in the text.

69. Clare Hanson, *Virginia Woolf* (London and Basingstoke: Macmillan, 1994), p. 29.

70. A signed article in the *Women's Leader*, 23 July 1920; rpt in *The Essays of Virginia Woolf*, ed. McNeillie, vol. III, pp. 241–5.

71. Cit. in Shaw, 'From a Room of One's Own to a Literature of their Own', 61.

72. Foucault, *The Archaeology of Knowledge*, p. 131.

73. *Ibid.*, p. 126.

74. Leonard Woolf, *Empire and Commerce in Africa: A Study in Economic Imperialism* (London: Labour Research Department, 1920), p. 316.

75. *Ibid.*, p. 21.

76. Foucault, *The Archaeology of Knowledge*, p. 127.

77. *Ibid.*, pp. 137–40.

78. Friedman, 'Uncommon Readings', 30.

CHAPTER 3: PENT-UP VOICES: *THE VOYAGE OUT* (1915), *NIGHT AND DAY* (1919) AND 'KEW GARDENS' (1919)

1. Virginia Woolf, *A Woman's Essays*, ed. Rachel Bowlby (Harmondsworth: Penguin, 1992), p. 176.

2. Alice Fox, *Virginia Woolf and the Literature of the English Renaissance* (Oxford: Clarendon Press, 1990), pp. 22–3.

3. Julia Briggs, '*Night and Day*', in *Virginia Woolf: Introduction to the Major Works*, ed. Julia Briggs (London: Virago, 1994), p. 40.

4. Hanson, *Virginia Woolf*, p. 30.

5. Woolf herself revised the 1915 text for an American edition in 1919. That text is an altogether tighter narrative than the 1915 version in which there is generally less overt authorial intrusion into the lives of the characters. See Louise DeSalvo, *Virginia Woolf's First Voyage: A Novel in the Making* (London and Basingstoke: Macmillan, 1980); *Melymbrosia: An Early Version of 'The Voyage Out'*, ed. Louise De Salvo (New York: New York Public Library, 1982).

6. The most persuasive case for *The Voyage Out* as a lesbian novel is offered in Patricia Juliana Smith, '"The Things People Don't Say": Lesbian Panic in *The Voyage Out*', in *Virginia Woolf: Lesbian Readings*, ed. Eileeen Barrett and Patricia Cramer (London and New York: New York University Press, 1997), pp. 128–45.

7. *Ibid.*, p. 134.

8. Helen Wussow, 'War and Conflict in *The Voyage Out*', in Hussey (ed.), *Virginia Woolf and War*, pp. 105–6.

9. *Ibid.*

10. Simon Ryan, 'Inscribing the Emptiness: Cartography, Exploration and the Construction of Australia', in Tiffin and Lawson (eds), *De-scribing Empire*, p. 116.

11. John Peck, *War, the Army and Victorian Literature*, p. 133.

12. Jane Wheare, '*The Voyage Out*', in Briggs (ed.), *Virginia Woolf*, p. 29.

13. On the decline of the empire, see Aaron L. Friedberg, *The Weary Titan: Britain and the Experience of Relative Decline, 1895–1905* (Princeton, NJ: Princeton University Press, 1988), and J. A. Gallagher, *The Decline, Revival and Fall of the British Empire* (Cambridge: Cambridge University Press, 1982).

14. E. J. Hobsbawm, *The Age of Empire, 1875–1914* (1987; rpt, London: Abacus, 1995), p. 57.

15. Between 1840 and 1875 the world's merchant shipping increased from 10 to 16 million tons. During the same period European exports increased fourfold and continued to rise from 1875 to 1914.

16. Woolf, *Empire and Commerce in Africa*, p. 24.

17. *Ibid.*, p. 22.

18. *Ibid.*

19. *Spenser Poetical Works*, ed. J. C. Smith and E. de Selincourt (London, Oxford and New York: Oxford University Press, 1970), p. 69. Woolf also drew upon Darwin's descriptions of the South American forest in *The Voyage of the Beagle*. See Gillian Beer, 'Virginia Woolf and Prehistory', in *Virginia Woolf: The Common Ground*, pp. 6–28.

20. Woolf, *Empire and Commerce in Africa*, p. 10.

21. E. de Selincourt, 'Introduction', in *Spenser Poetical Works*, ed. Smith and de Selincourt, p. li.

22. L. C. B. Seaman, *Post-Victorian Britain 1902–1951* (1966; rpt London and New York: Routledge, 1995), pp. 8–9.

23. Briggs, 'Night and Day', p. 34

24. *The Critical Writings of Katherine Mansfield*, ed. Clare Hanson (London and Basingstoke: Macmillan, 1987), p. 59.

25. Review published in the *Athenaeum*, 21 November 1919, 1227; rpt in *Virginia Woolf: The Critical Heritage*, ed. Robin Majumdar and Allen McLaurin (London and New York: Routledge and Kegan Paul, 1975), pp. 79–82 (see p. 82).

26. Lee, *Virginia Woolf*, p. 377.

27. *The Times Literary Supplement*, 10 April 1919; rpt *The Essays of Virginia Woolf*, ed. McNeillie, vol. III, 30–7 (p. 33). Later substantially revised as 'Modern Fiction'.

28. John Mepham, *Virginia Woolf: A Literary Life* (London and Basingstoke: Macmillan, 1991), p. 50.

29. Virginia Woolf, *Night and Day*, ed. Suzanne Raitt (Oxford: Oxford University Press, 1992), p. 9. All further references are to this edition and are given in parentheses in the text.

30. Phillips, *Virginia Woolf against Empire*, p. 85.

31. Briggs, *Night and Day*, p. 49.

32. Mazzoleni, 'The City and the Imaginary', p. 287.

33. Virginia Woolf, 'Kew Gardens', in *The Complete Shorter Fiction of Virginia Woolf*, ed. Dick, p. 95. All further references are to this edition and are given in parentheses in the text.

34. E. M. Forster, 'Visions', *Daily News*, 31 July 1919, 2; rpt *Virginia Woolf: The Critical Heritage*, ed. Majumdar and McLaurin, pp. 68–79 (p. 69).

CHAPTER 4: PRE-WAR ENGLAND: *JACOB'S ROOM* (1922)

1. Virginia Woolf, *A Room of One's Own and Three Guineas*, ed. Morag Shiach (Oxford: Oxford University Press, 1992), p. 365. All further references are to this edition and are given in parentheses in the text.

2. Zwerdling, *Virginia Woolf and the Real World*, p. 64.

3. John McCrae, *In Flanders Fields and Other Poems* (New York: Putnam's, 1929), p. 3.

4. Zwerdling, *Virginia Woolf and the Real World*, p. 66.

5. *The Question of Things Happening: The Letters of Virginia Woolf*, ed. Nigel Nicolson and Joanne Trautmann, 6 vols (London: Hogarth Press, 1975–80), vol. II, p. 71.

6. Elaine Showalter, *The Female Malady: Women, Madness and English Culture, 1830–1980* (1985; rpt London: Virago Press, 1995), p. 169.

7. Virginia Woolf, *Jacob's Room*, ed. Kate Flint (Oxford: Oxford University Press, 1992), p. 57. All further references are to this edition and are given in parentheses in the text.

8. Anonymous review, *The Times Literary Supplement*, 26 October 1922, 683; rpt in *Virginia Woolf: The Critical Heritage*, ed. Majumdar and McLaurin, pp. 95–7 (p. 96).

9. Anonymous review, *Pall Mall Gazette*, 27 October 1922; rpt in *ibid.*, p. 99.

10. Lee, *Virginia Woolf*, p. 296.

11. Hattaway, 'Virginia Woolf's *Jacob's Room*', p. 21.

12. Lee, *Virginia Woolf*, p. 296.

13. *The Question of Things Happening: The Letters of Virginia Woolf*, ed. Nicolson and Trautmann, vol. II, pp. 268, 271.

14. Lyndall Gordon, *Virginia Woolf: A Writer's Life* (1984; rpt Oxford: Oxford University Press, 1986), pp. 169–70.

15. *Rupert Brooke: The Collected Poems*, with a memoir by Edward Marsh (1918; rpt London: Sidgwick and Jackson, 1942), p. clvi.

16. Virginia Wolf, *Jacob's Room*, p. 63 and *Rupert Brooke: The Collected Poems*, p. lxxxiii.

17. Paul Fussell, *The Great War and Modern Memory* (Oxford: Oxford University Press, 1975), p. 278.

18. *Ibid.*, pp. 278 ff.

19. *Rupert Brooke: The Collected Poems*, p. cvi.

20. Zwerdling, *Virginia Woolf and the Real World*, p. 62.

21. *The Question of Things Happening: The Letters of Virginia Woolf*, ed. Nicolson and Trautmann, vol. II, p. 76.

22. *Rupert Brooke: The Collected Poems*, p. clv.

23. Mepham, *Virginia Woolf: A Literary Life*, p. 81.

24. James Brown, 'Education, Ideology and the Ruling Class: Hellenism and the English Public Schools in the Nineteenth Century', *Rediscovering Hellenism: The Hellenic Inheritance and the English Imagination*, ed. G. W. Clarke (Cambridge: Cambridge University Press, 1989), p. 176.

25. See, for example, Makiko Minow-Pinkney, *Virginia Woolf and the Problem of the Subject* (Brighton: Harvester, 1987).

26. Hanson, *Virginia Woolf*, p. 45.

27. See Jane Harrison, *Reminiscences of a Student's Life* (London: Hogarth Press, 1925), *Epilegomenao the Study of Greek Religion* (1921) and *Ancient Art and Ritual* (1913).

28. Lee, *Virginia Woolf*, p. 228.

29. *Rupert Brooke: The Collected Poems*, p. cliv. It is quoted here as translated from the Greek by Edward Marsh.

30. *Ibid.*, p. clv.

31. William R. Handley, 'War and the Politics of Narration in *Jacob's Room*', in Hussey (ed.), *Virginia Woolf and War: Fiction, Reality and Myth*, p. 115.

32. Fussell, *The Great War and Modern Memory*, p. 18.

33. Lee, *Virginia Woolf*, p. 292.

34. *Ibid.*, p. 293.

35. I am indebted here to Kathleen Dobie, 'This is the Room that Class Built: the Structures of Sex and Class in *Jacob's Room*', in Marcus (ed.), *Virginia Woolf and Bloomsbury*, pp. 195–207.

36. Hanson, *Virginia Woolf*, p. 51.

37. Zwerdling, *Virginia Woolf and the Real World*, p. 73.

38. Lee, *Virginia Woolf*, p. 296.

39. Gordon, *Virginia Woolf: A Life*, p. 170.

40. *Women's Leader*, 23 July 1920; rpt in *The Essays of Virginia Woolf*, ed. McNeillie, vol. III, pp. 241–5 (pp. 242–3).

41. Rebecca West, review, *New Statesman*, 4 November 1922, 142; rpt in *Virginia Woolf: The Critical Heritage*, ed. Majumdar and McLaurin, pp. 100–2 (p. 101).

42. Arnold Bennett, 'Is the Novel Decaying?', *Cassell's Weekly*, 28 March 1923, 47; rpt., in *ibid.*, pp. 112–14 (p. 113).

43. Hanson, *Virginia Woolf*, p. 53.

44. Angela Ingram, ' "The Sacred Edifices": Virginia Woolf and Some of the Sons of Culture', in Marcus (ed.), *Virginia Woolf and Bloomsbury*, p. 126.

45. Fussell, *The Great War and Modern Memory*, p. 21.

CHAPTER 5: 'NATIONAL CONSERVATISM' AND 'CONSERVATIVE NATIONALISM': *MRS DALLOWAY* (1925)

1. Virginia Woolf, *A Woman's Essays*, p. 148.

2. Bakhtin, *The Dialogic Imagination*, p. 252.

3. *Hanson, Virginia Woolf*, p. 57.

4. J. Hillis Miller, '*Mrs Dalloway*: Repetition as the Raising of the Dead', in *Critical Essays on Virginia Woolf*, ed. Morris Beja (Boston, MA: G. K. Hall, 1985), p. 62.

5. Virginia Woolf, *Mrs Dalloway*, ed. Claire Tomalin (Oxford: Oxford University Press, 1992), p. 93. All further references are to this edition and are given in parentheses in the text.

6. See, for example, *The Cambridge Cultural History of Britain: Early Twentieth-Century Britain*, ed. Boris Ford (Cambridge: Cambridge University Press, 1992), pp. 78–84 [originally published in 1989 as *The Cambridge Guide to the Arts in Britain: The Edwardian Age and the Inter-War Years*].

7. Jean Baudrillard, *Symbolic Exchange and Death*, trans. Iain Hamilton Grant (London: Sage, 1993), p. 156. [Originally published as *L' échange symbolique et la mort* (Paris: Gallimard, 1976).]

8. Ernest Jones, 'Mother-Right and the Sexual Ignorance of Savages' [1942], in *Essays in Applied Psychoanalysis*, 2 vols (London: Hogarth Press and the Institute of Psycho-Analysis, 1951), vol. II, p. 148.

9. Abel, *Virginia Woolf and the Fictions of Psychoanalysis*, p. 31.

10. *Ibid.*, p. 32.

11. *Ibid.*

12. Elizabeth Abel, 'Narrative Structure(s) and Female Development: the Case of *Mrs Dalloway*', in *Virginia Woolf*, ed. Rachel Bowlby (London: Longman, 1992), p. 94.

13. Alison Light, *Forever England: Feminity, Literature and Conservatism between the Wars* (London and New York: Routledge, 1991), p. 8.

14. John Taylor, *A Dream of England: Landscape, Photography and the Tourist's Imagination* (Manchester: Manchester University Press, 1994), pp. 121–2.

15. Light, *Forever England*, p. 11.

16. Taylor, *A Dream of England*, p. 124.

17. Virginia Woolf, *Between the Acts*, ed. Frank Kermode (Oxford: Oxford University Press, 1992), p. 6. All further references are to this edition and are given in parentheses in the text.

18. Taylor, *A Dream of England*, p. 132.

19. A. J. P. Taylor, *English History, 1914–1945* (1965; rpt Oxford: Oxford University Press, 1992), p. 166.

20. Virginia Woolf, *Diary*, vol. I, p. 35.

21. Alison Adburgham, *Shopping in Style: London from the Restoration to Edwardian Elegance* (London: Thames, 1979), p. 289.

22. Reginald Abbott, 'What Miss Kilman's Petticoat Means: Virginia Woolf, Shopping and Spectacle', *Modern Fiction Studies*, 38:1 (1992), 198.

23. I am indebted here to Reginald Abbott, who points out that the florist was a new phenomenon catering for the urban consumer who wanted corsages and floral arrangements for social events. *Ibid.*, 201.

24. Taylor, *English History, 1914–1945*, p. 171.

25. Julia Kristeva, *Strangers to Ourselves*, trans. L. S. Roudiez (New York: Columbia University Press, 1991), pp. 191–2.

26. Light, *Forever England*, p. 8.

27. *Ibid.*, p. 212.

28. *Ibid.*, p. 215.

29. Tate,'Mrs Dalloway and the Armenian Question', 475.

30. *Ibid.*, 472–3.

31. *Ibid.*, 472.

32. J. Habermas, *The Structural Transformation of the Public Sphere: An Inquiry into a Category of Bourgeois Society* (Cambridge: Polity Press, 1989), p. 27.

33. J. B. Thompson, *Ideology and Modern Culture* (Cambridge: Polity Press, 1990), p. 122.

34. Habermas, *The Structural Transformation of the Public Sphere*, p. 88.

35. Martin Phillips, 'Habermas, Rural Studies and Critical Social Theory', in *Writing the Rural*, ed. Paul Cloke, Marcus Doel, David Matless, Martin Phillips and Nigel Thrift (London: Paul Chapman, 1994), pp. 96–7.

36. Abel, 'Narrative Structure(s) and Female Development', p. 94.

37. Chambers, 'Narratives of Nationalism: Being British', p. 155.

38. Foucault, *The Archaeology of Knowledge*, p. 45.

39. *Ibid.*

40. Leed, *No Man's Land*, p. 204.

41. Foucault, *The Archaeology of Knowledge*, p. 45.

42. Showalter, *The Female Malady*, p. 192.

43. Leed, *No Man's Land*, p. 195.

44. *Ibid.*

45. Jacques Derrida, '"To Do Justice to Freud": the History of Madness in the Age of Psychoanalysis', *Critical Inquiry*, 20 (Winter 1994), 227–66 (233).

46. *Ibid.*, 234.

47. *Ibid.*

48. Duncan Kiberd, *Inventing Ireland: The Literature of the Modern Nation* (1995; rpt London: Vintage, 1996), p. 9.

49. Baudrillard, *Symbolic Exchange and Death*, p. 175.

50. Leed, *No Man's Land*, p. 204.

51. *Ibid.*

52. Baudrillard, *Symbolic Exchange and Death*, pp. 175–6.

53. Leed, *No Man's Land*, p. 196.

CHAPTER 6: WOMANHOOD AND DISCOURSE: *TO THE LIGHTHOUSE* (1927)

1. Virginia Woolf, *Mrs Dalloway*, pp. 212–13.

2. For a detailed history of the criticism of the novel see Jane Goldman, *To the Lighthouse, The Waves* (Cambridge: Icon Books, Icon Critical Guides, 1997). The groundbreaking study of the modernist, experimental nature of the novel is Erich Auerbach, 'The Brown Stocking', in *Mimesis: The Representation of Reality in Western Literature*, ed. Erich Auerbach, trans. Willard Trask (Princeton, NJ: Princeton University Press, 1953). It is reprinted, along with other essays primarily with an aesthetic focus, in *Virginia Woolf's 'To the Lighthouse': A Casebook*, ed. Morris Beja (London and Basingstoke: Macmillan, 1970). More recent critical essays are reprinted in *'Mrs Dalloway' and 'To the Lighthouse': Contemporary Critical Essays*, New Casebook Series, ed. Su Reid (London and Basingstoke: Macmillan, 1993). Psychoanalytic approaches to the novel as a feminist text, employing ideas from Freud, Lacan and Kristeva, are well illustrated by Rachel Bowlby, *Virginia Woolf: Feminist Destinations* (Oxford: Blackwell, 1988), Makiko Minow-Pinkney, *Virginia Woolf and the Problem of the Subject* (Brighton: Harvester, 1987), and Gayatiri Chakravorti Spivak, 'Unmaking and Making in *To the Lighthouse*', in *Women and Language in Literature and Society*, ed. Sally McConnell-Ginet, Ruth Barker and Nelly Furman (New York: Praeger, 1980).

3. See J. A. Lavin, 'The First Editions of Virginia Woolf's *To the Lighthouse*', *Proof*, 2 (1992), 185–211.

4. Louis Kronenberger, review, *New York Times*, 8 May 1927, 2; rpt *Virginia Woolf: The Critical Heritage*, ed. Majumdar and McLaurin,

pp. 195–8 (p. 195). Review, *The Times Literary Supplement*, 5 May 1927, 315; rpt in *ibid.*, pp 193–5 (p. 193).

5. Kate Flint, 'Virginia Woolf and the General Strike', *Essays in Criticism*, 36 (1986), 319–34.

6. Virginia Woolf, *Diary*, vol. III, pp. 131–2 (14 March 1927).

7. MS appendix A; cit Hermione Lee, '*To the Lighthouse*', in Briggs (ed.), *Virginia Woolf: Introductions to the Major Works*, p. 161.

8. Gayatiri Spivak, 'Unmaking and Making in *To the Lighthouse*', in McConnell-Ginet, Barker and Furman (eds), *Women and Language in Literature and Society*.

9. Lee, '*To the Lighthouse*', pp. 157–8.

10. *Ibid.*, p. 158.

11. For a discussion of Woolf's interest in Freud, see Lee, *Virginia Woolf*, and S. P. Rosenbaum, *Victorian Bloomsbury*.

12. Lee, '*To the Lighthouse*', p. 179.

13. Woolf's ambivalence towards the maternal heritage of the female writer is discussed in the postscript to Margaret Homans, *Bearing the Word: Language and Female Experience in Nineteenth-Century Women's Writing* (Chicago, IL and London: University of Chicago Press, 1986), pp. 278–87; abridged version published in Reid (ed.), '*Mrs Dalloway*' *and* '*To the Lighthouse*', pp. 130–41. See also Heather Ingman, *Women's Fiction between the Wars: Mothers, Daughters and Writing* (Edinburgh: Edinburgh University Press, 1998), pp. 125–44. The tension between maternity and androgyny, both active discourses in the 1920s, is a much-debated feature of Woolf's work. See, for example, Abel, *Virginia Woolf and the Fictions of Psychoanalysis*, pp. 156–7.

14. Margaret Homans, 'Mothers and Daughters in Virginia Woolf's Victorian Novel', in Reid (ed.), '*Mrs Dalloway*' *and* '*To the Lighthouse*', p. 133.

15. *Ibid.*, p. 135.

16. Abel, *Virginia Woolf and the Fictions of Psychoanalysis*, pp. 45–67 (p. 65). Alternatively, see Elizabeth Abel, 'Cam the Wicked: Woolf's Portrait of the Artist as her Father's daughter', in Marcus (ed.), *Virginia Woolf and Bloomsbury*, pp. 183–4. The essay is reprinted in Reid (ed.), '*Mrs Dalloway*' *and* '*To the Lighthouse*', pp. 112–29.

17. Homans, 'Mothers and Daughters in Virginia Woolf's Victorian Novel', pp. 130–41.

18. Virginia Woolf, *Diary*, vol. III, p. 106 (14 March 1927).

19. Abel, *Virginia Woolf and the Fictions of Psychoanalysis*, p. 46.

20. *Ibid.*, p. 49.

21. Lee, '*To the Lighthouse*', p. 171.

22. Minow-Pinkney, *Virginia Woolf and the Problem of the Subject*, p. 116.

23. Ingman, *Women's Fiction between the Wars*, p. 135.

CHAPTER 7: HISTORY AND HISTORIOGRAPHY: *ORLANDO* (1928) AND *THE WAVES* (1931)

1. Walter Benjamin, *One-Way Street and Other Writings*, trans. E. Jephott and K. Shorter (New York: New Left Books, 1979), p. 314.

2. Sheldon Sacks, *Fiction and the Shape of Belief* (Berkeley, CA: University of California Press, 1964), pp. 7–8.

3. *A Writer's Diary, being extracts from the diary of VW*, ed. Leonard Woolf (London: Hogarth Press, 1953), pp. 154–9.

4. Susan M. Squier, 'Tradition and Revision in Woolf's *Orlando*: Defoe and "The Jessamy Brides"', in *Virginia Woolf*, ed. Rachel Bowlby, p. 121. (This essay was originally published in *Women's Studies*, 12:2 (1986), 167–78.)

5. Mikhail Bakhtin, *Rabelais and His World*, trans. Hélène Iswolsky (Bloomington, IN: Indiana University Press, 1984), p. 72.

6. Virginia Woolf, *Diary*, vol. III, p. 131 (14, March 1927).

7. Terry Eagleton, 'Bakhtin, Schopenauer, Kundera', in *Bakhtin and Cultural Theory*, ed. Ken Hirschkop and David Shepherd (Manchester: Manchester University Press, 1989), p. 185.

8. Bakhtin, *Rabelais and his World*, p. 83.

9. *Ibid.*, p. 89.

10. W. B. Yeats, *Essays and Introductions* (1961; rpt London and Basingstoke: Macmillan Press, 1980), p. 365.

11. *Ibid.*

12. Virginia Woolf, *Orlando*, ed. Rachel Bowlby (Oxford: Oxford University Press, 1992), pp. 39–40. All further references are to this edition and are given in parentheses in the text.

13. Bakhtin, *Rabelais and his World*, p. 90.

14. *Virginia Woolf*, p. 522.

15. J. G. Merquior, *Foucault* (London: Fontana, 1985), p. 72.

16. Lee, *Virginia Woolf*, p. 513.

17. Denis Donoghue, *Yeats* (London: Fontana, 1971), p. 87.

18. See Homi K. Bhabha, 'DissemiNation: time, narrative, and the margins of the modern nation', in *Nation and Narration*, ed. Homi Bhabha (London and New York: Routledge, 1990), p. 295.

19. Bart Moore-Gilbert, *Post-Colonial Theory: Contexts, Practices, Politics* (London: Verso, 1997), p. 48.

20. Hobsbawm, *The Age of Empire, 1875–1914*, p. 285.

21. *Ibid.*

22. Seaman, *Post-Victorian Britain, 1902–1951*, p. 157.

23. Quentin Bell, *Virginia Woolf: A Biography*, 2 vols (London: Hogarth Press, 1972), vol. II, p. 132.

24. Sandra M. Gilbert, 'Orlando: an Introduction', in Briggs (ed.), *Virginia Woolf: Introductions to the Major Works*, pp. 189–90.

25. See, for example, Elaine Showalter, *A Literature of their Own* (London: Virago, 1978), pp. 284–305; and Gillian Beer, 'The Body of the People in Virginia Woolf', in *Virginia Woolf: The Common Ground*, pp. 48–73.

26. Hanson, *Virginia Woolf*, p. 107.

27. Squier, 'Tradition and Revision in Woolf's *Orlando*', pp. 121–31.

28. Virginia Woolf, *Diary*, vol. III, p. 168 (20 December 1927).

29. Squier, 'Tradition and Revision in Woolf's *Orlando*', p. 123.

30. *The Collected Essays of Virginia Woolf*, ed. Leonard Woolf, 4 vols (London: Hogarth Press, 1966, 1967), vol. I, p. 92; cit. *ibid.*

31. See, for example, Rachel Bowlby, 'Introduction', in Bowlby (ed.), *Orlando*, p. xlii.

32. Armstrong, 'Woolf by the Lake', p. 271.

33. Madeleine Kahn, *Narrative Transvestism: Rhetoric and Gender in the Eighteenth-Century Novel* (Ithaca, NY and London: Cornell University Press, 1991), p. 53.

34. Mepham, *Virginia Woolf: A Literary Life*, p. 139.

35. The obscenity trial of Radclyffe Hall's *The Well of Loneliness*, which occurred at the same time as the publication of *Orlando*, had an impact on *A Room of One's Own* that has been much discussed. Woolf was worried by the lesbian innuendoes in the text. Very soon after the publication of *Orlando*, she wrote her evocative essay on the friendship between Geraldine Jewsbury and Jane Carlyle. See, for example, Jane Marcus, 'Sapphistry: Narration as Lesbian Seduction in *A Room of One's Own*', in *Virginia Woolf and the Languages of Patriarchy*, ed. Jane Marcus (Bloomington, IN: Indiana University Press), pp. 163–88.

36. Frank Swinnerton, review, *Evening News*, 9 October 1931, 8; Louis Kronenberger, review, *New York Times Book Review*, 25 October 1931, 5; *The Times Literary Supplement*, 8 October 1931, 773; rpt in *Virginia Woolf: The Critical Heritage*, ed. Majumdar and McLaurin, pp. 263–8 (p. 268); pp. 273–5 (p. 274); pp. 263–5 (pp. 264–5).

37. John Mepham, *Virginia Woolf: A Literary Life*, p. 143.

38. Gerald Bullett, review, *New Statesman and Nation*, October 1931, Literary Supplement, x; rpt in *Virginia Woolf: The Critical Heritage*, ed. Majumdar and McLaurin, pp. 268–70 (p. 268).

39. Virginia Woolf, *The Waves*, ed. Gillian Beer (Oxford: Oxford University Press, 1992), p. 28. All subsequent references are to this edition and are given in parentheses in the text.

40. Judith Lee, ' "This Hideous Shaping and Moulding" ', in Hussey (ed.), *Virginia Woolf and War*, p. 184.

41. Fussell, *The Great War and Memory*, p. 136.

42. *Ibid.*, p. 118.

43. Jane Marcus, 'Britannia Rules *The Waves*', in *Decolonising Tradition: New Views of Twentieth-Century 'British' Literary Canons*, ed. Karen Lawrence (Urbana, IL: University of Illinois Press, 1988), pp. 136–62 and Phillips, *Virginia Woolf against Empire*, p. 181.

44. Martin Gilbert, *Churchill: A Life* (London: Mandarin, 1993), p. 335.

45. Phillips, *Virginia Woolf against Empire*, p. 154.

CHAPTER 8: PRIVATE AND PUBLIC SPACES:
THE YEARS (1937)

1. Virginia Woolf, 'The Mark on the Wall', in *The Complete Shorter Fiction of Virginia Woolf*, ed. Dick, p. 83.

2. Mepham, *Virginia Woolf: A Literary Life*, p. 151.

3. Ibid., p. 155.

4. Pamela Hansford Johnson, review, *English Review*, April 1937, 508–9; rpt in *Virginia Woolf: The Critical Heritage*, ed. Majumdar and Allen McLaurin, pp. 388–9.

5. Janet Montefiore, *Men and Women Writers of the 1930s* (London and New York: Routledge, 1996), p. 62.

6. *Virginia Woolf: The Critical Heritage*, ed. Majumdar and McLaurin, pp. 388–9 (p. 388).

7. Anonymous review, *The Times Literary Supplement*, 26 October 1922, 683; rpt in *Virginia Woolf: The Critical Heritage*, ed. Majumdar and McLaurin, pp. 95–7 (p. 96).

8. Virginia Woolf, *Letters*, vol. VI, p. 116.

9. Lynne Pearce, *Reading Dialogics* (London: Arnold, 1994), p. 152.

10. Ibid., p. 95.

11. Michèle Barrett and Mary McIntosh, *The Anti-Social Family* (1982; rpt London: Verso, 1984), p. 130.

12. *The Complete Works of John Ruskin*, ed. E. T. Cook and A. D. O. Wedderburn, 39 vols (London: George Allen, 1903–12), vol. XVIII, p. 122.

13. Zwerdling, *Virginia Woolf and the Real World*, p. 147.

14. Bernard Shaw, *Misalliance: A Debate in One Sitting*, in *Complete Plays with Prefaces* (New York: Dodd Mead, 1962), vol. IV, p. 85. Cit. Zwerdling, *Virginia Woolf and the Real World*, p. 147.

15. Clare Hanson, however, suggests that even though *The Years* is devoted to the horrors of family life, it is concerned with the family in a wider social and philosophical context. Hanson, *Virginia Woolf*, p. 150.

16. *Virginia Woolf and Lytton Strachey, Letters*, ed. Leonard Woolf (London: Hogarth, 1969), p. 43.

17. Foucault, *The Archaeology of Knowledge*, p. 126.

18. *Ibid.*

19. Zwerdling, *Virginia Woolf and the Real World*, p. 149.

20. For the distinction between social-paternalistic and domestic narratives of family I am indebted to Catherine Gallagher, *The Industrial Reformation of English Fiction 1832–1867* (Chicago, IL: Chicago University Pess, 1985), pp. 147 ff.

21. Alex Zwerdling suggests that works such as Morgan's *Systems of Consanguinity and Affinity of the Human Family* (1871), Westermarck's *History of Marriage* (1891; revised and expanded, 1921), Malinowski's books on sexual life in savage societies (1913ff.), Biffault's *The Mothers* (1927), and Margaret Mead's *Coming of Age in Samoa (1928)* were particularly influential (see Zwerdling, *Virginia Woolf and the Real World*, p. 146).

22. Bakhtin, *The Dialogic Imagination*, p. 247.

23. *Ibid.*, p. 245.

24. Judith R. Walkowitz, *City of Dreadful Delight: Narratives of Sexual Danger in Late-Victorian London* (London: Virago, 1992), p. 50.

25. David Bradshaw points out that it is ironic that, when North and Sara are having dinner together, Sara reviles Abrahamson, whom she can overhear having a bath, since she is living in a street named after a famous poet and libertarian (David Bradshaw. 'Hyams Place: *The Years*, the Jews and the British Union of Fascists', in *Women Writers of the 1930s: Gender, Politics and History*, ed. Maroula Joannou (Edinburgh: Edinburgh University Press, 1999), pp. 179–91, esp. pp. 187–8).

26. Baudrillard, *Symbolic Exchange and Death*, p. 90.

27. *Ibid.*, p. 89.

28. *Ibid.*, p. 90.

29. *Ibid.*

30. Mike Featherstone, *Consumer Culture and Postmodernism* (1991; rpt London: Sage, 1996), p. 79.

31. *Ibid.*, p. 78 ff.

32. Bakhtin, *The Dialogic Imagination*, p. 248.

33. *Ibid.*, p. 135.

34. *Ibid.*

35. *Ibid.*, p. 136.

36. *Walkowitz, City of Dreadful Delight, p. 19.*

37. *Ibid.*, pp. 15–16.

38. Foucault, *The Archaeology of Knowledge*, p. 126.

39. Walkowitz, *City of Dreadful Delight*, pp. 18–19.

40. Featherstone, *Consumer Culture and Postmodernism*, p. 79.

CHAPTER 9: THE LAST YEARS: 'THE SHOOTING PARTY' (1938) AND *BETWEEN THE ACTS* (1941)

1. Virginia Woolf, *Diary*, vol. V, p. 299 (27 June 1940).

2. Virginia Woolf, 'The Shooting Party', in *The Complete Shorter Fiction of Virginia Woolf*, ed. Dick, p. 255. All further references are to this edition of the story and are given in parentheses in the text.

3. Edwin Muir, review, *Listener*, 24 July 1941, p. 139, and B. G. Brooks, review article, *Nineteenth Century*, December 1941, 334–40; rpt in *Virginia Woolf: The Critical Heritage*, ed. Majumdar and McLaurin, pp. 443–5 (p. 443) and pp. 452–60 (p. 459).

4. Frank Swinterton, review, *Observer*, 20 July 1941, 3; rpt in *ibid.*, p. 442.

5. Hudson Strode, review, *New York Times*, 5 October 1941, Section 6.1.30; rpt in *ibid.*, pp. 446–7 (p. 446).

6. Karl Löwith, *Meaning in History: The Theological Implications of the Philosophy of History* (Chicago, IL: Chicago University Press, 1949), p. vii.

7. Robert Mackenzie, 'The Nineteenth-Century: A History' (1880), in *The Idea of History*, ed. R. G. Collingwood (Oxford: Oxford University Press, 1946), p. 146.

8. Linda Hutcheon, *The Politics of Postmodernism* (London and New York: Routledge, 1989), p. 62.

9. *Ibid.*, p. 66.

10. *Ibid.*, p .67.

11. *Ibid.*, p. 6.

12. Hayden White, 'The Fictions of Factual Representation', in *The Literature of Fact*, ed. Angus Fletcher (New York: Columbia University Press, 1976), p. 22.

13. Beer, 'Virginia Woolf and Prehistory', in *Virginia Woolf: The Common Ground*, p. 16.

14. *Ibid.*, p. 13.

CHAPTER 10: CONCLUSION

1. Jean Guiguet, *Virginia Woolf et Son Ouevre: L'Art et la Quête du Réel* (Paris: Didier, 1962); [Jean Guiguret, *Virginia Woolf and her Works*, trans. Jean Stewart (London: Hogarth Press, 1965)].

Index